THE LAST WILD ROAD

ALSO BY T. EDWARD NICKENS

The Total Outdoorsman
Best of the Total Outdoorsman
The Total Knife Manual
The Total Camping Manual

THE LAST WILD ROAD
Adventures and Essays from a Sporting Life

T. EDWARD NICKENS

LYONS
PRESS

Essex, Connecticut

An imprint of Globe Pequot, the trade division of
The Rowman & Littlefield Publishing Group, Inc.
4501 Forbes Blvd., Ste. 200
Lanham, MD 20706
www.rowman.com

Distributed by NATIONAL BOOK NETWORK

British Library Cataloguing in Publication Information available

Library of Congress Cataloging-in-Publication Data

Names: Nickens, T. Edward, author.
Title: The last wild road : adventures and essays from a sporting life / T. Edward Nickens.
Description: Guilford : The Lyons Press, [2021] | Includes index.
Identifiers: LCCN 2021931175 (print) | ISBN 9781493059645 (cloth) | ISBN 9781493071944
    (paper) | ISBN 9781493059652 (ebook)
Subjects: Nickens, T. Edward | Hunting—United States | Fishing—United States
Classification: DDC 799.2
LC record available at https://lccn.loc.gov/202193117

♾™ The paper used in this publication meets the minimum requirements of American National
Standard for Information Sciences—Permanence of Paper for Printed Library Materials, ANSI/
NISO Z39.48-1992.

For Julie, who kept it all together.

Contents

Foreword

At *Field & Stream*, we like to tell stories for the Total Outdoorsman, the kind of person who can do it all—hunt, fish, shoot, camp, and survive (and thrive) in the wild. And in the 13 years I've been with the magazine, I've often described T. Edward Nickens as our resident Total Outdoorsman, because the guy can do it all. When I say that, I'm not just talking about his sporting skillset; I'm also referring to his talents as a storyteller.

Nickens excels at virtually every kind of hunting and fishing story: how-to articles, adventure tales, gear reviews, personal essays, humor columns, and hard-hitting conservation reports. But if there is one kind of Eddie Nickens story that I like best, it's what we editors call a "come-along feature," a story in which the author and a buddy hit the road in search of wild thrills—and the reader gets to come along for the ride. No other writer comes close to Eddie on these stories, because no other writer makes you feel like you really are *there*—in the woods or on the water or riding shotgun—quite like Eddie does.

Of the many things I love about this book, the one that stands out most is how it feels like one big come-along story. And, for me, the journey down *The Last Wild Road* took place inside a time machine. One story after the next rekindled old memories of moments that I was lucky to have shared with Eddie:

- "The Ritual" reminds me of the Louisiana hog hunt Eddie and I took together. After I killed a pig—and word spread that it was my first—my cheeks were promptly smeared with wild blood.
- I can't read "The Meat Doe" without recalling the morning and afternoon I spent at Eddie's place, helping him butcher the doe he'd shot the evening before.
- "My Boy Jack" takes me back to one of the most formative editing experiences of my life, when Eddie and I sweated over the final draft, line by line, because we both wanted to get the story *just* right.
- Rereading "The Reunion Hunt," easily the most meaningful story I've ever collaborated on, jogs the memory of an indulgent dinner in Las Vegas that Eddie and I enjoyed together. After the meal, he began

telling me an unexpectedly emotional story of his first hunt. I was stunned at the end. "We have to tell that story," I told him.

I've worked with a lot of great writers in my career, so trust me when I tell you that it is rare for one writer to have so many stories that can trigger so many vivid memories. But then, T. Edward Nickens is a rare writer—one who can do with words what only the most gifted writers can do: Transport the reader. I have no doubt that I could share a memory from every single story in this collection, but I don't want to keep you any longer from enjoying my friend's book.

You're in for quite the ride.

—COLIN KEARNS, EDITOR-IN-CHIEF, *FIELD & STREAM*

ILLUSTRATION BY BRIAN EDWARD MILLER

"The danger of civilization, of course, is that you will piss away your life on nonsense."

—Jim Harrison

Introduction

I ran across the Jim Harrison line when I was years deep into my writing career, but it seemed to distill much of the yearning that had come before, and helped me focus more clearly on how I wanted my life to function in the future. Hunting and fishing—any moment in the natural world, really—help me take measure of the balance in my life, and point me toward how I might need to recalibrate the expenditure of time and resources. They help winnow away the less meaningful parts.

Not that everything outside the experience of the outdoors is nonsense. Hardly. I love a good college football game as long as one team is wearing Carolina blue. I love a rousing church hymn. I love the way my heart leaps when my daughter, Markie, holds on for that extra half second in a hug. I love how my son, Jack, holds the door open for his mother.

But it is true that my moments of purest clarity have come when I've put the sidewalk at my back and some piece of empty looming—water, marsh, forest, tundra—in front. There's a certain honing of spirit that comes in the pursuit of fish and game. I leave the woods or water with a more purposeful set of my shoulders, sharper of mind for having shed another shard or two of nonsense behind, like the metal grindings left on a whetstone.

Winnowing away the pieces that don't fit is also an apt description of what it is like to write a magazine story. For a full-length feature, I typically spend at least five days on the road. Most days begin at dawn and end in the black dark, with me ordering my notes and piecing together phrases, sentences, and paragraphs by the light of a headlamp. Before I put a single foot on the road, however, there are pre-trip interviews to help figure out what the story is in the first place, researching and reading, and a surprising number of phone calls to line up the logistics. Not to ruin the magic trick, but many of the seemingly serendipitous meetings with memorable characters on the road aren't serendipitous at all, but the result of weeks of phone work to weed out what drives the story and what gunks it up, and to make sure that the one-armed fly-tyer will be at the gas station when I arrive late one afternoon 13 days hence.

I nearly always wind up with enough good stuff to fill half a book, but 3,000 words is about the limit for a feature, a little better than 900 for a column. Like any creative endeavor, what ends up in the trash bin is a bit of a heartbreak. But just often enough, something meaningful emerges from all that planning and obsessing and 60 hours of sitting alone, stringing words on a chain.

I tell a story. And when I know I've told it well, it's quite a scene down here in the basement office. There is fist-pounding on the wooden desk upon which I have written for 37 years. There are whoops and hollers and much leaping about. Sometimes it looks like the end zone after a clutch catch. It's a little weird, since I am always alone. It nearly always frightens the dog. But the fact that I can do this—and that I get to do this—is still unbelievably exciting to me.

I was on the phone one day with my friend James Powell, re-hashing for the umpteenth time how wonderful it would be to take a long-discussed journey back to the southwestern desert rivers where James was raised and had first hunted ducks and geese with his father and stepfather. Our memories of our fathers had shaped us in similar ways. Along with our love for sunrises over marsh grass—and for storytelling in magazines—that shared experience lent us space for a kind of friendship honesty that I've always valued.

We talked about the places we would hunt, on this mythical trip, as we followed his childhood footsteps, and how meaningful it would be to explore that physical and emotional space together, and how maybe one day we'd actually pull it off.

Finally, James had had enough.

"You and I can talk about this story until one day all we can talk about is how much we wished we'd done it," my friend said. "Or we can hit the road."

We hit the road.

Chapter 1

Trailhead

ILLUSTRATION BY BRIAN EDWARD MILLER

THE REUNION HUNT

I'd forgotten about his long stride, how quickly he covered ground. I remember practically running behind Keith Gleason, holding one of those old olive-green periscope-shaped Boy Scout flashlights in one hand, a homemade climbing stand hanging the back of my legs as I tried to keep up. That was 40 years ago. Now, climbing a ridge in the North Carolina hardwoods, I'm determined not to lag behind. The logging road takes a sharp bend, and Keith stops for a breather.

"Look familiar?" he asks.

It's a curious question to pose in the dark, when there's nothing to see but inter-secting tree branches overhead and the next few feet of the path ahead. But I'm not sure that's what Keith means. I'm not even sure he expects an answer. He's quiet for a moment, then turns up the trail. We climb.

There's much of my childhood that I only faintly recall, but I remember this: Growing up, I dreamed of becoming a hunter. In some of my earliest memories, I am moving through the woods behind my house, a pellet rifle or small bow in hand, barefoot, feeling for twigs with the pads of my feet as I practiced stalking for whitetails. There was a jumble of busted-up concrete, dumped in the woods years ago, that gave me a vantage point across a small bottom. I called that spot the White Rocks. Perched there, I would watch for rabbits and squirrels. I would hope for a deer to emerge through the saplings.

Except it was all make-believe. Those woods behind my home were city woods. There wasn't a deer within miles. I never carried a real gun. I'd never seen a rifle. No one in my family hunted. None of my friends were hunters. I had never even met a hunter. While it's hard to overstate how badly I wanted to hunt as a kid, it's equally difficult to overemphasize how far-fetched it seemed that I would ever get the chance.

Nonetheless, by the time I was 10 or 11 years old, I was consumed by the idea of hunting. I was a walking preteen wannabe cliché: I squirreled away copies of *Field & Stream* and *Sports Afield*. I sent off for every free classified offer. I enrolled in the mail-in correspondence course offered by the old Northwest School of Taxidermy.

I've often wondered about the roots of this obsession. I was always drawn to nature, but early on I sensed a need to be more than an observer. Maybe it was linked to my early love of biographies. I devoured the tales of fur trappers and early pioneers. I knew Jim Bridger's and Daniel Boone's stories like kids today can cite Heisman statistics. Reading of their adventures was like living in a parallel realm—a reality that was just as real as my own, yet just out of reach.

I remember asking myself, over and over: Would I ever hunt?

Could I imagine a set of circumstances that would lead me to those places in the magazines, the woods where giant bucks ghosted in the morning, where ducks sprang from the marshes in a slanting rain? I could not.

Then, in the fall of 1974, everything changed.

～～

Our headlamps light up the late fall color along the logging road, as if we're walking through a kaleidoscope. The woods carry the sharp edge of tannin from the oaks, a slight tinge of decay. It's a two-track logging trail, and we start off shoulder to shoulder. But at some point I drop back a few steps, matching Keith's stride. We climb the ridge, incrementally, and as I listen to our footfalls in the leaves it occurs to me how different it was with Keith and me back then. There was nothing incremental about our meeting: There was a single defining shift at which my life took an irrevocable turn—and what I do now and the things I love and who I am changed because of that moment.

More precisely, there were two moments.

My father loved to fly. He saved part of a slim salary working at a brake shop in my native High Point, North Carolina, to pay for flying lessons. I was little in those days, 8 or 9 years old. When he was in the air on his first solo flight, my brother and I were playing behind the airstrip, climbing a steep mud bank. I fell on a stick and slashed my face. The control tower called my father on the radio to flag him back to the ground. He asked if the gash was life threatening. It wasn't, so my father flew. Stitches could wait. Dreams couldn't.

He also loved the woods and took my mother, brother, and me camping up and down the North Carolina mountains. I remember bear tracks in the mud beside our tent in the Great Smokies. I can see him skinny-dipping in a mountain stream. He was a kid with kids, a mid-20s Air Force veteran who played football with the rest of us in the backyard. When his flying career took off, he moved into flight instruction and small-plane sales. He could sense a dream within his grasp.

By the time I was 13, my father was working full-time for a small aviation company. And then, a turn in the road. I was walking home from school, rounding the long curve in McGuinn Drive, when I noticed a line of cars in my family's driveway. The plane had gone down in a field up near Pilot Mountain. My father's friends broke the news. They wouldn't yet allow me to see my mother, distraught in the back bedroom. Frightened and panicked, I fled to the woods. I was found there, some time later, standing on the White Rocks, staring into the trees.

A month after my father's death, Keith Gleason, a 25-year-old man in our church, asked my mother if he could take me squirrel hunting the next Saturday. Keith had helped my dad with the boy's group at church, and though he knew my father, there was no strong connection between them. He was fresh out of the Marine Corps, newly married, with time on his hands and enough intuition to know that a young grieving boy might need a distraction. My mother, grateful for the gesture, said yes.

I couldn't sleep. I could think of nothing else. The boys at our church already idolized Keith, this marine sharpshooter with the gorgeous wife and a battered Jeep Comanche pickup truck—the coolest rig ever. We hunted squirrels that Saturday, and again the Saturday after that, and again the Saturday after that.

And that's how it began: From junior high to college, I hunted with Keith from one end of North Carolina to the other. We chased squirrels, deer, bear, and groundhogs. We camped in plastic lean-tos in the Great Smoky Mountains and sweltered in canvas tents pitched beside cornfields in the coastal plain. He taught me to shoot a rimfire, a deer rifle, and a bow. We drove thousands of miles in the dark, unaware that the path we shared would lead me to a lifetime—and a career—of hunting and fishing across North America.

I lost my father. I found my way. A man I didn't know took me hunting. But once I left home for college in 1979, Keith and I never hunted together again. We reconnected for a time a few years after college, when I wrote a story for *Reader's Digest* on my first squirrel hunt with him. He invited me to hunt Eastern gobblers on his mountain place. We talked briefly about another try at groundhogs in the Blue Ridge. But by then my career was taking off. Plus, I had kids and a mortgage. I had excuses.

It seems inconceivable to me now that I let Keith slip out of my life with such completeness. So it was sheepishly, then, that I dialed Keith up with the idea for a reunion hunt. I should not have been surprised when he responded with unquestioned enthusiasm, as if we'd been hanging around each other for in recent years. We talked about one of the famed whitetail lodges of Alabama or Georgia. I made a few calls to friends in Kansas. Even Alberta was on the list. Deep down, though, we both knew where we had to go.

The Uwharrie Mountains rise from the west-central North Carolina farm country in rolling crests of oaks and hickories, rounded by the ages. Five hundred million years ago, they soared as high as the Himalayas, but they've been weathered to their bony foundations. Today, they are mountains in name only—the highest peaks are little more than 1,000 feet in elevation—but they wear their age like an old man in a rumpled quilt. Creeks cut deep under quartz bluffs, with rocky outcrops cresting long, loping ridges, and flat ground is as rare as the gold a few hardy miners still seek with a pan. The Uwharrie National Forest covers 50,000 acres of the biggest woods for miles around. Deer hunters hit it hard.

Keith has done his homework, scouting the area we'll hunt, which comes as no surprise. I recall his focus, forged in the Marine Corps. He has close-set blue eyes and tightly cropped salt-and-pepper hair; he's a big man, in great shape at 65 years old. He looks like Steve McQueen, who sits astride a motorcycle on a poster inside Keith's basement. He plays competitive soccer, skis the Alps, races ORVs, flies his own airplane, and rides a Harley.

He scouted this less-traveled corner of the Uwharries, the ravines and ridges where he took me deer hunting the first time, and many times after. While scouting, he bumped a nice buck and marked two treestand sites. After our mid-trail breather and another 20-minute walk, our headlamp beams catch a flag of orange surveyor's tape, and Keith pulls up short.

"Off in the woods here, maybe 20 yards, there's an opening where you can see pretty good," he whispers. "Good luck."

I step off the trail as Keith continues climbing, his headlamp blinking in and out behind trees. I find a promising pine and run the climber up. With each bite of the stand's blade, each foot I ascend in the dark, the years fall away like the bark scaled from the tree.

Keith had just been discharged from the Marine Corps when we first met, and I remember boasting to my friends that I was hunting with a marine sniper, fresh from Vietnam. I was enthralled by the fact that I was wingman to such a tough guy.

He was a disciplined, passionate rifleman, and early on rifle shooting became a bond that defined our friendship. We both loved to hunt ground-hogs in the pastures and farm fields along the New River. Keith was a grain-counting, reloading fiend who had tuned a Remington 700 Varmint Master to spit out .22/250 handloads that would crack a walnut at 400 yards. It was a bull-barreled beast of a gun that I had to carry with two hands, but there was no coddling from the marine. From our very first hunt, it was mano a mano. We traded shots at woodchucks from 200 and 300 yards or farther, and if it wasn't fair that a 13-year-old neophyte couldn't shoot as well as a jungle marksman, well, then, shoot better.

I used to get so balled up before our first hunts. At home, I would lie in bed in cold sweats, practicing trigger pulls in my mind. When I mentioned to Keith, the night before this reunion hunt, how I felt at the time that it was unfair to make a kid compete with a marine sniper, he laughed. "But it taught you to make that first shot count, didn't it?" he said. Then he added: "But I was never a sniper in the Marines. I don't know where you came up with that."

As Keith went on to explain, he never served in the war theater and was never shipped overseas. While he graduated at the top of his class at Parris Island, was known for marksmanship, and was given orders for Vietnam, a last-minute countermand switched his fate—and likely mine. He spent two Marine Corps years stateside, guarding ammunition depots with a top-secret clearance and shoot-on-sight orders.

I was surprised but not exactly stunned. It's a phenomenon I've read about: Memory is a poor historian. Psychologists speak of the retrieval processes in our minds that color what actually happened into what we remember happening. And trauma doesn't have to be a part of the mix. "History,"

Voltaire wrote, "is fables agreed upon." Tell a story long enough, and you start to believe it.

Somewhere along the way, I had layered the reality of Keith's military service with a veneer of myth, a lie of my own making. For 40 years, I would have sworn to anyone who asked that Keith Gleason was a Vietnam sniper. It had become truth to me, and a meaningful truth, for there was some added measure of healing in knowing that I'd been taken under the tutelage of a decorated veteran. Along the way I had fabricated in my head a kind of symbiotic relationship: Keith and I needed each other—the kid who'd lost his dad and the soldier who came home with a soul scarred by horrors he would not discuss.

I've run into this mythmaking of memory before. My father's plane crashed into a field at the base of Pilot Mountain, not too far from the Uwharries. At his funeral, our pastor spoke of his final moments—of engine failure and of my father steering the limping plane toward the salvation of a cleared field only to pull the craft back to the skies when he spotted a farmer on a tractor below. His dying act of grace was the gift of life for another.

I didn't question that story for years. Like the story of Keith's war service, it was a meaningful truth to me—something that illuminated a dark place and made other truths less painful and frightening. These were the stories I needed to calibrate a spinning compass. How much truth is in this story of my dad's final moments, I cannot say. But I wonder. I've gone as far as to find an online FAA report of my father's plane crash. I have it bookmarked on my laptop but have never clicked on the link. I'm not sure whether it's fear that holds me back. But I've been to the White Rocks before. I don't need to return.

I waited 40 years to parse out some of the truths of my relationship with Keith. I've yet to walk to the end of the path with my dad.

In a three-hour sit, all I see is a single whitetail, moving off into a thicket. Just enough of a deer to know that a deer is here. Just enough to quicken my heart and remind me: I am hunting. But it's early in the game, and it's no fun to tag out too soon. I clamber down and meet Keith on the fire road. On the way out of the woods he tells me something else I'd never known: This ridge was the very first place Keith ever hunted. He was after deer. His father wasn't much of a hunter, but his son was crazy to go, so he'd brought him here.

—⁓

For the afternoon hunt I find a promising setup: an old fire trail that dead-ends into a cul-de-sac in a saddle between two ridges. I climb a white oak, acorns raining down. It's a mixed omen. So much mast is on the ground that a deer could fill its belly and not move 5 feet, plus the rut is still a week or two off. But the best time to hunt is any time you can steal. I have four hours till the end of shooting light. It will be a long sit, but this is what I've come to love: the incremental stilling of my presence in the woods. The ripples of disturbance move out and flatten, my intrusion forgotten. It only comes with hours in a tree.

I have scant recollection of the years immediately following my father's death. I've long thought it odd, and a bit unsettling, that I remember so little of that time. From the age of 13 to about 16, I can summon very few memories. I've figured this for a protective cocooning of my psyche, or perhaps an outright excising of the trauma that visited the most formative period in a young man's life.

Except for those hunting trips with Keith. They've been preserved in a kind of spiritual amber, and I can summon up hunting memory after hunting memory in astonishing detail: a doe hanging from a gambrel in Keith's garage, its neck oddly canted with rigor mortis; the metallic tinge of C-rations eaten under a military tarp; the drum of rain on the plastic walls of a homemade bear-camp tent; the musky smell of an arrow smeared with blood and guts; following Keith as we tracked a fox in the snow, stretching my gait to place my boots in his footprints.

There: a deer. In the dog-hair saplings on the edge of the fire road. Not the whole deer, but the deer of memory—pieces and parts among the thicket. It's like a deer made of sticks, just the articulated forelegs, a curve of the chest. It moves into the thicket where it becomes less distinct, a brown blob, branches rocking with its movement, and then it is gone. My heartbeat slows. I wait and watch. When I was a child, I read many times that in order to see deer in the woods, you did not look for deer, but parts of deer—glints of antler, the horizontal line of a belly or back. In the woods behind my home, I would practice looking for whitetails. I forced myself to look between the spaces, between the trees, tunneling my eyes into the dark voids, training my mind to hunt, looking for the deer that were not there.

With 10 minutes of shooting light left, two yearlings step out into the fire trail's cul-de-sac. They are 50 yards away, and I track them with the scope, then pick apart the dog-hair saplings, looking for the mama doe. Getting a deer out of here would be a two-hour drag, but worth every step. The yearlings feed, never feeling the crosshairs on their chests, then slip back into the woods. I never see the doe. The woods are lit with moonlight as I make the hike down the ridge.

Later that night, in the hotel room, Keith and I quiz each other on what we remember from our years of hunting together. I remember, on a bear hunt to the Great Smokies, bathing in Fontana Lake with Lava soap, the only kind that would lather in cold water. I remember the old cars in the water, the remains of a copper mine. We both remember the Wise Potato Chips sign that marked the turnoff to the squirrel woods. We remember that one sunny October day when it seemed like rattlesnakes were everywhere. Keith remembers letting me smoke an occasional camp cigar. My mom would have killed him.

He asks if I remember the bear and the Indians. We were in the mountains again, this time with my church youth group, which Keith helped lead. I refused to get off the bus to shop through Cherokee, he says, because I was furious at the treatment of the black bears in the cages and the Indian "chiefs" who charged $5 for a photo. I don't remember any of that.

"It's amazing to me," I tell him, when the stories lull and the silence grows, "how much time we spent together." Then I let a question hang in the air, unspoken. Why did you do it? Weekend after weekend, year after year, why did you give yourself to this boy? Keith is quiet for a long moment, so long that I think this will simply be another of the unanswered questions. But he's sorting through a timeline I'm unaware of, and answers with a chronology I don't expect.

"You know," he says, "I don't remember anyone ever telling me: 'Hey, you should take that boy hunting.' I just knew you were going to need something. You wouldn't know this, but my dad had a real heart for helping the down and out. Money, food, places to stay. He was always trying to help people get back on their feet. I guess I have a little of that in me. One of my favorite Bible verses is Proverbs 27:17, where it talks about how iron sharpens iron, and how one man should sharpen another. That is so true. Just like me and you hanging out. We made each other strong, even back then."

<hr />

The next morning we hike back toward the ridge. At a dry creek bed, I tell Keith how to find my stand site from the previous evening. I walk 10 yards down the creek bed to my own climber, stashed in the woods. When I look back, Keith's headlamp flickers through the trees. It is the first time I've ever sent him to a treestand.

The eastern sky reddens as I ascend a ridge crowned with a sapling thicket. I'd scouted this spot at midday yesterday, trailing a line of fresh rubs, and it's the kind of place you recognize immediately—a hard interior edge deep inside the woods, just what a cruising buck likes to travel. I run the climber up a stout red oak and *settle in for the wait. It wasn't far from here, within a mile at most, where I used a climbing treestand for the first time.*

The woods begin to lighten, dark shapes appearing in the black void. I breathe deeply, settling into the stillness. I crave this feeling, when every moment is fraught: You must weigh the possible reward of movement against the possible cost of being discovered. I swivel my head, slow as drifting fog, and pick apart the spaces between the saplings, between the tree trunks, between the light and the shadow. If a deer suddenly appears in the open, I'll see it without looking for it. I focus on the interstitial spaces for the clues I might find there.

I have missed my father in all the ways one might imagine, and while I've made my peace with loss, I was blindsided not so long ago with a surprising resurgence of grief. As I grew into my 30s and 40s, hunting more frequently in distant locations, I began to meet fathers and sons at hunting camps, men and their boys who shared the stories of their days spent in deer stands and duck blinds together. I was staggered by waves of fresh anguish. I felt as if I'd stumbled across a foundation stone that was rotten and crumbling, one I had never suspected. The sight of a dad helping his kid out of waders would send me scurrying behind the truck in tears. For a few years, I would find myself weeping alone in my treestand or out in the woods beyond hearing and firelight, when faced with yet another reminder of what I never had. Thirty years after my father's death, this new aspect of what I had missed, and was missing still, sent me through a second mourning, a tough few seasons of a pain reawakened. And for the first time I was beginning to understand how much my father missed, as well.

It wouldn't take a psychologist to recognize my overcompensations. When it comes to spending time with my kids, I am a compulsive planner. Markie and I took our first father-daughter trip when she was in the second grade, spending a week on Oregon's Rogue River. I've hauled her to remote regions of Quebec, Honduras, Costa Rica, and a half dozen states. From September to February, my son, Jack, and I are near-constant companions in the field. I know what I'm doing. I'm not sure it's the healthiest approach to parenting, but I am haunted and shaped by the memories I do not possess.

So here is the clearest memory I have of my father: He was sitting cross-legged on the living-room floor when I leapt on him from behind, and in the midst of our father-son wrestling match, I wriggled free and took off running—out the back door, down the gravel road, to the woods. My territory. I couldn't have been more than 10 or 11. By the time he pulled his shoes on and took up the chase, I'd slipped down into the creek, and backtracked upstream like a deer on the run. I was panting, stifling my laughter, as I watched Daddy through the briers, just a few feet above, stalking the creek bank. Looking for me.

At 10:25, I'm thinking about climbing down, even though we'd agreed to hunt until 11 a.m. I get a text from Keith: "Let's stay till noon."

He is still one step ahead.

———

We can feel the clock ticking on our last evening hunt. We've seen few deer and joke about how it's just like it was in the old days. I started hunting with Keith when deer populations in the South were abysmally low, and we'd go a month without even seeing a whitetail. In fact, I have never killed a deer with Keith, and we both badly want to close the circle. The buck he'd bumped while scouting these woods earlier had been moving along a rub line, and Keith figured it was headed toward an overgrown clear-cut at the foot of the mountain. After lunch, we shoulder our climbers, and I move downhill as Keith climbs the ridge one last time, his orange hat enveloped in the riot of reds and oranges that mark the Southern hardwoods in October.

I work my way toward the timber cut and find a tall pine with views of woods on two opposing slopes. I fret for a moment that the evening's cooling air will pool behind me, scent-fouling the heavy cover along the creek, but I'm also counting on deer side-hilling the steep contours above, giving me a shot as they move into the oaks to feed. I clip a carabiner into a treestand harness, and as I've done countless times, in countless places, I breathe words of thanks: I am hunting.

Given our history, given the weight of this trip, if ever a time seemed destined for a deer, this is the moment. But hunting doesn't work that way. When a whitetail comes into view, feeding slowly along the hillside, it drifts into the dark timber before presenting a shot. I sit and watch and repeat the hunter's silent mantra as the shadows grow: It can happen. It will happen.

I remember this: Those first Saturday morning hunts, years and years ago, my mother would wake me in the dark, and I'd smell scrambled eggs and chipped beef on toast, and pull waffle-weave long johns on under blue jeans. Saturday after Saturday, until the years turned into a lifetime. And this, I will always remember: For a very long time, I could hardly believe it. I would not believe he was actually coming, until the headlights of Keith's Jeep washed across the glass panes of the back door, and my mother would hug me tightly before she set me loose into another world.

Twilight turns to night, and there is no deer. The hunt is over.

In the dark, as I work the climber down the tree, I'm overwhelmed for a moment with a wave of emotion. I'd come here to hunt with Keith to commemorate his acts of grace, yes, but also to tease apart the vines of grief and loss and gratitude that have gripped my relationship with Keith Gleason—and with my own father, Hubert Edward "Buddy" Nickens Jr.—for 42 years. By searching for a clearer vision of who he was and who we were together, I have a clearer vision of who I am still working to be.

Now we walk out of the woods—Keith and I, perhaps all three of us, together—quietly, as much to keep from spooking deer as to honor the grace of these last few moments. We've talked more in the last 48 hours than in the previous 40 years. Ahead in the dark, I am thinking that I can't believe we waited to do this for so long, and that I am ashamed of how little gratitude I've paid to the man who took me hunting, who changed nearly everything about the life I would have.

Keith whispers: "Man, I hate getting skunked."

"I know what you mean," I reply.

But it's a lie. I have never left the woods feeling that I've wasted my time. I have never walked out of the woods empty-handed. And it doesn't feel that way tonight. It has never felt that way, and never could, because of the man who walks through the darkness behind me.

LOCAL HAUNT

I caught the first fish in a small pool that clung to the rock face like lichen, 15 feet below the top drop of a double waterfall, just before the creek plunged over a 120-foot cliff. I was simply messing around as we took a breather before the trail's final descent to the bottom of the gorge. Nothing could live in there, I'd figured, as I halfheartedly rolled a yellow Sweat Bee fly into the hole.

The fly held less than two seconds on the edge of a foam line before a little brown trout smacked it like it was the last piece of a pizza at a frat party. The trout ping-ponged around the pool, with nowhere to go. I was just as surprised as the fish. It seemed incredible that a trout could live in this crack in the cliff. The fish must have washed down from upstream at some point, and unless high water swept it over the waterfall—and it likely wouldn't survive the ride—its life forevermore would be constrained by this one plunge pool hardly four steps wide.

Some days, we all know how that feels.

⚊⚊

Like a lot of us, I've been sticking closer to home lately, although thankfully my home is just a few hours' drive from both mountain and sea. And I've been charmed, tempted, and, admittedly, made a little jealous by the far-off and seemingly exotic, as I scroll through social-media pics of pals in their own necks of the woods—Montana trout streams, Everglades flats, Maine grouse woods. But being yoked to home ground has led me to think more deeply about the meaning of place, and about the hard-to-put-your-finger-on-it values of familiar landscapes. And on this quick camping escape to the North Carolina mountains, I edged a little closer to the hold home ground has on me.

From the ridgetop road, my buddy Matt Maness and I wound down the mountain on a trail that descended in long, sweeping switchbacks. When I finally got a glimpse of the creek below the falls, I could see a boulder-filled run, just wide and straight enough for a back cast. I've fished this stretch of the southern Appalachians for more than 30 years, but I'd never fished this stretch of creek. I could almost smell the trout. I looked over at Matt.

"Told you," he said.

We moved downhill, into a percussive growl of falling water that rose through rhododendrons on cool currents of air. At each turn in the trail, I could see down through tall red oaks and yellow poplar. It looked untouched and primeval, but I knew that wasn't the case. Across the Appalachians, from Alabama to Maine, nearly every slope of Eastern woodlands was once timbered, nearly every stream choked with slash. A century ago, these mountains were ground down to their bones and sinews and tendons, "sucked and gutted, milked dry, denuded of its rich primeval treasures," wrote Thomas Wolfe, who saw the destruction firsthand.

Yet today, there's a sense of forgiveness in these deep gorges and hardwood mountain coves, as if the forests have pardoned, for the moment, the sins of their oppressors. The towering forests over our trout creek disguised the sawn stumps that molder below. Trails that lead to many remote Appalachian trout runs or grouse coverts often follow the beds of long-gone logging roads. In the West, the value of wild places is partly writ in their expansiveness, their primal untouched qualities, the distance from the nearest hard road. But in these ancient mountains, beauty seems to root itself to an inextinguishable faith in the healing power of time. Wildness here is a deep, enduring temperament, not a metric measured by the mile. *Hang on*, these mountains seem to say. *Have faith*.

⌘

Matt and I traded runs until thunder grumbled over the ridge and the water started to rise. With time running out, I climbed toward a large pool hemmed in by a giant boulder slab that nearly spanned the canyon floor. With the fly rod in one hand, I felt with the other for fingerholds in rock smoothed by 12,000 years of moving water while my felt soles skittered on old-growth rock lichen. Three casts went ignored, but I knew there were fish to be had. When a small yellow caddisfly zipped by my face, I downsized my fly with the palest caddis in the box. Fish in these remote freestone streams aren't typically so picky, but fish tend to tell you how picky they want to be.

On the next cast, a wild brown trout slurped the fly. This fish had plenty of places to go, and plenty of line-breaking logs and ledges under which to hide. I steered it clear of the gnarly stuff three times, babying the light tippet, then cradled the wild, 10-inch trout in my hand as I backed out the hook.

When the fish slipped from my fingers, it held tentatively in the slow flow of the tailout, then darted upstream toward a mossed-over boulder that jutted like a gray-green knuckle into the pool. The fish knew right where it wanted to be. The trout finned to hold itself steady in the main flow of current, then slid sideways and out of sight. It was back in its place, and I turned around and headed downstream, searching, more intently than ever these days, for mine.

Scout's Honor

At one point I was on my hands and knees, squirreling through a tunnel gnawed in a curtain of greenbrier. For the moment it was the only way forward, and while it's hard to imagine that any creature larger than an opossum could make its way through this wormhole in the thicket, the deer tracks told a different story. The buck came this way.

That's the way it works with swamp deer. The fact that it seems nearly impossible to move makes it all the more likely that the deer came this way. The vines were chewed off in blunted ends; deer literally ate this trail. And the old rubs on the fattest saplings told me that at least one good buck knew about the route. I had been at it for an hour, and I was going to figure out where the trail led.

This is what whitetail deer hunters do. We wade the creeks, climb the ridges, scour the distant corners of the lease. We think like a deer. Look for acorns. Look for sheds. Look for gnawed-off honeysuckle. We obsess. All year long we wonder about the deer. Where are they feeding, drinking, sleeping, moving? How can I intersect their world? We walk deer ground when we can. We crawl it when we must.

That's what separates my deer hunting from my bird-watching and my canoe camping and even my fishing. I'm not here to spectate, to relax, or to have a good time necessarily. Not at the core. I hunger to enter this other world where whitetails sift through the thickets, where they breed and live and die. I want to play a part in that hidden drama and make my own mark, no matter how small.

It begins with scouting.

~

I only recently joined the Stillwater Hunt Club, so I'm the newbie. I have my work cut out. The club leases nearly 4,000 acres of swamp woods, pine plantation, and checkerboard farm fields, so it's difficult just trying to keep from getting turned around—not lost, never lost—much less trying to dial in on a couple of tucked-away stand sites that haven't already been discovered.

I started the way most of us do, the easy way: walking the field edges, the power-line cuts, and farm paths, looking for deer tracks, droppings, and subtle trail openings there. That didn't last long, though. I've never been much of a field hunter. I like to watch a deer move through the woods, weaving around the blowdowns, feeding on gum fruits, scratching an ear with a hind foot. Just being a deer. Often, there are long moments during which I don't even know if I'm going to pull the trigger. Sometimes the moment just doesn't feel right. What a pretty morning to be a wild deer in the woods. It's your lucky day, old girl. I can wait. I rarely regret it.

Other times I know the instant I see the whitetail that she's going home in the back of the truck. I rarely regret that, either.

I picked up this trail a few hundred yards away, in a creek bottom where a stand of wrist-thick trees grew as dense as the bristles on a hairbrush. This country doesn't make it easy. My buddies and I get a kick out of conventional deer hunting advice that prompts hunters to search out bedding cover, feeding cover, transition zones, and staging areas. In this neck of the South, two-thirds of the landscape is edible, and a deer can stand up from its bed—that's edible, too—and snack on basket-oak acorns, honeysuckle vines, persimmons, and fox grapes, then finish up with a fiber-rich mouthful of greenbrier, all while simply spinning in a circle. Pinch points? Funnels? In a 100-acre clear-cut?

That helps explain the allure of a beanfield. Which, for a guy who likes the woods, makes it that much more critical to find the spot.

—⁓—

I'd abandoned hope of dry feet early on, wading through waist-deep beaver sloughs, pouring the water out of my knee boots, and squishing through the woods. The trail, still faint but growing more distinct as more deer joined the flow, rose out of the creek bottom to arrow through an overgrown patch of pine plantation, then seemed to stop at the garish curtain of greenbrier. I was pushing through it, on hands and knees, when I fell forward hard on my elbows and tumbled into another world.

The brier thicket gave way, suddenly, to a small glade off a corner of the beanfield. When I looked around, I knew in an instant: Stepping gingerly out of the greenbrier, the deer would have their heads down. They'd make a slight right turn to get around a big water oak, then look toward the field edge, drenched with sunlight. That's the moment, I thought. I can climb that holly. Disappear in its swirl of branches, green all season long. Look down at the whitetail shaking off the last of the grasping thorns. Come November, this is the place.

Now, hidden in the holly, I carefully ease the bolt forward. It's been a long five months, dreaming of my spot.

THE HEALING HUNT

I didn't fully understand until later. Not until the day was done, and I was leaning against the truck and waiting for Tommy to walk out of the dove field.

It had been a rainy, nasty, post-hurricane dove opener. When I picked up Tommy Krisulewczs at his house, we both felt it. The storm was scrambling our plans. No one would spend the night at Stillwater. There would be no late night by the bonfire, no big feed with Greg's funky white Alabama barbecue sauce, and no caravan of trucks storming the field at dawn. There would be none of the pageantry and community that typically marks our opening-day dove hunt.

But I haven't missed a dove opener since 1980, when I went home with a college buddy over Labor Day weekend and shot my first dove. That bird spiraled down into cut corn and red clay mud, and there was laughter all around the field and a pig picking afterward. It was the first time I'd ever hunted in a big group. In the years since, I've hunted opening day when I had nowhere else to go but crowded public fields, and I've hunted when "hunting" meant pulling a pickup truck into a borrow pit and sniping doves as they flew in to pick grit. I never miss opening day. So it was just me and Tommy and my little Lab, Minnie, driving east in a hard, gray rain.

The storm wasn't the only thing that had fouled my mood. Work was a mess. I was behind on deadlines, juggling projects as all the balls fell at once. It didn't help that it was my first opening-day hunt in a decade without my son, Jack, who was away at his freshman year in college. There are times when you just feel sorry for yourself. I had worked till nearly midnight on Friday night and was staring at a laptop at 6:45 a.m. on opening-day morning. I opened the refrigerator for cereal milk, and the duck breasts and wild pig loin I'd planned to cook at the club were dull lumps on a plate. Outside, the rain pounded.

Tommy's phone call had been a pinprick of light. Hell or high water, he was hunting too. On the drive to the dove field, he told me that he'd just returned from three days at the Mayo Clinic in Minnesota—his third round in the ring with prostate cancer. I told him I was sorry, that I hadn't known. He said he needed a day under the sky, rain or no rain, and the smell of gunpowder and fresh dirt.

For the first time in days, I felt a little lucky: Minutes from the sunflower field, the rain tailed off to a mist. By the time we pulled the guns from the cases, the sky was clearing. The storm had passed. Minnie bounded ahead, so excited that she ran with a stilted, bow-legged gait, pissing on the run.

In a field turned sweltering and steamy, the birds went crazy. Bottled up through 36 hours of hurricane slop, they rained into the sunflowers low and fast. The shooting was stupid. Minnie held steady with each downed bird, flanks tremoring with anticipation before vaulting through the field.

On my 5-gallon bucket, I thought about that little dog and all our mornings together, and how lucky I was to have my farmer friend, Robert, who let us have his dove field after the club hunt fell through. I thought about the way a dove hunter can recognize a dove in flight a quarter mile away by its arrowed trajectory and the long tail feathers and stout chest that you sense almost subconsciously. I thought about Jack at his first college football game as a student. Slowly, like clouds breaking, I began to understand how wonderful it all was.

Across the field, Tommy whooped with every bird he shot. There was no ring of triumph in his shouts. Each sounded like a cry of gratitude, hurled to the sky for the gift of this day.

Minnie picked up fourteen of my fifteen birds. We walked back to the truck, and I leaned against the tailgate as she rolled in a cow pie, and I swear I heard my own voice: *Remember this. Remember what it feels like to lose yourself in the moment of the hunt, in the healing power of something that requires all of yourself—mind, body, spirit.* I thought of how Tommy hadn't whooped in the last few minutes, and how I bet he'd limited out too. I thought of how I hadn't fussed about work for one single second. *Remember what you never thought about.*

As I watched Tommy make his way through the sunflowers, my phone beeped. A text came in, a last benediction. "Happy opening day, Pops."

The Descent

The idea that there are two Alaskas came to me in a cold wave as my canoe was swept into the toppled trees and I was thrown overboard. I caught a glimpse of my pal, Scott Wood, sprinting toward me across a gravel bar, knowing that this was what we had feared the most. Wood disappeared into the brush, running for my life, and then the river sucked me under and I did not see anything else for what seemed like a very long time.

Every angler dreams of Alaska. My dream was of untouched waters, uncountable salmon and trout, and an unguided route through mountains and tundra. But day after day of portages and hairy paddling had suggested that mine was a trip to the other Alaska, a place that suffers no prettied-up pretense. The other Alaska is not in brochures. It is rarely in dreams. The other Alaska will kill you.

We'd had plenty of postcard moments, for sure: king salmon jetting rooster tails over gravel bars. Tundra hills pocked with snow. Monster rainbows and sockeye salmon heaving for oxygen as we held their sagging bellies. But day after day the four of us had paddled through the other Alaska, scared to death, except when the fishing was good enough to make us forget the fear.

Now the world turned black and cold as the Kipchuk River covered me, my head underwater, my arm clamped around a submerged tree, my body pulled horizontal in the hurtling current. Lose my grip and the river would sweep me into a morass of more downed trees, so I held on even tighter as water filled my waders. The river felt like a living thing, attempting to swallow me, inch by inch, and all I could do was hold my breath and hang on. But I am getting ahead of the story.

Give me a canoe, paddle, portage pack, and time, and I can make it down almost any river. For years I've considered this a given, and remote rivers have been my express route to fish that have never seen a fly.

It may be that no one had attempted what we set out to do last July: Complete a 10-day unguided canoe descent of southwestern Alaska's Kipchuk and Aniak Rivers. These are isolated headwaters in the extreme: To get bodies and gear on the ground required five flights in two-person Piper Cub and Super Cub bush planes. Our largest duffels carried 17-foot PakBoats—folding canoes on aluminum frames—which I figured to be our masterstroke.

This was part of the dream too: Instead of a ponderous raft, I'd paddle a sleek canoe, catching eddies and exploring side channels. Or so I'd planned.

There were four in the party: myself, photographer Colby Lysne, my friend Edwin Aguilar, and Scott Wood, who more times than not can be found in the other end of whatever canoe I inhabit. Dropping through tundra, we'd first negotiate the Kipchuk through a 1,000-foot-deep canyon. Then we'd slip into the Kuskokwim lowlands, where the river carves channels through square-mile gravel bars and unravels in braids until it flows into the larger Aniak. Some of the most remote country left in Alaska, it is the second-largest watershed in the state, with just a handful of native settlements. We timed our launch for a shot at four of the five Alaska salmon species— kings, pinks, sockeyes, and chums—with a wild-card chance for coho and the Alaska Grand Slam of salmon. We'd been counting our fish for months.

Truth be told, though, no one really knew what to expect on the Kipchuk. According to our bush pilot, less than a handful of hunting parties raft the upper river each year. He'd heard of no one who'd fished above the canyon, ever. As for the paddling conditions—well, he said, it all looked workable from the windshield of a Super Cub. But we weren't paddling a plane.

The first test came fast, just after put-in. A fallen spruce blocked the channel, with barely enough room to shoulder past. The obstacle looked easy enough to handle, but the water was swift and heavy, and the laden boats were slower to react than we'd imagined. Wood and Aguilar fought to cross a racing tongue of current and were carried straight for the spruce. Watching from upstream, I could hear Wood barking over the rush of water—"Draw right! Right! Harder! Harder!"—as the canoe slipped closer to the tree. They cleared by inches. Wood glanced at us, knowing what we were in for.

"So," Lysne said, his eyes on the water. "That didn't look so good."

Already we were feeling our handicap. With a flyover scouting report of no whitewater, Wood and I had dialed back the level of paddling experience we expected from our partners. Lysne and Aguilar had plenty of remote camps in the bag, but they'd never been whitewater cowboys. Cocksure with a canoe paddle, I figured—as did Wood—that we could handle whatever came up from the stern. What came up was a paddler's worst nightmare: miles of strainers. Where sharp turns occur, the current undercuts the channel's outside bank. As the bank collapses, trees fall, wedging against the shore. Water gets through, but a canoe carried into a strainer has little chance of remaining upright—and a body slammed into the underwater structure has little chance of escape.

Rattled, Lysne and I slipped into the fast water and tried to crab the boat sideways with short draw strokes. A big-handed North Dakota hockey player, Lysne tackles obstacles with a brawler's bravado—a frame of mind that would pay off later. I started to yell as we neared the strainer, and for a second I caught Wood's concerned look, knowing that in the next moment, the boat would tangle sideways in the spruce and our fishing trip would turn into a rescue operation.

I paddled the strongest half dozen strokes of my life as the spruce boughs raked across Lysne's shoulders and caught me in the chest. We pulled away, inch by inch. My heart was pounding. We sidled up to the other PakBoat.

"We cannot capsize," Wood said, his face intense. "You know that. We simply cannot capsize."

That night we calmed our nerves with Scotch and pan-fried Arctic grayling, whose bodies had spilled out whole mice when we cleaned them a few hundred feet from our campsite. Wine-red shapes coursed up the pool—king salmon that ignored our flies. But it was early. With each paddle stroke, the fishing should only get better, the paddling easier. I crawled into the tent feeling like a dog clipped by a car. Tomorrow, we figured, it would all come together.

But tomorrow was the day the canyon closed in.

This stretch of the river was filled with more dread and sweat than we'd bargained for—and far less fishing. Every turn in the Kipchuk was a blind bend. Every bend was lined with downed trees. And each time the river narrowed, a chute of blistering midstream flow formed a hard wall of current that threatened to flip the boats.

We were also running a different kind of uncharted waters. Though Wood and I have been to spots where getting through the country proved difficult and dangerous, never had we experienced day after day of serious peril. We wanted the Alaskan wilds, and we didn't mind pain and sweat for a payoff of unknown country. A taste of fear was part of the price. But on the Kipchuk, we were gagging on terror.

～

"There was a time," Wood said, standing on the bank three days into the canyon, "when I liked being scared in the woods. It made it all seem so . . . real." His voice trailed off, and his gaze followed downriver. I knew where his thoughts were taking him. Mine were already there. Home. Wife. Children. "I don't like being scared anymore," he said.

Lysne and I pushed the canoe into the river without saying a word. I could only imagine what he was thinking. Lysne never complained, never pointed out that he'd signed on to photograph a fishing trip, not an adrenaline rush down a rain-swollen river. I didn't voice the thoughts coursing through my own head. The cheerful scouting report notwithstanding, I'd had no business putting inexperienced paddlers in such remote, unknown water. My arrogance was shameful, and the dangers were accruing. Humping gear and dragging boats through 20-foot-tall thickets, where a feeding bear would be invisible at 10 feet, was a necessity. But that's the seduction of wilderness travel. Each time you come back, you think you can handle more. Until you can't.

Downstream, the river disintegrated. On the banks, water boiled through 10-foot-tall walls of downed timber as the Kipchuk careened around hairpin turns. Time and time again we roped the canoes around the roughest water, but too often the only choice was to carry everything. To portage the hairpins, we bushwhacked through thickets, taking turns as point man with the shotgun and bear spray. We hacked trails through streamside saplings. We fished in spurts—10 minutes here, 15 there. It took all we had just to keep going.

One night I crouched beside the campfire, nursing blisters and a bruised ego. My back felt like rusted wire. Lysne limped in pain, his toes swollen and oozing pus. I was tired of portaging, tired of paddling all day with little time for fishing, tired of fear. I watched Lysne take a swig of Costa Rican guaro.

"I have to be honest with you," he muttered. "I've had some dark times the last few days. Been f---ing scared and I'm not afraid to say it."

The night before, he said, he'd dreamed that we were paddling through a swamp, but it was inside somebody's garage, and a fluorescent alligator attacked the canoe.

"Weird, huh? I wonder where that came from."

The next morning I dragged myself out of the tent with a mission. Somewhere, downriver, the other Alaska waited.

"Today we paddle like madmen," I suggested.

"Yeah," Aguilar groused. "We need to quit being such slackers."

A few miles downstream we lined a run and dragged the canoes to the head of a deep pool the color of smoke and emeralds. A half dozen large fish held near the upstream ledge. I slid a rod out of the canoe. The first cast landed a pink salmon. My second brought in a chum. I hooted as Aguilar fumed and glanced at his watch.

"Ten minutes!" I pleaded. "I promise, just 10 minutes!"

He huffed and grabbed a rod. Fishing chaos broke out. Wood, Lysne, and I worked a triple hookup on salmon, our lines crossing. We fought sockeyes, kings, and wolf-fanged chum salmon. We landed a 3-pound grayling and a solid 26-inch rainbow. One fish ran up the rapids at the head of the pool, leaping like a silver kite. Another was so close that it splashed me. For the first time I felt the pieces coming together. The pull of strong fish was a poultice for ragged nerves and sore shoulders.

Eleven salmon steaks, slathered in chipotle sauce, sizzled over the fire that night.

"We deserved today," Aguilar said, lying back on a bed of rocks.

"Fishing is fun," added Wood. "We should try to do more of it."

—— ——

Late the next afternoon, we beached the boats to fish another salmon-choked pool, and in less than a minute we were shoulder to shoulder, working a quadruple hookup. Lysne cackled as my king ran under his bent rod.

It was a fine place to camp and a good time to call it quits, but I'm not fond of camping above a hairy rapid. Just below the pool, a pair of fallen spruce trees leaned over the main channel, then the river bent hard, the bank combed with strainers.

"Let's get this over with," I muttered. "We can celebrate when there's clear sailing ahead."

"Sure," Wood replied. "But we were first on the last horrible, terrible, death-for-certain river bend. You're up."

The next half minute, Wood would later say, seemed to last an hour. Entering the river, Lysne and I lined up with the route we'd hashed out. Once the laden canoe sliced into the main current tongue, however, it was propelled downstream with terrifying speed. Draw strokes didn't budge us. Pry strokes and stern rudders proved useless. I lost my hat as we rocketed under the timber. The craft arrowed into a wall of downed trees and suddenly we were tangled in branches, broadside to the current, water boiling against the hull.

"Don't lean upstream!" I screamed. Lysne didn't, but in the next instant the river swarmed over the gunwales anyway. The boat flipped, violently, and disappeared from view. The current sucked me under. I caught a submerged tree trunk square in the chest, a blow buffered by my PFD, and I clamped an arm around the slick trunk.

I can't say how long I hung there. Twenty seconds, perhaps? Forty?

For long moments I knew I wouldn't make it. With my free arm, I pulled myself along the sunken trunk as the current whipped me back and forth. But the trunk grew larger and larger. It slipped from the grip of my right armpit, and then I held fast to a single branch, groping for the next with my other hand. I don't remember holding my breath. I don't remember the frigid water. I just remember that the thing that was swallowing me had its grip on my shins, then my knees, and then my thighs. For an odd few moments I heard a metallic ringing in my ears. A vivid scene played across my brain: It was the telephone in my kitchen at home, and it was ringing, and Julie was walking through the house looking for the phone, and I suddenly knew that if she answered the call—Was the phone on the coffee table? Did the kids have it in the playroom?—that the voice on the other end of the line would be apologetic and sorrowful. Then the toe of my boot dragged on something hard, and I stood up, and I could breathe.

Wood crashed through the brush, wild-eyed, as I crawled up the bank, heaving water. I waved him downstream, then clambered to my feet and started running. Somewhere below was Lysne. The big-handed hockey player had gone overboard farther midstream than I had and vanished beyond the strainers. Stumbling through brush, I heard Wood give a cry, and my heart sank. I burst into sunlight. Wood was face down on a mud bar, where he'd catapulted after tripping on a root. Aguilar battered his way out of a nearby thicket. A few feet away, Lysne stood chest-deep in the river, with stunned eyes and mouth open. In his hand he gripped the bow line to the canoe, half sunk and turned on its side, the gear bags still secured by rope.

Our ragged little foursome huddled by the river, dumbstruck by the turn of events. For a long time we shook our heads and tried not to meet one another's gazes.

Wood finally looked at Lysne. "I can't believe you saved the boat."

"It was weird," Lysne said, his voice rising. "I popped out of the water and saw another strainer coming for me, and I just got pissed off. I was yelling to myself: I ain't gonna drown! I ain't gonna drown! I went crazy, punching and kicking my way through the trees. Then boom: I saw the rope, grabbed it, and started swimming."

I'd lost a shotgun, two fly rods and reels, and a bag of gear, but everything else that went into the river came out.

Aguilar sidled over, quietly. "You okay? I mean, in your head?"

Only then did I feel the river's grip loosen from my legs. I began to shiver, and no one said a word.

———

"Salmon. Salmon. Salmon-salmon-salmon." I was counting the kings passing under the boat. Sunlight streamed into the water, lighting up 15-, 20-, and 30-pound chinooks. Downstream, the Kuskokwim lowlands flattened out—no more canyon walls, no more bluffs: slow water and flat country and easy going.

In the bow, Lysne watched the fish and shook his head. "I just spent a week on the Russian River, shoulder-to-shoulder combat fishing," he said. "I can't believe nobody's here. And nobody's been here. And nobody's coming here. Amazing."

I settled into a cadence of easy paddling, the sort that lets the mind drift free. So far, the price of admission to a place where nobody goes had come close to a body bag. I wondered how much longer I'd be willing to shell out for the solitude. Back home were two kids and a wife and a life I've been lucky to piece together. With each year I have more to lose. I'm not ready for an RV and a picnic table, but I couldn't help but wonder if it was time to dial the gonzo back. I didn't know. I won't know, until I hear of the next uncharted river, the next place to catch fish in empty country, and ask myself: What now?

———

Late in the afternoon we slipped into a deep pool unremarkable but for the fifty kings, pinks, and chums queued up, snout to tail. For 15 minutes they ignored egg-sucking leeches, pink buggers, Clousers, mouse flies, saltwater copperheads, and even a green spoon fly, the go-to choice for hawg bass back home. Downstream, salmon darted across a gravel bar. We could see them coming from 100 yards away.

Wood reeled in and stomped off. He is not one to be snubbed by visible fish. "I'm gonna think outside the koi pond," he said, following grizzly tracks up the sandbar. Ten minutes later we heard a whoop from inside shaking willows. The tip of a fly rod protruded from the thicket, arcing into the water. "Bring your cane poles, boys," Wood hollered.

Worming his way through the brush, Wood had flipped a fly into the gravy train of salmon. It didn't work right away. But ultimately, a pig king had sauntered over to slurp it. No casting, no stripping was required—you just had to keep the fly away from the tykes and hold on. Some of the fish were enormous. Dangling my rod over the salmon, I tried five drifts, ten, no takers, fifteen drifts with the pink leech jigged fractions of an inch from the mouths of fish. They stared, looking, looking, l-o-o-o-king, until one sucked it down.

Cackling and howling, the four of us caught king after king, taking turns in the hole. No one cared that this was artless fishing. Dumbed-down salmon whacking was what we needed. A half hour later, Lysne hooked a brute of a king. The 30-pound chinook never showed until Lysne fought it into the shallows. I went in up to my armpits to land it. My hands barely reached around the base of the tail. Lifting the fish was like pulling a log out of the water. When I handed it to Lysne, he groaned. "We've got to camp right here," he said and grinned. "I don't think I can lift a paddle after this."

Behind him, chum salmon leapt in the air, and kings sent more rooster tails skyward, their backs out of the water. We flopped on the sandbar and fired up a stove. Mist turned into rain as we scrounged the food bag, poured out the juice from a can of smoked mussels, and sautéed jerk-seasoned sockeye in the makeshift frying oil.

Not 3 feet away, a single chum salmon labored upstream. This one was far past spawning. The sight struck me silent: The fish was rotting, its flanks pale and leprous, the spines of its dorsal and tail fins sticking out above the flesh like the shattered masts of a toy sailboat.

<p style="text-align:center">~~~</p>

The next three days brought the Alaska of my dreams. Now the fish came in schools so large that they appeared as burgundy slicks moving up current. There was nothing easy about coaxing them to a fly, and nothing easy about bringing them to hand. We killed one fish a day, enough to eat like kings. One afternoon I was lying back on rocks near grizzly and wolf tracks so fresh that the prints had not yet dried. "This is what I thought it'd be like every day," Aguilar said. "But now, just one day of it feels so-o-o-o good."

We'd had moments of fish chaos—multiple hookups, the Cane Pole Hole, outrageous rainbow trout. But fishing remote Alaska isn't about the numbers, or the variety of species. It's about the way the fish are seasoned with fear, sweat, miscues, and the mishaps that are the hallmark of an authentic trip in authentic wild country.

On the night before our scheduled pickup, we camped at the juncture of the Aniak and a long, sweeping channel. After setting up the tents, Lysne cooled his heels. His toes were swollen and chinook-red from day after day of hard walking in waders.

"I can't even think about wading right now," he said. "I'm just gonna lie here and fish in my mind."

Wood, Aguilar, and I divvied up the water: They headed off to hunt rainbows down the side channel, while I fished a wide pool on the river.

Since I'd lost my rods and reels when our boat flipped, I fished a cobbled-together outfit of an 8-weight rod with a 9-weight line. It was a little light but heavy enough for the fish we'd landed over the last few days. In an hour of nothing, I made fifty casts to an endless stream of oblong shapes. Then suddenly my hot-pink fly disappeared. Immediately I knew: This was my biggest king, by far. The salmon leapt, drenching my waders, then ripped off line and tore across the current.

The rod bent into the cork, thrumming with the fish's power. I'd have a hard time landing this one solo, so I yelled for help, but everyone was long gone.

So I stood there, alone and undergunned, and drank it all in. It no longer mattered if this was my first or fifteenth or thirtieth king salmon. What mattered was that wild Alaska flowed around my feet and pulled at the rod, and I could smell it in the sweet scent of pure water and spruce and in the putrid tang of the dying salmon. I felt it against my legs, an unyielding wildness. Part of what I felt was fear, part of it was respect, and part of it was gratitude that there yet remained places so wild that I wasn't sure I ever wished to return.

Then the king surfaced 5 feet away and glimpsed the source of his trouble. At once the far side of the river was where the salmon wanted to be, and for a long time there was little I could do but hang on.

SOMETHING IN THE NIGHT

Since neither of us were old enough to drive, my buddy Vernon Hedgecock and I would walk to Oak Hollow Lake, jump the locked gate, and fish from a dock's dark end where the security lights didn't reach. Many a night I lay there half asleep with one eye cracked open for a patrol car and the fishing line between my toes so I would wake up with the bite. I cut my fishing teeth in the darkest hours of the night, and I still love to pound a lake or creek when it's just me, the bats, and a few bellowing bullfrogs. I love wading in the dark. I love the scary feel of the canoe bumping some unseen log. DEET in my nostrils brings back delicious memories. Some from years gone by. Some from just last week.

August is the time to roll out when the sun goes down. It's the time to find a whitefly hatch on a bronzeback river and work popping bugs in the black dark. It's the time to lob big, nasty streamers into big, nasty log-jams where big, nasty brown trout prowl. It's the time to work a Jitterbug over every square inch of a 2-acre farm pond—its *gluk-gluk-glukking* the soundtrack of a summer childhood. Few things can beat sunrise on the water. One of them is moonlight.

~ ❦ ~

Mr. BoBo turned me on to night fishing, which is a little odd since I never fished with him. Most of the neighborhood kids knew of Mr. BoBo because he was once bitten by a copperhead but refused to see a doctor. He sat on his front porch for weeks while his foot swelled up and split open like a watermelon you dropped from your bike. This was back before zombies and video games and even Tammy Faye Bakker, and the sight of human flesh in gruesome condition could keep young boys up at night.

But I was intrigued by Mr. BoBo's overnight disappearances. He'd head out early on Friday evenings, and I'd watch the tips of his cane poles and fiberglass rods wave as he drove away, sticking out of the rolled-down rear window of his Ford Galaxie 500. Some nights I'd sprawl out in bed and imagine that mysterious world of lantern light and men's hushed voices, cigarette smoke and fish pulling hard in the dark.

On Saturday afternoons, Mr. BoBo would pull back into his driveway, and I'd bolt out the screen door and run over to peer into a 5-gallon bucket slam full of catfish, bass, bluegills, and the occasional eel. What I remember most was Mr. BoBo nailing those cats to a pine tree with eightpenny nails, slicing around their heads with a Case jackknife, and pulling off their hides with steel pliers. Mr. BoBo recognized a kindred spirit, and long before I ever globbed a worm on a hook I learned to skin catfish at the old man's side.

Which led me straight to the lonesome dark pier on Oak Hollow Lake. Night fishing was a simple affair back then. Vernon and I carried two rods apiece, max. A tin of hooks and lead split shot we mashed with our teeth. I don't carry much more today. If I'm on the move, I take one rod and a small chest pack loaded with a half dozen lures. That old Jitterbug still does the trick, and a big black spinnerbait is good medicine for covering lots of water fast. I'm not a big fan of snap-swivels, but they're handy in the dark. If I'm hunkered down, old-school style, on a dark dock or pier, I'll upgrade to circle hooks. I land more fish and gut-hook virtually none. A small LED rod-tip light will alert me to a bite. I no longer worry about tipping off the po-po.

It doesn't take long to get back into the groove of night fishing—it's like riding a bike—even after a long winter in the deer woods and spring's six-week mish-mash of chasing turkeys and shad. I walk to the water's edge and fire off a cast. I hear the line zinging through the guides, and I'm so in tune with it all that I can feel the lure arcing toward the stars and darting back down to earth. I don't even have to hear it hit the water.

It all takes me back to those Mr. BoBo days. And those nights, shared with fireflies and cicadas and my first Ugly Stik, and my mind skipping like a stone between how I was going to pull off the three-point turn on my driver's test and whether Jill Zimmerman would say yes to a Friday-night football game date or shoot me down cold. Heavy thoughts in those fast-moving days. A lot on my mind for an August night, and—Whoa! My toes are tingling. I think I have a bite.

MY BOY JACK

As we turn our backs to the glow of the truck's headlights, the still deer lies half darkened underneath our shadows. Blood flecks its muzzle like beads of rain. Mud coats the hindquarters—it was no easy drag up the hill. The air is steeped with the earth-and-sweat musk of a buck in rut.

My 7-year-old son, Jack, holds one hind leg as I open the belly with a knife turned blade up. The skin tears open with the sound of a zipper. Jack's eyes are like moons. He talked nonstop during the long sit in the stand and during the hour after the gunshot and the dragging to the old barn. But he has not said a word since I handed him the hoof to hold. He has seen deer before in the wild, hanging under the deck, on the butcher table in our basement, and on his dinner plate. He has not seen deer like this.

I point out the liver, the bladder, the windpipe, and the rope of intestines. "Where's the heart?" Jack asks.

With one hand I part the red lungs, clasped together like a mussel shell. The bullet tunneled through the upper lobes, pulverizing the tissues that stain my hands and wrists. I remove the heart and wipe it clean of blood. It is dark and hard, unlike the other organs that seem to quiver of their own accord.

"That's a heart?" he asks.

I nod. He looks at it for a moment.

"Cut it open."

This is a startling request, and I hesitate for it seems almost sacrilegious. But when a little boy is struck with wonder, there's no time to trifle, and I want this moment to go wherever my son wishes to take it. I cleave the heart with the knife, top to bottom, so the two halves sag open in my palm. The hollows of the interior chambers are dark. I squeeze the heart to show Jack how it works—how it pumps blood from the lungs through the heart and then out the arteries that branch, again and again, into the dendritic vessels that feed each cell of the body.

He's quiet at first, and I fear I've lost him. "Just like ours?" he asks, low and husky like he speaks sometimes. I hear in his voice the man he will become.

"Just like ours," I say.

━ ～

An hour earlier Jack and I had decided, independently and simultaneously, that this hunt was a disaster.

After only 15 minutes in the stand, Jack is miserable. The joy and adventure of driving to the farm and walking to the stand wear off quickly, like bad paint. The unexpected glee of watching the woods with a bird's-eye view lasts 10 minutes, the challenge of staying still becomes a tiring game after another five. Then the fidgeting begins in earnest.

Jack is a world-class fidgeter. Tell him to hold his hands still, and he will twitch his legs. Admonish him for that, and he will move his lips, tongue, or eyelids. Next he begins tapping the curtain of camouflage netting at the front of the blind with the toe of his boot. The perforated sheet ripples in waves.

"Be still, Jack." I whisper. "You have to be still."

"I'm trying, Daddy."

This buys a half minute of stealth. Suddenly he pivots to the left, arms flying.

"Didja hear that?" he asks. "Is that a deer?"

On the forest floor I see the shadow of a squirrel scurrying up the shadow of an oak. I close my eyes and exhale. "Jack." My stern tone surprises even me. "*Still.*"

"I am. *I am, Daddy.*"

He wants so much to enter the late-light, live-action, loaded-rifle world of my hunting life. It's the only aspect from which he's absent. Together, we scout before the season, check the ladders on the tree stands, and visit the places where I tell him, *One day, I bet this is where you'll get your first deer.* He rushes to the truck when I return from evening hunts. "Whaddup, Dad? Get one?" Headed for bed, he spies my gear piled by the front door. "High-five, Dad," he says. "Good luck tomorrow." But it's not the same as being there.

Still, I've fretted that this is all happening too soon. He is only 7 years old. Most of the time, I can't imagine that he could stay still long enough for a deer to wander into range. I wonder if he is ready for the visceral reality of a deer on a gambrel. I finally relent. The reason is simple: He is my son, and I want him with me as badly as he wants to go.

Jack's body and mind continue to revolt against the strictures of stealth. He cannot be still. He cannot be quiet. Nobody's having fun, and nobody's going to kill a deer. But I decide to ride it out, because the last thing I want is to make Jack feel as if he's ruined our first deer hunt together. I figure we'll suffer through an hour of falling light and possibility, and head home.

What also keeps me in the stand is the perfect scene below us. It's the last week of October—a time when nights are cold and dew blankets the grass at dawn. So many acorns are on the ground that we turned our ankles during the walk in. The woods floor is pocked with patches of pawed earth. Rubs glint yellow-white along the creeks. It is prime time to catch a buck off guard and paying little mind to fidgets. It's also a good time to hunt hard and long and make few movements and fewer mistakes.

Jack taps the shooting rail with the button of his sleeve. *Clink. Clink-clink.* I clench my teeth. It's not about me. I remind myself. This is all for him. But my desire to show him a deer from this stand is much greater than his own to see one, if only for the fact that Jack doesn't yet know the thrill of watching a whitetail buck wind through the woods at 100 yards, nose to the leaves, prodded by urges this young boy cannot appreciate.

Clink.

"Be *still.*" I hiss. "Please, Jack. Please."

"I'm trying, Daddy. I promise."

He looks up at the sky, lips quivering. I didn't want this to be hard. I wanted Jack to want every aspect of the hunt. But I had moved too quickly in one other aspect of mentoring a hunter. Not long after giving Jack a BB gun at Christmas, I let him shoot my aptly named Remington Speedmaster. After our carefully paced sessions with the lever-action BB gun—and constant safety lectures—Jack stood on a creek bank, my arms cradling his own, hip-firing the .22 semiauto into a mudbank with monumental glee. The appeal of a single-shot BB vanished. I had shown him too much, too soon.

Now I'm worried I've made the same mistake with deer hunting. Long minutes creep by. There is little to keep Jack interested. A woodpecker stops for a moment on a nearby snag. A chickadee visits. But that's all. It is the season of shortening days, falling leaves, and fattening up for the coming winter, but there is not so much as a squirrel in view. Eventually, I decide that this is ridiculous. We are both miserable, and relief is as close as a five-minute drive to the White Swan for some sweet tea. I start to rise and glance down at Jack. His head is drooped to his chest. His fingers, finally stilled, are interlaced in the overly long netting of camouflage gloves. I elbow him in the shoulder.

"Jack," I whisper. "Hey, don't fade out on me."

He throws up a quick hand in a quieting gesture. Another few seconds pass before he looks up through the gap in his face net. "I wasn't sleeping, Dad," he says. "I was praying to God to send us a big buck."

I throw an arm around his shoulders and hug him. For the moment, the trees could turn to 10-pointers and flee at the offending movements for all I care.

— —

Jack is eventually dragged down by boredom and slumps across my left thigh, resting his head in my lap. I rub his back in small circles, feeling the swell of his breaths in my palm, and for a moment I think, *A busted hunt and a wasted afternoon, but let's make the best of what's left.*

One of the most rewarding skills a father can develop is an ability to recognize, as he receives them, the unexpected and often inscrutable gifts from his children. I am only nudging my way into an understanding of this. The headline payoffs of parenting are hard to miss: the bedtime stories, the impromptu hugs, the finger-painted Father's Day frames constructed of Popsicle sticks. Not so obvious are the more cryptic gestures of love: the unquestioning faith that you can fix the toy, the searching glance toward the bleachers to make sure that you made it to the game. As I rub Jack's back, 16 feet high in a tree, with his body against mine, and an autumn sunset seeping into the woods, it suddenly seems a richness of experience that I can hardly bear. It shames me for my earlier impatience. Who but a hunter could rate such a gift? Who but a hunter's child could give it?

Then, a movement, unexpected yet instantly recognized, occurs. I tense as adrenaline floods my veins. A small doe enters my field of view at a slow run. She's just to the right of dead ahead—80 yards out and moving to the left, out of the thick ridge of brush and into the open cypress bottom. I watch her for a few seconds as she lopes through the open woods before I trace her route backward to the edge of the tangled brush. I let my eyes wait there. I have a good idea about what's coming.

"Get up, Jack," I whisper. "Ease up, man. Deer."

Jack rises with a startle, and we see the buck at the same time. He bursts into the open woods without a moment's hesitation: nose to the ground, hot on the track. He is purposeful and, thankfully, keenly concentrated on the young doe ahead.

"A buck, Dad! I see it!"

I already have the rifle up and the deer in the scope. He's moving steadily, visible only in the lanes between the big trees. I spot a sweeping curve of caramel-colored antler beam, which is long enough to quell any thought of passing on the animal. A nice buck with Jack to see it all—this could be an amazing moment.

Jack starts to giggle. "When are you gonna shoot it, Dad?" he whispers.

"Shhhh! Quiet, Jack. He needs to stop."

The buck is too far to even think about a moving shot. This needs to be a clean, quick kill and all the more so with Jack by my side. I whistle. The deer keeps moving. I whistle again. The buck skids to a stop. I search through the glass. A broad, dark pillar of bark is where the deer should be. I pick apart the jumble of branch and leaf in the scope. There. A mound of rump sticks out from the right side of the tree. I track the crosshairs left. A few inches of tine extend from behind the trunk. I hold on the far edge of bark and wait.

"Are you gonna shoot, Dad? What are you waiting for?"

"Quiet, Jack, he's looking for us."

"He's going to get away, Daddy! Shoot!"

"Jack, shut up!"

"Dad! You know we're not supposed to say that!"

The deer takes a step from behind the tree, and I fire. The buck runs again, keeping its same course, nose to the ground. A miss. What'd I hit? The tree? Some sliver of branch unseen through the scope? I jack the bolt and track the deer again. He moves right to left and angles slightly away. Suddenly, inexplicably, the buck stops in the open, and I sweep the scope across his flanks. I pull the trigger the moment the crosshairs settle on the ribs.

Fortune turns swiftly for the patient hunter. One moment there is only immobility, frigid toes, strained eyes, and second-guessing the long hours that could have been spent a hundred other ways. The next moment there he is, antlers gleaming, the animal that suddenly changes it all. So often it changes this way, and you can only wonder. *How?*

The deer lies on the ground, head and shoulders obscured by a tree. I watch through the scope. He is still. When I turn to Jack, his mouth is open wide. For a few moments he is silent. He looks at the deer, looks at me, and looks at the deer. His reverie doesn't last.

"We got him, Dad! We got him! Look! Ohmygosh! I can't believe we got him! We got him!" He throws his arm around my neck.

"Easy, Jack," I say, laughing. "Watch the gun."

"I can't believe it. Can we go see him? Right now?"

I glance at the still form on the forest floor. Of course we can.

We kneel next to each other beside the deer and pray as the wet woods seep into our knees like bloodstains. We offer thanks for the life we took and the life it gives, for the woods, for the yearning inside that leads us to places like this. If ever there were a time for ritual, this is it. It is as unselfconscious a moment as I can recall.

From here on out, the rest is work: the dragging, the lurching, the snagging of briers across arms and face. Jack insists on pulling his own weight, so I tie a small loop in the drag rope. He slips it over a shoulder. I grab a tine. We grunt all the way to the road.

Then we turn our backs to the truck's headlights, the still deer half darkened underneath our shadows. I pull out the knife and hand Jack a hoof. "Hold this," I say.

Later, as we climb back into the truck, Jack is still under the influence of utter amazement. "Dad, this is the most awesome thing to happen to me in my whole entire life."

I laugh. "It's pretty high up on the list for me, too, son." Then we turn off Rose Dairy Road and onto the hardtop, headed toward home with a gift that we will never again receive—our first deer.

CONSTANT COMPANION

It had to be one of the first ones made. Bear Archery produced its Black Bear recurve bow from 1972 to 1978, and for Christmas '72 I scored one as part of a set, with arrows, that my parents ordered from the *Sears Wish Book*. The first time I shot it, I was standing in the backyard in my pajamas, the Christmas Day sun barely over the treetops as I flung an arrow at a hay bale my daddy had placed there. With a 50-pound draw weight, the bow was too much for an 11-year-old to draw and hold, but I'd insisted on one heavy enough to kill a deer. And inch by inch, day by week by month, I worked into full draw. From then until I left home for college, I shot that Black Bear bow nearly every day.

For much of my youth, little mattered as much as a tight arrow group. When I could Robin Hood one cedar shaft with another, I stepped back five strides and started again. This was inside city limits, and kids rolling by on their way to football practice would holler out "Nature boy!" in derision. I shot through the jeers. Fifteen yards, 20 yards, 25.

I joined the Fred Bear Sports Club and roamed the woods behind the house, shooting stumps. I killed rabbits, squirrels, and a single dove I felled in flight with a flu-flu arrow tipped with one of those giant wire bird heads. I shot and shot—through acne and junior-high angst, and through the grief of my father's early death. Shot through the tears when Denise Gurley dumped me for Bill Jarrett. Thirty yards, 35. I shot until "nature boy" became a badge of honor.

I never killed a deer with that bow, but how I tried. In the 1970s, deer populations were rebounding in North Carolina, but getting one in bow range was no easy task. I hunted from the coastal plain to the Uwharrie Mountains, scaling trees with a homemade climbing stand. I eventually capitulated to a three-pin bow sight, and I honed Bear Razorheads on an Arkansas whetstone. But the closest I came to an arrow-killed deer was pulling up with my mentor, Keith Gleason, to a Gates County cornfield in the dark. Our pal Ed Crabtree stepped into the truck's headlights and held out an arrow smeared tip to nock with the blood of a deer he'd shot. During all those hours in the backyard, the concept of killing a big-game animal was abstract. But there's nothing abstract about a bloody arrow. I was so excited that after the next morning's hunt, I set up a portable target beside that very cornfield and shot and shot and shot.

In time, I upgraded to a compound bow and relegated that beloved Black Bear to bowfishing. Later in life, I stored it in an old hard case and hauled it from house to house. For more than 20 years it lay in dark corners of various basements, until I hung the bow in my son's room when he was little, a sort of talisman that I hoped had a power that could cross generations. I would pull it down now and then, after bedtime stories with Markie and Jack. In the dim glow of a night-light in the hallway, I would draw the bow, relax my grip, and aim an imaginary arrow.

That bow opened a door that led from my backyard inside city limits to a limitless world of woods and prairies and tundra. But it did more than turn me into a hunter. It taught me discipline. The value of process. The burden and reward of a single-mindedness of purpose.

At one point, early in my education as an archer, I wrote on an index card the steps to follow for a good shot and taped it on the flat of the limb that faced me at full draw so I could read them. That was more than 40 years ago, but some things don't change. Firm stance. Concentrate. Smooth pull. Follow through.

And take five steps back when the challenge is gone.

THE OUTER LIMITS

We drove south from Albuquerque, trailing the cottonwoods along the Rio Grande, down the old Spanish royal road that once stitched old Mexico City to old Santa Fe, down to the funky town of Truth or Consequences, and then east, over the high, piney Capitan Mountains to drop through the black lava fields of the Valley of Fires, the land of crusted ember.

It was a strange place for a duck trip. We sortied toward the Pecos River and Roswell, a town that attracts conspiracy theorists, UFO believers, and tourists who flock to gift shops selling alien dolls and scorpion-filled lollipops. We hunted hard and a little mean in a great southern arc across New Mexico's Chihuahuan Desert because hidden in the heat shimmer, in the sage, mesquite, rubber rabbitbrush, and wolfberry, in the marshes along the Rio Grande and Pecos Rivers, were the ducks.

And the ghosts. We never were far from the ghosts.

For my friend James Powell, this was a homecoming. He was born in Roswell and spent his early years in Albuquerque. He hunted mule deer with his father in the big woods around the family cabin near the iconic peak of Sierra Blanca, and his stepfather took him on waterfowling trips to the Bosque del Apache National Wildlife Refuge, on the Rio Grande, when he was 6 years old. At the White Sands Missile Range, where Powell worked as a young biologist, he ran vegetation transects across creosote flats and rattlesnake dens. He learned to love the marsh, he told me, "because when you're raised in the desert, a wetland seems like a miracle."

The passion paid off in unexpected ways. Powell is now chief of communications for Ducks Unlimited, and he and I have hunted together for years. We have a lot in common: jobs tied to a vibrant natural world, sons who share our love of feathers and marsh muck, and memories of fathers whose passion for the outdoors set the rudder angle of our own lives. Powell had been thinking of this road trip for a long time, and he regretted not pulling it off sooner. His father had passed away three years earlier, and James Powell the elder would have loved sharing this road again, and a few more desert sunrises, with his son.

"Now you and I can talk about this trip until one day all we can talk about is how much we wished we'd done it," Powell told me. "Or we can hit the road." He didn't have to ask twice. Shooting ducks, sharing old stories, and looking shoulder to shoulder into the past are precisely what friends are for.

Our sprawling loop traced a rough line along Powell's own history here, jumping from duck hole to duck hole from the Rio Grande to the Pecos. Each waterway is a long, linear oasis in an arid landscape. Enormous marshes unfurl for miles between the rivers and nearby mountains. The ducks, geese, and sandhill cranes that get this far south have their backs against the wall. They put down roots for the winter, and they get smarter with each passing day.

Which makes chasing waterfowl here a bit of a crapshoot. There's a lot of dry land between one decoy set and the other, which requires a lot of time behind the windshield—and a lot of miles and hours to muse on where the ducks might be out here in cowboy-and-alien country.

⚊ ⌒ ⌒

The first ducks were close, willing, and easy—although they required a down payment of sweat and scramble. Two hours before sunrise, we followed our guide's pickup truck down 2 miles of off-road switchbacks, deep into a half-dry lakebed, headlights boring through dense stands of mesquite and yucca. In the dark, we buried one truck to its chassis in soft sand. Digging it out put us way behind schedule, kicking off a mad sprint to beat the sunrise. Worn out before we even uncased the shotguns, we crawled into a pair of layout blinds half sunk in the muck. The lake's receding water left behind a crazy plain of sprawling cocklebur fields pocked with silty potholes. We were hemmed in by cactus and rock cliffs. It was as un-ducky a spot as I'd ever seen. And then the predawn light seeped up from the east.

Our first duck dropped in like every mallard should: early, courteous, and straight into the decoys. Powell and I fired together and rolled the drake into the muck. Duck number two was a northern shoveler. Hoisting it into the sun, I felt like I always feel about this ugly cousin of puddle ducks: Not the sharpest knife in the drawer, but it would be on every hunter's wall if not for the garden trowel attached to its face. A single pintail followed, dropping low from a flock of five, just in range. I can't tell you where the wigeon came from. One moment I was scanning the sky, on high alert. The next moment five birds were already in the decoys, wings set, like they were spat out of a deep mountain cave in the volcanic ridges above us. Powell and I scrambled to get a shot off, but the birds cartwheeled wildly behind us when they saw us move. My shotgun stock wasn't even near my shoulder when I pulled the trigger.

"All yours," I said to Powell, rubbing my bicep, when he brought the duck back to the blind.

"That's a nice bird."

Five ducks, five species. I started getting greedy. This far south, it's possible to shoot birds that rarely venture farther north. *Come on, cinnamon teal*, I thought. *Bring it on home, Mexican mallard.* A pale hunting moon hung high in the sky, and I took it as an omen that our luck would hold.

But it was the sun that did us wrong. At first it was a trio of pintails that flared off the layout blinds, and I consoled myself with the thought that it was just pintails acting like pintails. Then flocks of mallards gave us a wide berth. I looked around. Our layouts cast black shadows 5 feet long. The decoys were as lifeless as roadkill. Now even the wigeon swung far to the south to skirt out of range. For the next hour, not a single duck gave us a look as we broiled in the sun. Powell and I made a pact: One more duck, and then we'd jet for the nearest air conditioning.

An hour and a half later, a single bird rocketed over the slough from behind, startling Powell and me out of a half-snooze. I watched the single make a great, looping flight far beyond our boot tops, lost it against the dark bulk of a tall mesa, and then grinned when it rose into the blue sky, its slender silhouette turning on scimitar wings. Powell chuckled. "All yours," he said.

"Hello, Mr. Spoonie," I said, slipping the shotgun to my shoulder. "It had to be you."

After our mixed-bag hunt outside Truth or Consequences, Powell and I stepped on the gas. We had a four-hour drive to Roswell and the marshes along the Pecos River, but it's a road tripper's dream route: In San Antonio, we ate at the Owl Bar & Cafe, whose famous green-chile burgers fueled the work of atomic scientists in the mid-1940s as they fine-tuned the world's first nuclear bomb. We scouted the Smokey Bear Historical Park, where the eponymous bruin was rescued as a cub after a fire in 1950 and laid to rest 26 years later. We took a tour of Lincoln, its buildings still bearing bullet holes from Billy the Kid's 1878 jailbreak. Then, falling out of the Capitan Mountains, the world turned to bunchgrass, rocks and dirt, and busted windmills. Soybean fields sprouted old adobe houses and abandoned Minuteman missile sites with their silo doors rusted open. I saw the first alien on a billboard a few miles from town, grinning over an ocotillo cactus. "Welcome to Roswell," Powell said. "It's feeling ducky already."

And feeling more like home to Powell, whose father attended the New Mexico Military Institute in Roswell. "Believe it or not," he said, "they still had a cavalry unit when he was there."

As it turned out, we could have used a few mounted scouts. Our next stop was Bitter Lake National Wildlife Refuge, which straddles the Pecos River where the Chihuahuan Desert butts up against the Southern Plains. The refuge can hold tens of thousands of ducks and geese, but we had meager intel to help us narrow our search. We scrambled in the late afternoon—all that green-chile-cheeseburger eating and Smokey the Bear rubbernecking had put a dent in our scouting time. With the sun dropping fast, we followed a coyote trail through big bluestem and head-high gamagrass on a hunch that yodel dogs would have as keen an interest as we did in finding a decent duck hole. Our hunch played out when we stumbled, literally, into a lush cattail-ringed marsh. It was duckless at sunset, but the pressure was on, so we rolled the dice the next day.

By midmorning, we hadn't felt ducky in hours, and we'd run out of patience, cold water, biscuits, and things to talk about. We were in one of the most promising-looking spots I've ever hunted, with a truck full of gear and a few square miles of empty to explore. But nothing was flying at Bitter Lake. There were no birds on the slough, the sky was so clear and blue it hurt to look up, and there wasn't enough wind to make a candle flame twitch. It was one of those days where you'd stay home if you were home. But we were on the road and, ducks or no ducks, we were there to hunt.

I sat in our cattail sauna and stewed. I could feel the bad mojo rising inside. I take a lot of pride in preparation. I have a Plan A, Plan B, and multiple variants of Plan C queued up at all times. There's something about ducks that hits me differently than any other quarry. I don't like to work so hard for nothing. Beside me in the marsh, Powell thumped his shoulder against mine. "I feel Bad Eddie coming on," he said. We've hunted together enough for him to recognize the dark clouds. "Nobody wants to see Bad Eddie."

"One duck, man," I said. "That's all I'm asking for."

So we sat and hoped, and then I ran out of hope too.

"Give me an hour," I said. "Then we can go." I stood up, grabbed my pack, and pulled three decoys out of the spread. I headed up the slough, sloshing toward a meager cove a few hundred yards away. A small point of thick willows pushed into the open water. I'd been chewing on the spot for an hour.

Maybe that's all it would take. Shake things up. Change something, if just our angle on hope. I tossed two decoys into the main slough and a single into the cove, then hunkered down in a scrim of dead willow in the water. No bucket, no call, just three decoys and a pocket of shells. Over the next two hours I saw only two ducks, each one zipping up the far side of the slough. I got down lower, making myself as tiny as possible, until the water lapped over the back of my waders.

The choice was either hunt or bail. For another two hours, I hunted.

That night, Powell and I smoked cigars on our inn's porch while I tied large snap swivels to black paracord, fashioning a jerk cord, so tired from five days of burning both ends of the candle that I could barely work my fingers. I was kicking myself for not having a jerk cord in my pack that morning. It might have been all I needed. Could have pulled both those singles in. I couldn't remember the last time I hunted ducks without a jerk cord in a pack pocket. I sulked in a cloud of cigar smoke, spiraling downward into a foul duckless mood.

"How you doing over there?" Powell asked. "I think I might have to have some kind of intervention."

My friend knows me too well. I sat back and took a deep breath. Tighten up, I heard Bad Eddie say. We didn't come all this way not to kill ducks.

Waterfowling, of course, is an eternal fount of hope: Every night could be a migrating night. Every dawn brings another chance. Our last crack was at Bottomless Lake State Park, a complex of deepwater desert sinkholes and sloughs on the far side of the Pecos River outside Roswell. Months earlier, I'd put my fingers on a Google Earth image of the place and thought, *I bet we could kill a duck there*. I scrolled across the satellite map, following a dirt road to a path through the scrub, which skirted a green marsh. From there it looked like a straight shot of maybe 300 yards to a blob of open water. Might be a few trees in the way, I figured. Maybe a ditch or two. It didn't look too bad. Such is the delusion of the long-distance duck-hunting road tripper. From 1,500 miles away, everything looks easy.

Now, in the asphalt-black desert dark, I blinked at the OnX map in my hand. Where was the freaking water? We were sweating and breathing hard, and feeling a little stupid, dragging decoy sleds across hundreds of yards of crunchy bunchgrass and crumbling desert dirt. But after 45 minutes of searching, the eastern sky was going from black to blue. We had no options. Back toward the truck was a sliver of reflection, so we spun 180 degrees and headed for the only water we could find in a scrub desert of Pecos sunflower and salt cedar.

A half hour after daylight, we knew it wasn't going to happen. We put in a long sit filled with jokes and sweat-soaked shivers, but we were going through the motions. Neither of us wanted to quit, and we weren't just being hardheaded. On days like these, you stay in the marsh not so much because you think your luck will change, but because you know that something inside you will change if you fold the cards too early.

A few hours later, while dragging the decoys out of the desert marsh, I pulled ahead in the scrub, moping. There was no way around it: It had been a hard six days, and all we had to show for the trouble were eleven ducks that would fit into a single six-pack cooler. I was feeling licked and demoralized, and had no interest in bantering back and forth on the hump back to the truck. And that's when I remembered what another pal had said one time as we walked out of a deep hardwood cove in the Alabama turkey woods with nothing to show for our sweat.

"There's a difference between leaving the field empty handed," he said, "and leaving the field beaten."

Bad Eddie was wrong. We didn't come all this way just to kill ducks. We came all this way to chase good memories and pay our respects to the long roads behind, the ones that led us to lives filled with crazy dreams like an epic duck slam in the desert. Any road trip with a good friend brings a harvest you can't put on a plate.

And I couldn't leave the field beaten when I thought of some of that harvest. Like the gadwall that nearly took my head off. Remembering the moment, I laughed out loud for the first time in two days.

It was our third morning on the road, and I'd crumpled the duck high over the decoys. "Incoming!" Powell yelled a half second before I threw my arms over my face as the bird thumped like a meteorite into the muck 2 feet off my right shoulder, dead center between my layout blind and Powell's. By the time I poked my head out from under my arms, the gadwall was off like a roadrunner through the cocklebur.

I pushed out of the blind in hot pursuit, my unbuckled waders sagging around my knees. The duck crossed a slight rise, 40 yards away, silhouetted for a quick moment like a mule deer making a break over a ridgeline. Powell howled with laughter as my shot puffed sand a foot off the duck's right wing.

I pulled up my pants and chased the bird for another 50 yards, through cocklebur and mesquite, until I pinned it down with a wader boot and finished it off with a twist of the neck. Hands on my knees, blowing hard, I thought it all looked like some scene from a spaghetti western—the desert and sand flats, the sun rising over rocky mountains, a dead body at my feet.

But it wasn't the duck at all, nor a memory from a blind or a desert marsh, that will stay with me the longest from this New Mexico road trip. It was a moment on the drive from Bitter Lake to Roswell. The sky over Capitan Peak was going from orange and pink to deep blue and black, and long skeins of sandhill cranes coursed overhead. Powell pointed toward the tiny town of Ruidoso, in the Sierra Blanca Mountains, where his family had their cabin in the pinyon pines and junipers.

"That's where we brought Dad," he told me. "Where we spread his ashes. We knew that's where he would want to be. Hard to believe it's been three years already."

Powell looked out the window toward the dark plains, up to the high country, to the north, to that place where the ducks and the cranes and the geese come from.

That's what I would remember after six days on the duck-hunting road. Not the easy birds or the tough mornings, but my friend in the dark, face awash in the weak green light of the truck's display panel, missing the man who helped him love to hunt in the desert.

HAND-ME-DOWN GUN

Kirk McInnis died too early and too hard. Scott Wood and I cut cattail stalks for his casket spray, swatting mosquitoes in the late-summer heat, and couldn't believe he was gone—Kirk with his Sure-Shot Yentzen call, his wire-rimmed glasses, his old-school gruff ways that never quite hid a gentle inner spirit.

It was nine years later when another in our little circle of swamp duckers stopped by the house. Tom Valone rang the doorbell, and I could see through the wooden shutters that he was holding something. I waved him in. Tom was uncharacteristically solemn. As he unzipped an old camouflage gun case, he said: "Let me tell you a story."

In 1965 when Kirk turned 12, Tom began, his uncle gave him a shotgun. The uncle had bought the gun for his wife, and had the stock cut and outfitted with a recoil pad, but it turned out that she liked the country club better than clays. Kirk hunted with the gun for five formative seasons, then retired it.

"It's a little bitty thing," Tom said, and what he pulled from that gun case was a stop-the-traffic beauty—a 1958 Browning Auto-5 Light Twenty, with a round-knob pistol grip. The wood was burnished and worn, and the bluing was in fine shape.

Kirk was a good friend of mine, but he was Tom's best friend. Two months before Kirk died, when Tom's boys, Fielder and Sam, were 12 and 10, Kirk gave the gun to Tom. He wanted Tom's boys to grow up with it, to learn how to lead a bird with that Browning, and for it to be a small part of their own friendships forged in a duck swamp. And it wouldn't hurt, Kirk said, for those kids to know that the man who owned this gun made some poor choices in life, and left the world too young.

Fielder and Sam shot doves and clay targets with that gun, listening to the A-5's long-action ka-thunk of a recoil as the barrel slammed back and forth, and learned to love its quirks. Then they did what young boys do: They outgrew it.

Which is what brought Tom by my front porch. Kirk had plans for that shotgun. "When your boys outgrow the gun," Kirk told Tom, "they have to pass it on to another kid. I don't want the gun to ever have an owner. Its role is to teach."

"He was very specific with his directives," Tom told me. "And very adamant. And if you'll agree to Kirk's wishes, then I want your boy to have this gun."

I was speechless, my gratitude rooted in Kirk's memory. That wasn't the scene when I showed the gun to my son, Jack. He howled in delight. Jack shot his first wood duck, mallard, and dove with that gun. He shot clays and cans and sycamore leaves floating down Black Creek. The seminal moments of Jack's young, wild love affair with hunting were tied intimately to that historic Auto-5. I remember watching him stalk doves feeding in soybean stubble, and when the birds flushed and he connected he held that gun to the sky and whooped with joy. I remember a certain mallard—"the mallard," as it came to be known. We'd jumped a pond and I missed that greenhead three times before Jack fired Kirk's gun once, and rolled the duck into the water. For a long moment he stared at that gun as though he'd pulled King Arthur's sword from the stone.

Jack shot Kirk's gun longer than he should have, hunched up over that humpback receiver like a grown man with a Red Ryder. He was loath to give it up, for Kirk's gun was the key that had opened a new world. But when it came time to hand it down, there was no question where it would go. Scott Wood had known Kirk even longer than I did. His boy, Alex, had a birthright to that Browning. He shoots it to this day, although soon enough he will pass it along.

Counting Kirk, that's five young hunters who have learned to shoot with his gun. Five young hunters who have layered their own dings and scratches on that old wood stock, who stared down sunrises and screaming wood ducks along that barrel. I think Kirk realized that there's a season for the shiny new things, a time and a purpose for the latest and the best. But he saw a growing number of new young hunters with their $1,000 starter shotguns. He knew there are connections we are in danger of losing, and that his old humpback Browning could offer kids a chance to sink their own roots into a legacy that would never pass away.

This time of year I'm scouting duck swamps, despite the fact that it's hot and awful outside. It's when I miss Kirk the most, when I remember my armfuls of cattail stalks from that October day 15 years ago. And at this time of year I can picture Tom, standing in my living room, holding an old gun case. When he finished telling me the story, Tom slid the shotgun back in its case. "That's about it," he said, but we both knew the story wasn't over. There was new life, and another new beginning, for Kirk's old hand-me-down gun.

LAST CALL

It's late-afternoon light, melancholy and gold in the tops of the shortleaf pines, but it leaves the creek bottoms in moody shadow. It's the kind of light that lets you know the hunt is just about over. My arms are tired from carrying the gun, my face is windburned, and my legs are worn out from a million high steps through a million blackjack oak tangles. We could have quit an hour ago, but my buddy George Dixon and I know what quitting means. This deep into the season, this far into February, stopping might not mean just calling it a day. It might mean the end of it all—the last hunt of a season that reaches back nearly half a year. Back through birds and ducks and deer and geese, all the way back to September doves when it all started and never stopped.

The dogs feel the end of the day just as keenly, but theirs is a different response. While Dixon and I dawdle every chance we get, catching our breath, resting our knees, they're ranging farther than ever, hunting harder, sensing the time tick away. We call them in, time and again, but they push the limits, knowing there's little time to waste. The big pointer, Smokey, courses through fire-blackened pines. Boy, a setter, quarters through curtains of river cane, throwing caution to the wind. The falling sun only sharpens their senses and heightens the urgency. They pant with a cadence any hunter can interpret: Where are the birds, where are the birds, where are the birds?

That's when the quail explode beneath my feet, whirring wings and frantic, black-hooded heads flung from some subterranean wormhole. It's a tattered late-winter bobwhite covey—seven, maybe eight birds at most— overrun by the dogs, and when they flush one is so close I feel wind from its wings brush my cheek. The first shot is wide of the moon, but I check my nerves, find a single quail streaking on the edge of the pack, and string it together: butt, belly, beak, bang. Another miss.

I shake my head in disappointment. "Now don't get all whiny," Dixon says. I'd been on a streak over the past two coveys. "You've had a pretty good run these last few hours."

Which is the point. I don't mind being bested by birds, but I want to go out on a high note. Today, more than most, I want to sink the last shot.

<hr />

We're gnawing the bones these days, scratching out a last few hunts in the seasons that remain open. It's mostly a small-game gig this time of year, and nothing comes easy. Rabbits are run ragged. Squirrels are loath to risk a day-time stroll along leafless branches. Left in the woods are the quick and the crafty. Still, this is one of my favorite times to hunt. Late winter lays bare the woods' secrets. More than a few times I've cut a deer hunter's half-hidden trail while stalking a squirrel cutting nuts, and followed wisps of surveyor's tape to oak stands I never knew existed. I've watched mallards bomb into overlooked pocket swamps. I don't forget such honey holes. I'm likely to sketch a tiny map on the back of a wadded-up biscuit receipt. I'll be back.

I hadn't hunted quail in years when I picked it back up the season before last. I fell in with a crowd of wild-quail enthusiasts who pour heart and soul into managing their land for bobwhite quail. The hunting isn't easy. You can pretty much forget about classic open-field points. Twenty-first-century bob-white quail have adapted along with everything else, and they're more likely to inhabit a nasty half-grown clear-cut than a cornfield border. Dixon and I spent much of our morning plowing through briery hedgerows and pushing through brush to get reluctant bobs to use their wings instead of their legs, and the afternoon has settled into a bit of a lull. But it ain't over till it's over, and there's nothing like a bird dog to remind you of that.

We're heading back to the truck, the sun slipping fast, when Smokey locks up. Dixon and I give each other a nod and move in, throwing elongated man-shadows on the ground as we close the distance. For a moment I wonder if those spectral shapes might unsettle the birds, and in the next moment the covey flies.

Dixon is first on the draw. He downs a bird with his bottom barrel as I swing and fire with my own, a puffball of feathers signaling a hit. My second shot is not so lucky. The rest of the covey scatters like confetti, singles strafing above the broom sedge and bluestem.

After the retrieves, we whistle in the dogs. "No bird, no bird," we call. "Let 'em go." It's too late in the season to hunt down loners. The nights are cold and long, and during the morning's frigid hours it might take until lunchtime for a bobwhite to find a breakfast's worth of seed. We leave the birds to roost up and gather their strength. Dixon and I turn back to the truck, a half mile away. There's not a ray of sun left in the treetops when we pass an old tenant house moldering in the pinewoods. Its day, like ours, is done.

Dad's Cans

I've carried them from my childhood home to my college dorm room, to the duplex I rented after graduation, to my first home and my second and now my third. They don't take up much space.

We parked by the side of a dirt road and scrounged up two cans from the ditch. Daddy shot first: His blast obliterated the Pepsi can, leaving the top and bottom barely connected by a metal strip that would fail, despite my years of efforts to keep it together. I went next. It was the first time I'd ever pulled a trigger, and I almost missed the Budweiser can: Three pellet holes pocked the bottom half. We left the woods—but not without the targets.

That was the only shot I would ever share with my father, our only time afield with a gun. He died a few months later, unexpectedly. He never got the chance to buy me a gun. Instead, I carry our cans from place to place—for 41 years now—like the embers from a fire.

Chapter 2

Passages

ILLUSTRATION BY MICHAEL HOEWELER

SENSE OF PLACE

When I pulled up to the end of the farm path by Dead Dog Field, I checked the map on my cell phone before turning toward Stillwater—and that's when I realized this had gotten out of hand. I knew to turn left to get to my deer camp; I had driven out from Dead Dog a million times. But there it was, in my hand, my cell phone with the little blue blip that marked my location on a digitized satellite image. I had checked it without even thinking.

This time of year finds me in the deer and duck woods almost as often as during deer and duck season, because it's a great time to scout with the leaves still off the trees. I had spent the morning stomping up and down the creek, marking locations on my mapping app. Buck rubs, creek crossings, duck swamps, oak groves, climber trees, beaver dams—all those waypoints and hash-mark routes glowing on the phone screen gave me the feeling that I'd figured out the big woods by Dead Dog Field. Then I drove out to the hard-top and couldn't even make a simple turn without looking at my phone. It was instinctive by then. A habit. Faced with the simplest navigational choice, my first impulse was to pull out my phone instead of using my noggin. This had to stop.

There are plenty of funny stories—and horror stories—about folks who wander off-trail while their eyes are glued to their cell phone maps. That's not the problem I worry about; I hope I'm smarter than that. And my concerns run deeper than the old saw about what I'm going to do if my battery dies. I carry a small backup battery pack. Some problems are easy to fix. But turning our back on paper maps has sown the seeds of a more insidious problem.

With a paper map, you have to pay attention to your surroundings before you can calculate where you are, or how to get to where you want to be. You have to find yourself on the map before you can find yourself in the field. You need to know whether you are, generally, east of the ridge gap or south of the hard road. You need to be able to translate a map's features to the landscape around you. Digital maps, however, put us at the center of the world by default, always, everywhere, and in real time.

On the smartphone, the world revolves around us, a known entity. There's no need to keep track of which shoulder the sun is setting behind. North is no longer a true direction from which all other directions and routes emanate or orient. It's an icon on a screen. With my map app, I cede to the little black box in my hand the vigilance I used to keep with regular check-ins to a map and compass. And I don't learn the woods like I used to. I don't have to remember to angle left at the gum tree with the busted branch that looks like a bear's face. I know I can always get back here. But over the last couple of years, as I've built a dense database of waypoints and track logs, I fear I'm losing touch with where here is.

These apps are great tools—irreplaceable for many tasks. But as with any tool, using them too often is like using a favorite hammer too much. You can use it to pull the staple out of the fence, but a pair of pliers would work better and not leave a mark. You wind up looking at your phone to confirm what you've known intuitively for a decade: Turn left, you idiot, to get back to Stillwater.

—◦—

Perhaps the most intensive navigational experience I've ever had was on a weeklong canoe trip in far northwestern Ontario with my buddy Scott Wood. We paddled a complex of rivers and miles-wide lakes all connected by small sloughs and unmarked portages. With the map and compass in the bow paddler's lap, we called out the intricate details of the shoreline.

"That point has a little hook in it. See that?"

"Got it."

"Looks like a creek there, but does that ridge look right?"

"Keep going. It's the next bay past the marshy cove."

If we missed the bay that led to the cove that drained into the fir-lined outlet slough, we'd lose hours if not days of travel time. It was nerve-racking and exhilarating. A digital mapping program would have removed the work—and the anxiety—of knowing exactly where we were. But it would have also removed our constant communication and our steady check-ins with the land around us, which built a feedback loop that tied us to one another, to the water, to the woods, and to the cadence of the canoe moving across a remote wilderness. There was a sense of capability and accomplishment in moving by map and compass, for sure, but each time we navigated to the correct little stream outlet, it felt like we had not only found our way across the landscape, but also deeper into it—like a friend had confided a secret or passed along some nugget of wisdom that opened up a different way of looking at the world.

So, I'm going to work on this. I'm going to be more mindful about which old skills I let go of, and how I bring technology into my relationship with the wild. It's a powerful feeling to hold the entire world in one hand, and to be able to find my way to the very waypoint that marks the tree beside the slough that leads to the beaver pond that no one else in camp knows is there.

But more often these days, what I really need to do is find my way back. Back to camp, certainly. But back, also, to a place where I listened to the creek more intently, and noticed the shiny slickness of fresh deer droppings, and watched for the telltale dip in the silhouette of pine woods against the sunset to tell me it was time to turn west toward home.

Gone, for Good

The tom arrowed down through the piñon pines of the Aldo Leopold Wilderness. We were hunting public land—a national forest in New Mexico—and the bird's challenging cries rang from the canyon walls. I could hear every gobble and step yet couldn't get a visual on the bird. But Ted Koch could. He was 15 feet to my left, in a spare brush blind, hands on a traditional bow, and when I saw him drop his eyes to the ground, I knew the tom was closing in—and very close to dead.

Then, in an instant, everything that was right turned not quite right. The gobbler stepped into view and froze, head erect and eyes alarmed. I tried to stymie every possible movement—my eyes, my chest rising with each breath—and then the air came out of the turkey like a punched tire. Where once stood a full-blown strutting gobbler now appeared a slender reed of a bird, and a bird making himself smaller by the second. As he turned to run, I brought up the gun, but it was too late. The chance was lost.

I had schemed on this trip for a year with my buddy Koch, who recently retired from running the US Fish and Wildlife Service's endangered species program in the Southwest. We planned to take mules and horses deep into the Gila National Forest to hunt Merriam's turkeys. The Gila is America's first wilderness area, proposed for designation in 1924 by Aldo Leopold, author of *A Sand County Almanac* and long considered the father of modern wildlife management. The area shares a boundary with the 202,000-acre Aldo Leopold Wilderness, designated in 1980 in Leopold's honor. Together, the landscape of soaring rimrock and deep canyons runs for 27 miles north to south and 39 miles east to west, roadless but for a single gravel Forest Service road. There are few better places in which to lose yourself in raw, wild country, and navigate the days based on whatever such country throws your way.

On a mid-April morning, with skies spitting snow and sleet, our packer, Mike Root, helped Koch, photographer Tom Fowlks, and me into the Aldo Leopold Wilderness. Mule hooves clattered on stony trails that wound through cottonwood canyons and along cactus-clad ridges. We pitched two tepees beside a creek and bid Root and his pack string goodbye for five days. We had gear, food, and maps—and not a clue where turkeys could be found in the big nowhere that unfurled around us. We couldn't have been more excited.

When that first gobbler bolted from near-certain death, he kicked off a day and a half of patience-shredding, run-and-gun turkey hunting for henned-up toms. I watched one hen wade a shallow creek for 45 minutes while Koch called to her mate, hidden in the cliffs above. The gobbler answered everything Koch threw at him, but neither he nor the hen wavered. They only had eyes for each other. Half a day later, with another bird gobbling on demand, I pushed my luck. With a shotgun in one hand, a turkey fan in the other, and a push-button yelper clenched between my teeth, I belly-crawled for an hour as Koch hung below a ridgeline and rattled the bird with yelps, cutts, and gobbles. A dozen feet away, a coyote stalked the same bird, so transfixed by the near-constant gobbling that it never saw me huddled on the ground. I pulled up 75 yards away from the henned-up tom and let him have it with two calls. He gave it right back—without budging an inch. I finally gave up and crawled back down the ridge. Koch and I conferred on the creek, shoulders slumped.

"Knowing that they're henned up," he said, "I feel a little better about being ignored."

"Maybe," I replied. "But it sure hurts my feelings to strike out."

It seemed like we needed a change of scenery, so the three of us struck off on a long-distance scouting venture. A mile and a half up the creek lay a long, wide canyon. On the map it appeared to be a turkey nirvana—a flat valley floor cut with side canyons, meadowed and timbered. Getting there required dozens of creek crossings, and at one point the canyon narrowed to a 10-foot-wide pass between soaring cliff walls. We clung to the rocks, edging over the water, plunging through dog-hair stands of willow and alder.

But the canyon was a bust. Recently burned, it was a chasm of fire-blackened logs, dead snags, and sandy, bleached soils where a turkey could see us working through the barrens from a half mile away. Koch and I sent a few yelps up the side canyons in case one might hold the odd bird, but the canyon felt empty and lifeless.

We turned around to hoof it back in retreat. Dead ends and scuttled plans are a part of hunting backcountry—especially unknown country—but working our way out of the canyon and back downstream, the waste of precious hours and energy gnawed in my gut. With every stream crossing, I seemed to fret more about the tough birds and the waning days. Willows crowded the streambank. We all lost sight of each other in the streamside thickets as we strung out along the narrow canyon floor. Suddenly, I heard a violent splash, and a deep groan from upstream.

I whipped around and bashed through the willows. Fowlks was lying in the creek, cradling his right arm in his lap. He groaned again, his eyes glassy and fixed on his wrist.

I hollered for Koch and helped Fowlks to his feet. He winced in pain. The injury wasn't life-threatening, but I could tell from the contorted wrist, twisted like an owl's head and sheared at a sickening angle, that we needed to deal with this quickly. Koch and I whittled willow splints for Fowlks' arm, wrapped them in duct tape, and assessed our options. Looking back, it's still surreal how fast everything changed. We started walking. The hunt was over.

※

When Aldo Leopold first traveled to this rough country in 1909, he was 22 years old and fresh out of the Yale School of Forestry. A farm boy from Iowa, Leopold was a birder and hunter, but he must have been wild-eyed at the raw Southwest. New Mexico and Arizona were still US territories, and one of his early assignments was to kill bears, mountain lions, and wolves in Arizona's Apache National Forest to placate the ranchers, who loathed the animals. It was the killing of a wolf there that kicked off a tectonic shift in Leopold's perspective on ecology, and led him to frame a concept of wildlife management that deeply informs both science and land ethics today.

He and a survey team were eating lunch on a high cliff in the Apache when they spied a mother wolf and her pups. "In those days, we had never heard of passing up a chance to kill a wolf," he wrote, decades later, in *A Sand County Almanac*. So they didn't. The young men opened fire, then hiked down to the foot of the rimrock. Leopold reached the mother wolf, an "old wolf," he wrote, "in time to watch a fierce green fire dying in her eyes. I realized then, and have known ever since, that there was something new to me in those eyes—something known only to her and to the mountain."

Around our campfire, on our first night in the Aldo Leopold Wilderness, a Dutch oven hissed in the coals while a single Merriam's gobbled for an hour on the ridge above the tepees. Koch, Fowlks, and I wrangled with the challenges presented by Leopold in his essay on that wolf killing, which he titled "Thinking Like a Mountain." We'd come to this country to hunt turkeys, but we also wanted to steep ourselves in Leopold's writings and pay homage to his pioneering expression of our moral responsibility to the natural world, be it the backcountry or a city creek. Our plates were heaped with a stew of wild duck, country ham, and vegetables blackened in an iron pot, and we ate as the gobbling and the campfire died away.

The place and role of wolves in the wild is a complicated, multifaceted issue, but Leopold's writing has deeper resonance than predator control. *A Sand County Almanac* is a call to a type of ethical arms every bit as relevant today as in Leopold's world. "Thinking Like a Mountain" is about the killing of a wolf, certainly, but it is also about the severing of humanity's ties to a world where wolves can remain, and the ragged strands such a rending leaves behind. His work hints at the conflicts of living in an overly tamed age, and it explores the losses of living in a world where fewer people value the mountain's point of view. Or even seek it. Leopold recognized the too-much of the civilized life—just as I recognize the starved bones of my own soul when I stray too far from a connection to the wild world.

"We all strive for safety, prosperity, comfort, long life, and dullness," he wrote in *A Sand County Almanac*. For many of us, wild country is the only antidote for that dullness. But out there, as I learned when Fowlks slipped in the stream, we don't always get to choose how that dullness is abated.

It took nearly 30 hours of careful hiking and climbing, plus a midnight dash to Albuquerque to get Fowlks to a hospital. My chance at a wild Merriam's was lost, and I don't know if I'll ever return to Leopold's wilderness to hunt one again. I'd like to think I will—to close all the circles left open by our sudden evacuation—but as we were walking Fowlks out of the woods, my mind kept going back to a moment when I felt most connected to this place, and what we were trying to do here beyond the killing of a turkey.

Three days earlier, scouting on the afternoon before the Monday morning opener, I hiked out of our campsite meadow to climb a steep ridge that led to a knife-edged hogback ridge. I sat against a piñon pine and glassed the steep canyon below. I could smell the conifers, hear the wind, and see to infinity. I pulled out a notepad and began to write.

Everything before me was pure wilderness. I watched a bull and cow elk sift out of the timber and move through a meadow harrowed by a flock of turkeys. The landscape felt permanent, unyielding, and wholly disconnected from the world beyond the horizon, but I knew what these mountains could not know: The future of such wild places lies far beyond the horizon, in a world where lines on a map and words on paper—laws and policy and the human lust for treasure—defines its fragile reality.

Thirty-five years after he killed that mother wolf and her pups, Leopold wrote: "I now suspect that just as a deer herd lives in mortal fear of its wolves, so does a mountain live in mortal fear of its deer." The natural world is a cosmic, living Jenga tower, and Leopold understood the ineluctable forces that push against balance. No piece or part is without value. To think like a mountain means to live as a citizen of the landscape, he wrote. Not its conqueror.

On my own seat in the rimrock, not so far from Leopold's historic perch above the wolves, I understood more deeply the fear that has taken deep root in my own spirit: That all wildness will be pruned away from this world—ingested by concrete, scored by roads, pocked with drilling rigs and cell towers—and human experience defoliated of the lushness of the empty and roadless places. We spend too much time striving for dullness, and not enough in places so remote and removed that both renewal and peril are a possibility with every step across a stream.

Leopold wrote of the deep relationship between mountain, wolf, and deer, and of the similar symbiosis reflected in the human experience with blank places on a map. Every hunter feels this. I felt it as I hiked back down the ridge that evening, moving into the dark night as if wading into baptismal waters. And I recognized it on our first night in camp, when that lone tom on the ridge behind the tent gobbled like crazy, in a place so wild that I wondered if any other human had ever heard his challenging cries.

There was something in those eyes known only to the wolf and the mountain. Perhaps that something is, ultimately, unknowable to the modern hunter, no matter how passionately we pursue it. But to those of us who still feel the heat of the wolf's fierce green fire, this we know: It is these last untrodden places that fill our souls with understanding and purpose. The lessons they teach us, just like the journeys we take there, are often surprising and sometimes unwelcome. But with each diminished connection to the world of wolves and elk and wild turkeys gobbling in the starlight, we lose a tenuous handhold on our journey toward who we might be at our very best.

THE YALLERHAMMER

The old man called the fly the "skull crusher" because the brook trout would come after it so hard and fast that they'd bash their heads on boulders. He tied them with one arm, in the cool of the little store in the shadow of Grandfather Mountain, not far from the creek where he'd first heard of the fly when he was a kid, some 75 years earlier.

I thought I knew all about the Yallerhammer, arguably the most traditional of the old Southern Appalachian fly patterns, but this was news to me. The region has birthed a number of homegrown fly patterns—among them the Thunderhead, Jim Charley, Sheep Fly, and Tellico Nymph, the region's true breakout to fame and widespread use. But the Yallerhammer is the fly that seems to hold the fancy of local anglers. Its history is as shrouded in mystery and lore as these old North Carolina mountains are in their famed blue mist. Some say the pattern was devised by the Cherokee. Others figure Scotch-Irish pioneers dreamed up the bug. It was originally tied from the split wing feather of a yellow-shafted flicker—what the old-timers called a "yellow hammer," a large woodpecker once common across these mountains—but these days, of course, it's illegal to shoot a songbird such as a flicker. Most of the flies are tied with dyed mourning dove feathers. You hardly ever see anyone fish it. The Yallerhammer is an attractor pattern, sort of a Bob Evans–buffet kind of offering, which tends to offend the purest of fly anglers. And the Yallerhammer was traditionally fished as a wet fly, although those have fallen out of favor these days.

None of this mattered to me. I was hunting for Yallerhammers because of their historic and cultural significance. If they caused trout to bang their heads on the way to the hook, all the better. I bought the last four the old man had in stock, size 14s. "I'm fixing to tie some 10s when I get around to it," he said, apologetically. But I couldn't wait, because I was fixing to turn off the hard road and onto the Forest Service gravel, and climb high enough into the Southern Appalachians to leave behind cell service and stocked fish alike. Four Yallerhammers seemed like plenty to gamble the day on.

The last time I counted, there were 1.6 billion trout fly patterns, with more on the way, options made increasingly numerous through an ever-evolving array of new synthetic fly materials—stuff like holographic chenille, UV polar flash, translucent midge tubing, and photo-imprinted foam.

I'd hardly be called a traditionalist, with my graphite rod and sling pack, and I'm a sucker for sexy articulated streamers. Who wouldn't want a Sex Dungeon in the fly box? But when it comes to tiny brook trout in ancient brookie water, there's something to be said for dressing up in your Sunday best, fly-wise. Beloved though they are, rainbow and brown trout are interlopers in these parts, the rainbow hailing from western America, and the brown from the waters of Europe. Only the lovely little brook trout, whose name Salvelinus fontinalis means "dweller of springs," can boast of being a true Southerner, hanging on in the highest headwater creeks since the last glaciers turned tail in retreat from Dixie heat. Drive far enough into these mountains and hike high enough into these headwater creeks, and chunking some gaudy postmodern polar-ice chenille fly at a fish like a wild Southern Appalachian brook trout seems a little off, like wearing Versace ankle boots to a rodeo.

With the classics in my chest pocket, I drove past the stocked section of the creek and past the delayed-harvest waters, parked at a sign that designated the stream as catch-and-release/artificial lures only, and started hiking. Up and farther up, until the trail petered out and the rhododendrons were too thick to crawl under. Until it was time to fish.

By then, the creek had narrowed to a meager shimmer in the boulders. It's hard to imagine a trout even living there, but this is where these Southern Appalachian brookies have to stay, hunkered down against the browns and rainbows that will outcompete them for food and the warmer waters in lower, less protected crannies. There's no room for a real cast, but I've never been an old-school dabbler, dipping flies into tiny pocket water like a mayfly laying eggs. So I moved through the crazy-tight cover without concern of scattering fish, threading the rod through the rhodos, holding my hat to my head, until the creek straightened out just enough.

I roll-cast a Yallerhammer into the foamiest part of the water and took in the slack line. The heavily palmered fly "sort of spins and twirls in the water," the old man told me earlier, "and that drives the trout nuts." I tried to imagine the fly doing just that, tumbling in the washing machine of the pour-over, then drifting in the calmer water, like something dazed and confused but still alive. And edible.

The fiberglass 4-weight bent deep, and the tip jerked like a dowitcher pointing fish. The little bugger ran straight at me, and I glimpsed a small slip of orange-on-white and green vermiculations just as it spun a 180 and darted back to the plunge pool. I took a half step forward, protecting the light tippet, then coaxed the brawler to hand.

The yellow fly was nearly the size of the brook trout's head. The fish struggled in my palm with violent wiggles, leaping from my loose fingers twice before I could get the forceps on the hook and back it out. Forget all that stuff about swishing fresh water through the gills and babying a fish until it gathers back its strength. This little pig had gumption and attitude to spare. It burst back into the deep water, trailing orange sparks like a bottle rocket. If it could have flipped me a pectoral-fin bird, I'm sure it would have. Everything else was in miniature—the water, the rod, the fly, the cast—except for the outsize heart of that 12,000-year-old beast, its life a struggle, its future a stacked deck, but its fight and tenacious lust for life no mystery at all.

THE MEAT DOE

I removed the tenderloins when I field dressed the doe. These are the deer's filets mignons—slender, butter-tender cuts that don't need to age—and I like to grill them as soon as possible after pulling the trigger. To savor a meal when my boots are still muddy from the drag out of the woods and the tinge of entrails lingers on my hands is my doxology for the hunt, for the deer, for the blessing of both.

That was five days ago. Now the doe hangs from my deck like a tawny chrysalis, hindquarters spread by the gambrel, head in a bucket. The butchering table is clean, the knives are sharpened, and pans for meat and scraps are ready. My first cup of coffee is half empty. I'll need four hours to render this doe into vacuum-packed parcels stacked in the freezer. Both dogs are at my feet, licking their lips. It's a happy day for them, too.

I butcher my own deer because I like the end product: finely trimmed boneless cuts that I instantly recognize months down the road. I never wonder if venison from my deer is mixed with that of other hunters. I never question my meat's cleanliness, or worry that it will be freezer-burned and soured from improper cooling, handling, and packaging. And I've come to believe that those last hours with a knife and grinder are something of a sacrament, closing the circle of a hunter's self-sufficiency. I've had a hand in every part of the process, from oak flat to table. There's a lot of satisfaction in that.

Pride in my butchering skills took time to develop. Early on, I was daunted when faced with a whole hindquarter. I didn't grow up in a deer hunting family, so my first year or two of home butchering involved a fair serving of trial and error. If it took me a few seasons' worth of oddly shaped roasts, fine. Even those hacked-up meals were delicious.

To begin, I slice the skin on the inside of the legs, work the hide down like a too-tight jacket, and saw off the head. The disrobed carcass always gives me a start. There's nothing graceful about it. There is sinew and meat and bullet-blasted bone. The bloody exit wound kicks me into a mental shift, away from my recollection of this nimble forest creature slinking through the river bottom. This is food. I trade the big skinning knife for a blade with a piercing tip.

The backstraps are the first cuts to come off. Long and lean, these muscles give a deer its ability to vault fences and twist out of the way of a slashing antler. I start at the hip, with a shallow cut close to the spine, working the blade along the bony processes, then deepen the cut to feel the knife tip bump along the sharp angle in the vertebral arch. When I move the incision out toward the flanks, the backstrap begins to sag away from the carcass under its own weight. At this point my foot starts tapping. This is my favorite cut of venison, and when it comes free of the deer, I hold 2 feet of lean meat draped across my palms. Trimmed of silver skin, this alone balances out the long sweaty drags and frigid mornings in a tree.

I tackle the shoulders next. This is my least favorite part of the undertaking, and I want to work through them before my back aches and my concentration lags. I slice hunks of stew meat from the scapula, filleting the flat bone clean as a dinner plate. One shoulder I leave whole, bound for braising with apples and turnips.

With the hindquarters in sight, I take a break and stretch my back. The next few minutes reap big rewards. I separate one quarter from the pelvis, then fillet out an entire boneless ham. The major seams between the big muscle groups define a foursome of roasts that line up on the table: sirloin tip, top round, bottom round, and eye of round.

Now I'm no longer working with indistinct hunks of meat. I can see individual meals coming to life. I set aside the choicer backstrap for Thanksgiving. I line up steaks I can grill in 10 minutes for a midweek dinner squeezed between kids' soccer games and helping with homework. There's a big heap of stew meat. I don't want to wish away a single day of deer season, but already I look forward to long Sunday afternoons in February, fussing over a bubbling black pot. This is what I miss when I turn a deer over to a processor—the chance to relive hunting memories, and relish the memories to come.

I start to run out of steam about now, and I know I could do better when it comes to rib meat, neck rough, and those lower leg cuts I refer to as shin-derloin. I used to scavenge the carcass for stew and grinder meat like a half-starved raven, and I appreciate folks who utilize every edible component. Now I high-grade what I can off the flanks and neck. There's still enough grinder meat to fill a big pot.

By lunchtime, I have enough vacuum-packed venison for at least thirty-five family-size meals, plus jerky meat. While I didn't butcher this beast with a knife I forged in a fire, I feel a warm kinship with a few centuries' worth of my forebears. Now each package bears the date, the cut, and a detail— "big swamp 8" or "last-day doe"—that will bring back a rush of sweet memory. That's the last of the 9-pointer I had to drag across the creek. That's Jack's first buck.

I close the freezer door. Walking up the steps, I catch myself humming: "Praise God from whom all blessings flow."

FAMILY MEAL

The dusky grouse came from the big slopes of the Flathead and Kootenai National Forests, behind Tom Healy's house in the Northern Rockies. When Fast Eddie, Healy's wirehaired pointing griffon, locked up along an edge of pines, Healy knew instantly and intuitively that it was no ruffed grouse. "The big duskies like that sunshine, that open ground in the big woods," he says, standing in the deep shade of a wall tent, stirring a mixture of grouse meat, elk meat, and wild rice. "I knew what was coming."

Healy harvested this wild rice too, with his wife, in a canoe deep in Minnesota's Boundary Waters. Now he stirs the dirty rice in a black iron pot as he describes arrowing through the dense rice stalks in the canoe, knocking the grains loose with short wooden batons so they fell into the boat.

There is elk heart in Healy's dirty rice mix too, and elk sausage from a cow he killed eight days into a Big Hole Valley backcountry hunt. He had a .270 in camp, he recalls, but he carried a slug gun that day. "I wanted to force myself to get a little closer," he says. "Make it a little more real."

I glance around the tent. Nearby, a tall, bearded, cowboy-hatted guy sears mallard breasts from a Rocky Mountain spring creek. Another outdoorsman debones a Bristol Bay salmon. There is snowshoe hare and Idaho chokecherry sauce and goose confit in the works. On an open fire outside the tent, skewers of lynx meat sizzle.

Getting closer to the heart of the matter seems to be the dish of the day. I'm in Boise, Idaho, at what is arguably the world's most impressive wild-game meal: The Backcountry Hunters & Anglers field-to-table dinner, held during the group's annual Rendezvous. Each year, some of the country's best wild-game cooks put on a fundraiser feast so fine, it's been written up in gourmet-cooking magazines.

I wander from camp stove to fire pit, sampling beaver meatballs and smoked Lahontan cutthroat trout. I quiz the chefs about each dish, but what I hear most isn't the merits of wild plums versus the grocery-store variety, or why jackrabbit is underrated on the table. Instead, everyone tells me a story about the harvest. I hear how warm it was that January day on the Boise River when the trout were biting, how the moon lit the trail on the tough hike out with the elk quarters.

It's been this way, always. This might be one of the fancier wild-game gigs I've ever attended, but I've felt this same kinship in Cajun squirrel camps, Yukon duck camps, and my deer camp back home. It's what we do.

The earliest art, religion, and connections between human communities were all rooted in the things we chase, kill, and eat. And share.

Here's another story: A few years ago, my wife, Julie, and I had new friends over for dinner. I smoked a chunk of pronghorn backstrap and served it with Gouda cheese and red peppers blackened on the grill. It was not terribly different from our normal wild fare. To our guests, though, antelope was the most exotic meat they'd ever eaten. They gushed about its tenderness and sage-tinted bite. They wanted to know where I'd killed it (Wyoming) and how (arrowed from behind a decoy). They asked about my other hunts. They were surprised to learn that I butchered my own deer and aged ducks in the refrigerator's vegetable crisper. They were unaware of the modern hunter's connection to this ancient cycle, that wild meat still nourishes soul as much as body.

I asked if they'd like to meet their meal, since the antelope's head was hanging on my office wall. They politely declined, but still, that one simple meal sparked a conversation about hunting, sustainability, and the honesty of eating what you kill. They still talk about it. Not every wild-game dinner is a conversion experience, to be sure. Sometimes you just want to chew on a squirrel leg. But there's no doubt that a grilled backstrap is as fine an argument for hunting and fishing as any philosophical treatise.

At the BHA chow-down, I hover over Idaho chef Randy King as he works up a dish of spring rolls stuffed with goose confit. Always a sucker for a good goose recipe, I'm about to ask for the particulars of the dish, but King tells a different story. "This is kind of funny," he says, "in sort of a bad-funny way." He tells me that he and his 12-year-old son, Cameron, hunted these geese from a southwestern Idaho farm ditch last winter. Cameron was shooting a single-barrel 20-gauge, the kind with an exposed hammer, and with the first shot, the hammer bit the boy on the cheek hard enough to require stitches. Blood gushed. "I felt awful," King says, "but he is so proud of that scar, you wouldn't believe it."

But I would, of course. What hunter wouldn't? It's the kind of story that seasons a meal and life long after the hunt, and makes every day on this Earth a sweeter bite of life.

HEAVY METAL

The kid was 8 years old, a Cajun boy from the Louisiana big woods, and he was killing me at blackjack. It was past 10 p.m., and we had been hard at it since well before dawn, chasing squirrels so far back in the swamps that we had to be on the ATVs an hour before sunrise. I was deep into my cash and ready to fold for good, but my concerns did not amount to a puddle of tears. An hour earlier my hosts had capped a 12-quart black pot with its battered iron lid and slid a half dozen squirrels into the oven.

"This is what we call *puttin' it on drink*, Mr. Eddie," they said. Beer tabs popped like somebody was two-stepping on Bubble Wrap. "Ain't no hurry. Now we jus' enjoy ourselves."

In other words, supper would be ready when it was ready. You can't rush black magic. My freckle-faced adversary grinned across the table and shuffled the deck. I pulled out my thinning wallet. For the time being, the Dutch oven held all the cards.

That raucous, late Louisiana night was hardly my first brush with a Dutch oven, but it was the one that kicked off an obsession. When those squirrels came out of that black pot—seared in bacon grease, simmered in their own rendered fat, and braised alongside the Cajun holy trinity of onion, green pepper, and celery—everyone in camp dropped what they were doing and vanished to the kitchen, as if they'd been raptured to the dinner table. The scene, not to mention a belly full of bayou squirrels, sparked in me an intense love of filling a Dutch oven with wild game and then marveling at the result.

It's easy to get worked up over the magic and alchemy of a Dutch oven, and I'm as guilty as anyone. It's really not all that mysterious: Cast iron is slightly porous, so preventing the metal from rusting and keeping food from sticking to that grainy surface requires slicking it with a tough, nonstick covering—what cast-iron aficionados refer to simply as the seasoning or patina. It's nothing more than oil smeared on the metal and baked in temperatures hot enough to polymerize the fat. The molecules rearrange themselves in the high heat to form a hard, lacquerlike layer.

Once that base layer is down, something truly marvelous happens over time. A Dutch oven's seasoning improves the more you use the pot. It blackens and slickens and thickens with near microscopic layers—bacon fried for an opening-day breakfast, doves seared in butter, cubes of venison shoulder browned for stew, fish fried with potatoes and onion. Each meal takes from every previous meal a bit of its character and flavor. And it passes on its own

DNA to infuse the dishes to come. As long as the pot is cared for and fussed over just a little bit, tonight's fried rabbit could sizzle on a surface whose foundation was laid in your grandmother's kitchen.

It's happening right now, in fact. A half hour ago, I seared three plucked Nebraska mallards in a stovetop beast as squat as a toadstool. Stirring the grease in the bottom of that black pot was like looking into a reflection of the past. Maybe it's only in my mind, but I can taste a little bit of green-chili chicken from a favorite Florida Keys campsite each time I fry ham in that Dutch oven. There's a hint of northern pike fried on spruce twigs when I bake French toast in the fire. Venison on the stove in a Cape Lookout fish camp. Fresh-picked blackberry cobbler baking under a halo of oak coals. Jack's Mountain Man breakfast on a Virginia river sandbar—he cooked it all by himself and wasn't yet 10 years old.

After my black-pot epiphany on the bayou, I laid in a pretty good store of Dutch ovens: a couple on spider legs so I could set them on coals; others good for oven and stovetop use; even a pair of lightweight aluminum Dutch ovens that some consider blasphemous, but then they're not the ones who portaged them across a mile of Ontario granite. But I still play favorites. This banged-up old soldier with the bent bail handle was my first Dutch oven. It lives on top of the freezer, close at hand and ready for rapid deployment.

I slide the oven off the burner and add cut-up onions, green peppers, summer sausage, garlic, and Cajun spices. Then comes an oddball pair of secret ingredients: half a can of Coke and a one-second squeeze of pancake syrup on top of each bird. Over the next three hours, at 300 degrees, something beyond my understanding takes place inside that black cauldron. The duck fat, cheap syrup, seasoning, and cola mingle into an amber broth that tastes as though you'd liquefied marsh grass, whistling wings, and gas station honey buns and poured a duck-blind sunrise over rice.

But not for a while. The lid goes on with the same soft clank that's meant the same thing over the centuries, in fur trapper's cabins and cattle driver's camps and deer woods across the country: Dinner's coming, but in its own sweet time. I slide the Dutch oven into the heat, and put it on drink.

No Surrender

We're picking up a few good fish, rainbows and cutthroat trout with fat bellies and black-peppered flanks. No one's complaining, but we also know the fishing could be better—a lot better. I'm running a double stonefly nymph rig when my guide, Dave Deardorff, scratching a few days of stubble, ponders a pale morning dun hatch that's so light I have to stop casting and squint to see the bugs. "Let's switch things up," Deardorff says. He swaps out the stones for a small Yellow Sally and PMD nymph. My next cast feels spot-on. Hopeful. Sometimes the subtlest shifts can make it happen.

When you're drifting down one of the most revered pieces of trout water on the planet, Idaho's South Fork of the Snake River, it's pretty tough not to fish with high hopes. Framed by grassy, rolling buttes that give way to 700-foot-tall canyon walls, the South Fork carves a twisting football-field-wide course through the western slope of the Rockies. Fly anglers lock down the best South Fork guides a year in advance. There are 6,000 trout per river mile here, with the largest native cutthroat population outside of Yellowstone, which makes every scoreless cast feel a bit like a screwup. I cast up and across, pounding every dark hole and cut bank. Ten casts and nothing.

"Keep at it," Deardorff says.

I cast again and mend the line, managing its drift and my own expectations.

— ⌣ —

I'd scheduled a two-day, 28-mile float to take in the South Fork's wild and roadless canyon stretch, with a bunk at the South Fork Lodge's private canyon campsite. It's a sweet spot shaded by cottonwoods, with cabin tents, woodstoves, and a monstrous fire pit, and overnighting on the river lets us skip the frantic dawn hatch of drift boats at the Conant Valley ramp. Deardorff and I launch at a civilized 10 a.m., and for the entire first day's float, down some of the most coveted trout water on the planet, we see only two other parties on the river. Hours into the float, though, the fishing stays slow. On a river revered for its dry-fly fishing, the hatches are spotty and sparse, hampered by rain.

Trout fishing has a long register of bucket-list rivers, but fishing an icon like the Snake has its baggage. Famous trout water is trout water nonetheless. It can turn off in a second, or it can never turn on. Any decent angler knows that any day can be a bust, and that there's more to fishing a legendary stream than big fish and big fish numbers. But I'm starting to struggle with a demon that can bedevil any big trip to big-time waters: What happens when it doesn't happen like you hope?

By the time Deardorff oars us to our camp, I'm a bit beat down from chunking streamers and nymphs for nearly seven straight hours. Within minutes I have a bracing drink in hand, a steak searing over the fire, and new friends around me. But later in my tent, as I drift toward sleep, the South Fork's purling chorus reminds me of the gulf between the fishing I'd hoped for and the fishing I'd experienced. Try as I might, I can't shake a nagging expectation that lingers just shy of presumption. It's unfair to the fish and the river, I know, and it robs each moment of its precious, peculiar gifts.

~ ~

A third of the way through the second day's float, basalt cliffs crowd cottonwoods to the water's edge, and the river braids into a half dozen channels. The skies are bruised and broken, sending out sheets of rain one minute, then thunder and sunlight the next. "This is the mother of all riffles," Deardorff tells me, back-oaring into a deep emerald run that knifes through the gravel. When the first bugs appear, I figure them for fluffs of cottonwood. Deardorff sits bolt upright.

"Those are yellow PMDs," he says.

"There's a mahogany. See it?"

Within two minutes, the hatches explode. We round a bend in the braid to find legions of mayflies springing from the water. There are blue-wing olives, green drakes, and PMDs. The river is frantic, cobbled with the rain but boiling, as well, with trout snouts, fins, and tails. I scramble to tie on flies, my fingers shaking. This is what I'd imagined, but I can't believe it's happening now.

"This is unreal!" Deardorff hollers, as the storm drowns out his voice.

It seems impossible that an insect could hatch and fly in such a downpour, but the bugs won't be denied, and the fish follow. An 18-inch brown clears the water four times before coming to the net. Rain nearly batters my fly into the drink, but in an hour and a half I rise who-knows-how-many fish. I land eleven trout in a 15-minute stretch, with rivers of rain running off my hat brim. One long cast puts my fly a half foot up the riverbank— "the emerging minnow presentation," Deardorff says—but a half breath after the fly goes wet, a 16-inch cutthroat boils underneath. The strike happens so quickly that the details sharpen only after the fact—a flash of crimson slashes right to left in a dark hole where the fly was floating, and then my rod comes to life.

We get a solid two hours of what the South Fork can be, wrenching brown trout from the grass banks and cutts and rainbows from bubble lines that gyre below the riffles. By the time the bite peters out, we're in the river's slack section, and Deardorff cranks a small outboard to push us home. I lean back in the drift boat, stow the rod, and shake my head with gratitude. I got what I came for, and it was all the sweeter for what I knew in my heart: This time, it was more than I deserved.

Extreme Panfishing

"What do you think?" Sam Toler asks. "Far right, maybe?" But Toler has already made up his mind, for I can hear him in the stern of the canoe, shoving gear out of the way. Just ahead, a downed river birch blocks the creek. We can't get under it, and lifting the boat over the huge trunk would be no picnic. "Looks like a little hole beside that broken limb," he says.

I grin and nod, tuck the rod tips under the gunwales, fold my seat down, and turn my hat backward. "The usual full-speed entry should do it," I say, then we dig the paddles hard into Swift Creek's languid flow. Ten seconds later we crash into the treetop like a train off its tracks. A jagged limb rips my shirt, drawing blood. Half a dozen spiders rain down my back, their webs a wet slime across my sweaty face. And a handful of turtles and at least one snake hit the water. Then the canoe screeches to a halt, held tight in a crotch of the tree.

"Snap, crackle, pop!" Toler hoots. "This is my kind of canoeing! Hey, you use the machete. I've got a bow saw around here, somewhere. That wasn't bad at all, was it?"

Well, no, I think. Not when I consider the little piece of paradise that lies just beyond the blowdown. It's a pool of panfish water tucked into the outside bend of the creek. The bank shines with mussel shells, and an ironwood tree lies low over the stream just beyond the gold of a submerged sandbar. In two minutes we've cut our way free of the tree, and I scramble for my ultralight rod, buried under the half cord of firewood now stacked up in the boat. But Toler is a step ahead. He is short and powerfully built, his scratched and bleeding forehead covered with a battered straw hat. Despite his thinning hair, comparisons to Huck Finn are impossible to avoid. Within seconds of clearing the tree he's fired a short-stroke, cross-the-chest shot that sends a Panther Martin spinner across the creek with the trajectory of a belted magnum. It banks off a cypress stump and lands in a dark eddy. He's immediately playing a fat redbreast sunfish on 4-pound-test line. It's fish No. 43 and we haven't stopped for lunch yet.

"Oh, son," he says, loading up that single word with more syllables than a water snake has ribs, "let me tell you something. I dragged my bass boat up and down the highway for 20 years. Left at 3 a.m. to fish some reservoir all day long just to come home with five bass and brag about what a great day I had." Then one day, he explains, a coworker took him on a panfish float down a tiny, winding creek in a small fiberglass johnboat. They caught scores of redbreast sunfish, one of the most ornately colored freshwater fish on the planet. Known throughout the region as a "robin," it's a scrapper that loves clean streams and comes out of the darkest holes glowing with a sky-blue back and its eponymous firecracker-red belly.

Toler sold his sparkle sled a few weeks later and now owns six canoes and johnboats. "I see wild, wild country not an hour from my house. Never wait in a boat-ramp line. Get to act like Lewis and Clark. And catch one hundred fish a day, easy. No more big water for me. Uh-uh. From now on, I'm in the creeks."

—◆—

After a scant few hours in Toler's battered canoe, I'm convinced he's onto something. Toler's home waters are the slow, black, swampy creeks and streams of eastern North Carolina, but similar small waterways are everywhere and just about universally ignored by all but bridge anglers. Pull out a topographic map of rural country near your home, and it's likely that a webbing of smallish blue lines veins the landscape. They're apt to be chock-full of creek-loving panfish—not pond-happy bluegills but intriguing quarry like the South's venerated redbreast, rock bass in the Missouri Ozarks, and warmouths in Texas. "Draw a 50-mile radius on the map around here and you could spend a lifetime trying to fish all the creeks close to home," Toler says.

It would be difficult to imagine a scene further removed from a big-water reservoir than this one. Swift Creek uncoils like a muscadine vine through the hardwood bottoms of eastern North Carolina. In places the skinny stream isn't as wide as our canoe is long. When we pulled off the side of the road 100 yards from the bridge, Toler ran down to the water and hooted up through the brambles: "Goo-ooo-oood-ness, the creek is low-low-low. I don't know who I feel sorrier for—us or all those fish we're getting ready to catch!" We carried the canoe through 40 yards of brush littered with a soggy sofa, busted glass, bags of garbage, and a pickup-bed's worth of old roofing shingles. At the water's edge, cinder blocks, beer bottles, and Y-shaped rod-holder sticks suggested we weren't the first ones to drown a cricket in Swift Creek. Toler seemed oblivious to the trash. "You just wait," he said. "Soon as the bridge is out of sight you'll be in another world."

Ten paddle strokes are all it took to carry us underneath a canopy of tall river birch, gum, and swamp chestnut oaks. Cypress stumps and knees line each bank like teeth in a comb. Snakes drip from the trees; painted turtles and yellowbelly sliders plop with all the stealth of a loosed champagne cork.

Once we leave the bridge, signs of human presence are relegated to jet contrails overhead and the occasional whine of distant logging machinery.

Fishing this water requires guerrilla casting tactics. I take two paddle strokes, grab the rod, and flick a spinner beneath undercut banks, into deep water on the far side of sandbars, and across the slack flow between buttressed cypress trunks. Backhand, forehand, underhand—most often there's only time for a cast or two before I have to grab a paddle and steer clear of vines, briers, blowdowns, or sandbars. And most times I'm well rewarded. I make a cast: a robin. Another cast: another robin. Next a small bass with an oversize attitude smacks a Beetle Spin so hard that lure and largemouth come out of the water together. Just downstream, Toler's rod is divining a 2-pound chain pickerel, what locals call a jack. It's essentially a Southern-grown version of a northern pike, small but with a similarly scaled wallop and teeth.

<hr />

The fish are willing but there's a price to be paid—wading in dank muck, sharing a 15-foot-wide body of water with 4-foot-long snakes and spiders beyond counting. One time I feel something crawling up my thigh and glance down at three arachnids of varying species and ranging in diameter from dime-size to I'm-trying-not-to-think-about-it. I smash the most garish looking of the lot with my elbow in the same movement I use to flick a backhanded cast. It's multitasking, extreme panfishing style.

And the bills come due in the form of blowdowns, logjams, and treetops felled by beavers and the hurricanes that have ravaged the region in the last few years. At times we paddle for a half hour or more with our feet in the boat. Other times we're in and out again and again in a 20-minute stretch, hauling the canoe over or around moss-slicked logs and slashing our way through snags by means of various edged weapons. "People hear where I've been and they say, 'What? You went down that little thing?'" Toler says, laughing and hacking at a thigh-thick branch. "When I tell people how much fun I had, they look at my arms all scratched up and bloody and say, 'Uh-huh. That looks like fun.'"

Halfway through our route we take a lunch break on a sandbar scored with turkey tracks. Munching on boiled eggs and venison jerky, Toler sketches out his strategy for finding out-of-the-way panfish meccas. He pulls state government geological survey maps off the Internet and looks for long stretches of creek and stream between rural bridge crossings. They come with seductive names: Pig Basket Creek. Lick Log Branch. Devil's Gut. He looks on topographic maps for waterways hemmed in with green-inked banks instead of white splotches that denote clearings and farm fields. The longer the run between bridges, the better, because high numbers of logjams turn back all but the most obsessed robin hunters.

"Ninety-nine percent of people will give up 59 minutes of pleasure because of one minute of pain," Toler figures, when marveling at the lack of fishing pressure. But what fun it is. The rest of the day is a carbon copy of the first four hours, each grunt-filled haulover opening the door to yet another run of first-class robin water. We scatter heavy-bodied whitetails with antler nubs in velvet, and beavers give us weird looks, holding green saplings in their teeth.

When we hear a vehicle rumble across the narrow bridge somewhere ahead, we know the end is at hand. We tally up the score: In 7 miles of stream we'd been forced to haul the canoe over obstacles twenty times. One rod broke in a crash dive through a treetop, and I must have smashed at least thirty spiders into my arms, legs, belly, and noggin. We'd not seen a human footprint or a piece of trash. Along the way we'd landed 175 redbreast sunfish, fifteen largemouth bass, a dozen bluegills, three jacks, and a pair of suckers. And I'd be home in time for supper.

I ease Toler up to one last lie, a huge cypress stump lording over a sandbar that gives out to a licorice-colored run. "Oh, son," he says. "I know a big one's in there. Give me a minute to tie my shoes on tight. I don't want that robin to take me away."

But they already have a pretty good grip on me.

DEER CENTRAL

On a satellite image, this little piece of ground—39°33′16.49″ N, 96°25′56.87″ W—lies slightly downhill of a knuckle of pasture grass and cedar shrub that juts into a Kansas alfalfa field, up where Pottawatomie County nudges toward Nebraska. The slope falls into a deep draw, timbered with thorned wild plum trees, exactly 1.32 miles due west of Kansas Route 99. This is big farm country, big pasture country, a three-hour drive from Kansas City, about 4 miles north-northwest of Blaine, once a bustling railroad stop along the Santa Fe line and now a near ghost town. I had stared at the spot for hours. This land was either hallowed ground—or a colossal waste of my time.

To an American deer hunter, any place that harbors whitetails is a special piece of ground. There are places where deer are overpopulated, certainly, where folks hold a gardenia-grubbing buck in scorn. But to most of us, a patch of dirt with deer tracks is a seat of magic and a trove of mystery. That's what I was thinking better than a year ago, and that line of reasoning led me to this: If deer hunting is special everywhere, then what about deer hunting at the precise, scientifically calculated dead center of the whitetail deer range in America? Would Deer Central hold a distillation of everything we love about chasing whitetails? Or would it be just a blip on a map, a meaningless spot generated by some inscrutable computer algorithm?

And could I even find it? That was the surprisingly easy part. Last summer I had a geographic information systems (GIS) specialist crunch current range data for the whitetail deer in the US, using maps compiled by the International Union for Conservation of Nature. She e-mailed me a Google Earth satellite image marked with a bright yellow electronic thumbtack at the center of the range. There was no reason for surprise, really. It was planted in what is easily one of the best counties in what is arguably the best big-deer state in the entire country: Pottawatomie County in Kansas.

To be exact: 39°33′16.49″ N, 96°25′56.87″ W.

Next, to hunt down the landowner of America's Deer Central, I spent three days on the phone calling local town halls, chambers of commerce, and conservation officers. Finally, I hit pay dirt. I tracked down the closest taxidermist to Deer Central and rang him up.

"Lots of folks around here have really big deer—170s, 180s, you name it," Scott Schwinn said. Schwinn also happened to be the local sanitation officer. He knew every dirt road in Pottawatomie County. I sent him my map, and he sent me a name: Robert Christener.

Of course, Robert Christener wouldn't have known that his family had come to own and care for the spiritual center of deer hunting in a nation increasingly obsessed with deer. But long before he learned about Deer Central, he knew his land was special. The Christeners love to hunt, and they even manage a half section of land where they put out preserve pheasants for a few paying hunters. "I want my boys to have a taste of what I had growing up around here," Christener told me when I called him. "But birds are one thing. We don't let anyone but family hunt the farm for deer."

I kept the phone still and held my breath. Deer Central, it turned out, was just for family. And, just this once, for me.

On November 11, 1869, Robert Christener's great-grandparents made landfall in Kansas—in a covered wagon, family tradition holds. They claimed 160 homestead acres of rolling ground crosshatched with wooded draws, and over the years the family's holdings grew. These days, the Christeners own four tracts scattered about Deer Central, and another 1,500 acres or so around Frankfort, Kansas, 10 miles to the north.

The Christener family is as Heartland, USA, as you could imagine: Robert is 53 years old, lean and boyish and rugged; a flap of brown hair peeks out from under his blaze-orange cap. His wife, Janet, runs a day care and is no stranger to a bolt action. They have two sons, Donnie and Mike, and a daughter, Melissa. They share farm chores. They dote over elderly family members. They say grace before meals. And they struggle with the challenges faced by rural families across the country.

The afternoon sun casts long shadows when I pull up to a white, two-story clapboard farmhouse to meet Robert's boys. They've both come straight from work, and their differences are telling. Mike, 23, lives here and is just in from the farm. He is brawny and big and wears battered coveralls, mud-splattered boots, and a hooded sweatshirt. Donnie, 26, has just driven in from Kansas City, where he manages mutual funds for a Luxembourg-based firm. Gym-fit, he sports an outfit he's anxious to change now that he's home: black jeans, a black pinstriped shirt, and black square-toed shoes.

Mike tried college for a semester, at an agricultural school in Nebraska. "But I just can't sit inside too long," he says. "One day I was in class learning about how to drive a tractor and I knew that was it. I'd been driving a tractor all my life. I came home."

Donnie's horizons always seemed a little farther out than the Pottawatomie County line. "Mom and Dad always encouraged me to try something else," he says. "They told me that the farm would always be here if I wanted to return." But college and career have taken their toll. While Mike has filled a room with crazy-big deer, Donnie's had few chances to score. The Kansas rifle season always seemed to coincide with college exams. Getting away from work is never easy. He grins sheepishly. "To tell you the truth, I haven't shot a buck since high school."

That's putting a bit of pressure on Donnie, and we feel it the next morning, on our first hunt together. Donnie and I are 10 minutes from the truck when the worst possible scenario emerges on the dark horizon: Four does scramble to their feet, silhouetted against the sky. We hit the deck. We have another quarter mile to cover before shooting light, but we grind our faces into the dirt, pinned down on open ground near a pencil line of locust hedgerow. Donnie groans. "That's exactly where we want to be," he says.

Fifteen minutes later the whitetails bolt across the field into the broken cover beyond. Donnie and I take a stand on the field edge and wait for the sun, but I know the chances of a buck ignoring the fuss and stepping into range are nil and none. When we limp back to the truck after three hours of watching an empty field, our only solace is the fact that getting busted is perhaps the single most unifying experience in the entire realm of deer hunting in America.

<hr>

The next day, I have one of those -could've-should've-would've moments that haunt every deer hunter. Behind Mike's farmhouse is a 60-acre cornfield, edged by a sharp bend in Clear Fork Creek. Across the creek, an overgrown pasture cloaks a gentle slope. There's a thicket up top, a wide belt of oaks, and an ankle-deep trail of deer tracks scored into the bank. I'm hunkered down by midafternoon, back against a big oak, a cut cedar at my feet to break up my silhouette. In 36 years of deer hunting, I've never watched a more perfect deer funnel.

What blows me away is how rarely this spot is watched. Mike sleeps with his head on a pillow exactly 1,013 yards to the north, but he hardly ever hunts this crossing. I realize that I've brought my own baggage to Deer Central, expecting an obsession with whitetails that infuses every aspect of life. I find something like that. But it looks very different from what I'd imagined.

By and large, deer season on the Christener farm is embraced in a subtle fashion. Suddenly, one morning, blaze-orange vests appear on truck seats. Binoculars find their way to dashboards. Many locals hunt in whatever grease-grimed coveralls they wore to rebuild the combine thresher; in five days of deer hunting I will not see a single item of camouflage clothing other than my own. And guns are always at the ready. During the ten-day Kansas rifle season, rarely will a member of the Christener family travel farther than the woodpile without a centerfire within reach. Here, deer hunting is a seamless part of a day on the family land.

From my perch I watch a pair of does feed across the pasture slope, dark shapes like cloud shadows. Geese call overhead. About an hour into the sit, a spike buck bumbles down the trail, sparring with saplings, unaware of the crosshairs that rest on his ribs. I'm not tempted, but still my heart starts to pound. Then, as the last of the sunlight creeps up the trunks of nearby trees, a shape forms in the upper right quadrant of my peripheral vision. At first, I am not completely aware of it, only of a vague sense that another being has entered my orbit, and I realize that I am fondling the checkering on the gunstock with my index finger.

The buck slips along the pasture, just as I had hoped, and turns toward the creek crossing, just as I had planned. He stops, 70 yards away, nose to the ground, on a narrow gravel island. When the buck turns to the right I see that he is bigger than I first thought. The main antler beam extends almost to the nose, and the tines tower over his head. It's a deer I should shoot, and I should figure out just where that will happen.

The whitetail steps behind a big sycamore tree, and I wait for him with crosshairs centered on the other side. For the next half minute, I search frantically through the riflescope for an ear or antler or patch of white belly hair. But the moment is gone. The buck simply disappears into that unseen hole in the forest floor where deer often fall, and vanishes.

Later, Robert will smile and tell me about the side trail along the dry creek bed, the one that slips just out of sight beyond the gravel island. It's a trail a hunter might know about, if this land was his land. It's one that the buck knows, since this is his home.

It's the next evening that it all comes together. The buck walked out of the big woods to the west of a cornfield where a long stone wall channels deer from one farm section to another. Donnie tells the story while standing in the field stubble, stars twinkling overhead. Robert and I have just driven up in Robert's pickup, and Donnie's words are still rapid-fire, still breathless an hour after a big whitetail went down.

When a single doe stepped into the field, Donnie and Mike, sitting about 5 feet apart, backs to the woods, exchanged glances and shrugged. You think she's alone?

When they looked back toward the field there were four does and one of the biggest bucks Donnie had ever seen. It happened just that fast.

"But I've always had a hard time judging deer," Donnie says. Mike makes a face and nods. "So I looked back at Mike and his eyes were bugged out, and he gave me a little head shake like, Are you going to shoot that deer or what? That's when I really knew what was standing out there."

Donnie took two shots with a .270 bolt action, his arms shaking. The buck took a few steps and went down in a heap.

"Oh man!" Donnie says. "So there we were, high-fiving and whooping it up on the field edge, but you know you're not supposed to walk out there right away. That was the really awesome moment. You know the deer is out there, lying in the stubble, but you really don't know what you have yet."

What he had was a brutish 11-point buck, wide racked and neck swollen, with a single hole in the shoulder.

Robert and I follow the brothers in Mike's truck to the Christeners' sprawling farmstead a few miles away and pull up to a soaring barn shoehorned between feedlots and corrals. It takes a tractor to unload Donnie's trophy, and as the headlights wash across the barn interior, they light up another pair of big Kansas whitetails. There's a 10-point buck Janet shot two evenings ago when she and Robert were getting hay for the cattle. Her deer hangs beside a 12-point beast with split brow tines that Mike shot the next morning. He saw the whitetail while ticking off farm chores.

It is impossible not to feel a bit envious. This is a trio of monster whitetail deer, and Donnie shot his buck not 300 yards from where I had been snookered by my own Deer Central buck. The whole family comes out to marvel. Mike drapes his heavy hunting coat around his sister's shoulders, and I feel my outsider status keenly. The Christeners are warm hosts, but this is a family moment, a time to remember.

Inside, around the dining room table, we chat about Robert's side business hauling cattle, and Melissa's upcoming volleyball schedule. Janet has fixed pot roast, plates piled high with steaming vegetables. As I hold hands with the Christeners while Robert says grace, I can hear the mama cows shuffling in the feedlots outside. With my eyes closed I see the three Christener whitetails hanging in the barn, towering overhead, each one the end of a winding trail leading to one special place, and I tell myself that this is how it should be.

—⁓—

Two days later I hike across a half mile of CRP grass as stars streak across the sky, and burrow into a frost-sheathed haystack. It is 14 degrees and everything is right: the wind quartering in my face, a killer setup commanding a half dozen wooded draws. Everything except for the complete lack of deer.

I'm halfway through a five-day hunt, and I haven't seen a mammal in three hours. Dejected, I drive back to Mike's place, warm a pot of five-hour-old coffee, and plop down in the living room to make myself feel better with a giant bowl of Cap'n Crunch. This doesn't work, either. I am surrounded by reminders of what could be.

On one wall, there's a huge 11-pointer with a branched brow tine, next to another 11-point buck with midbeam mass fat as a cottonmouth back home. Directly over my head: 12- and 14-pointers. Framing the door to my bedroom: a soaring 10-pointer with overlapping main-beam points and a garishly tall 12-pointer with a triple-branched G2. Whoppers are propped in corners like forgotten mops. The TV stand looks like a voodoo supply closet: skulls and antlers in a heap. Within 20 feet are twenty sets of whitetail antlers so large that most American hunters would carry their photos around in their wallets.

"I like 'em with some character, I guess," Mike said earlier, trying not to smirk as I gawked at his dropped-tine, branched-tine, misshapen-beam trophies.

I take a drive down to Hofman Farm Supply, in nearby Blaine. Back in the day, Blaine sported a bank, hotel, stockyard, grocery store, and bar. "This was a real community," Elaine Hofman says. "Folks thought we were really something for a while." Hofman has run the store with her husband for 37 years, since the day after their wedding. These days, the old farm-supply store is mostly stocked with auto parts and tires, a reflection of the lack of farm business here once the railroads literally pulled up the tracks. Dressed in packer boots and a snazzy red jacket with a Christmas tree brooch, Hofman is tickled pink to hear about Deer Central. "It's remarkable that we're noted for something up here. The town's just about all gone now."

It seems that the changes and challenges facing the Christeners are reflected in what's happening elsewhere in Deer Central. This rolling, pastoral countryside keeps a tight grip on the hearts of its residents but has a harder time holding on to the people themselves. There were thirty-two seniors in Mike's graduating class at Frankfort High School. Melissa's class is half that size. For now Deer Central serves as Christener Central, too, a time and place where the family's diverging paths are wound back together.

In the dark the next morning, Robert describes what we'll see when the sun comes up. "This is a half section, 320 acres," he whispers. In front of our pop-up blind, a deep draw leads into grassland, thicketed with plum and dogwood. There are beanfields to the south and alfalfa in the field behind us, but the land still hews to its pioneering history. To the north, native pasture rolls out of sight. "There's big bluestem, little bluestem, buffalo grass. Prairie that's been here, basically, forever."

Now the wind comes up with the sun. By shooting light the gusts are ripping better than 30 miles per hour. They knock the pop-up blind around like a thin bush and whisk through the shooting windows we've closed to meager slits. It doesn't take long to start a slight shiver.

When I set out on this long-shot quest, my intention was to spend a cold morning or two in the heart of deer hunting in America, and roll the dice on the gift of a deer in such a place. I've found all I could want in a deer hunting spot, no doubt. But more compelling than my discovery of Deer Central has been my encounter with the family that loves this place, that shepherds the very ground that sustains their bodies and souls and knits their family together. Glancing over, I see Robert's face silhouetted in the dark shadows of the blacked-out pop-up. His eyes are fixed somewhere out on the rolling hillsides of his family land, and it occurs to me that no matter how hard I look, I will never see what he sees.

Robert shuffles his feet and arches his back in a long stretch. "When you called me and told me about the idea of Deer Central," he says, "I felt like it was a real privilege to have something like that on our land." He is quiet for a moment. "I really want you to shoot a big deer, Eddie. But seeing my boy with that buck the other night, him and his brother together, after so many years for Donnie." He shakes his head and glances over, almost apologetically. "Well, that's just everything to me. I sure hope you understand that."

If I didn't, I think, I wouldn't be here.

On my last morning in Pottawatomie County I follow fence posts in the dark until a line of plum trees runs out along an alfalfa field. I worm under a barbed wire fence, snip thorns from a plum's trunk and lower branches, and hunker down in the grass. I am invisible. I prop my boots up on the lowest strand of barbed wire, and wait for it to come together in Deer Central.

Three hours later, I have no choice. I'm faced with a three-hour drive to a 2 p.m. flight. A trio of western meadowlarks flies into the tree overhead, chipping nervously. I take it as a Kansas farewell. I've had my chance.

When I stand up, there he is. A very big deer, an 8-pointer, at least, and likely larger, with a neck like a sack of cattle feed. He must have been stepping out of the plum thicket as I crawled out of my hide, within rifle range with a steady rest, but by the time I get the scope on him I figure it's 250 yards, and he's loping through broken thicket cover, aware of danger but not yet crazy-spooked. I seethe with frustration and disappointment. Five days of hard hunting and I needed but five seconds more. I center the buck in the glass, then move the crosshairs ahead of his shoulder, and in my mind I empty the rifle's magazine. But already I'm shaking my head. This deer deserves better.

I ease the rifle down. He's crossing pasture now and pours it on. With each vaulting leap he covers 15, maybe 20 feet of open ground, and seems to belong to both earth and sky. A part of me knows he belongs to the Christeners as well, and that he's not meant to be my deer. For the moment he is, quite simply, a marvelous thing to behold, and when he vanishes into a distant wood's edge I realize that I am smiling.

NO LONG SHOTS

I'd been in the treestand for an hour and a half when the doe walked into the field. It had been an hour and a half of pure bliss. The trees were painted in fall colors. The blue sky was so crisp, it was hard to look at. I'd seen the tail end of a small buck cross the back field not long after I'd settled into the stand, so my head was on a swivel. The hunt had an air about it that anything could happen. It was one of those sits where you feel like you could sit forever.

I watched the doe cross the pasture, undisturbed, tail flicking, pausing to browse after every few steps. The deer was just what I wanted. A decent doe, alone, with no young around. Out in the open. Loading would be a snap. It doesn't get any easier.

So I watched her for a minute—then two, then four—and I knew what was happening inside my head. There are times when I take the easy shot and I'm thankful for it, and there are times when I will drive an hour and climb a tree and watch a deer through the scope, finger on the trigger, and tell myself, over and over, boom and boom and boom, but the rifle never bangs. I shoot when it feels right. Sometimes I just never know.

I was struck recently by something a friend said. "I love everything about hunting—up to that moment," he said. "And I love everything about hunting that happens after that moment. But I don't love that moment."

Boom.

I totally agree. I structure my life around everything that happens up to the moment of the kill, and everything that comes after. I love packing up and driving out to my deer lease in the late-afternoon light. I love climbing into a stand. I love the turning of the trees and the pregnant feel of the air during the rut. I love the hands-and-knees tracking, the pit in my stomach as I work to find the deer, then hauling it out of the woods. I even love the bloody parts—the field dressing, the butchering, the works.

I especially love the trigger squeeze. I will sit at my office desk, rack a bolt, and squeeze the trigger ten times in a row. When you know a rifle and its trigger, there is something intimate about taking a shot. I love moving the crosshairs into play and watching them settle. I love the feeling as I exhale and try to still my heartbeat before the trigger squeeze. I love every single moment of it all—except what happens in the fraction of the second after the trigger sear releases, the striker hits the firing pin, the powder ignites, and the bullet leaves the barrel. I want what comes next over and done with as quickly as possible.

I watched the doe take the shot and bolt toward the woods. I tracked her in the scope. She ran maybe 40 yards before she crumpled on the field edge, kicked three times, and died.

In nearly 40 years of deer hunting, I can only remember two deer I shot at that I didn't bring home. This is not a boastful statement. You might even call me a timid rifleman. But I am a very good shot at the shots I take. I just tend to shoot deer fairly close—inside 150 yards, almost always—and in the open. I don't take chances.

It's not that I'm incapable of longer shots, but this isn't about numbers. I'm not talking about distance, really. My 200-yard stretch might be your 700-yard chip shot. I'm just being super honest with myself about my abilities and experience, and super fair to an animal that could pay a gruesome price for my hubris and carelessness.

I think we could use more of that self-reflection in the woods. We hear all too often of hunters who stretch it out. Who sight in their rifles only after they miss a deer. Who muse about a miss without accepting the fact that they likely just wounded the animal. Who come back to camp with stories of overly long shots at big deer just because. A whitetail buck that's lived that long, sneaked past that many hunters, and moved like smoke through that many dawns deserves the most carefully considered shot, not some why-the-hell-not-Hail-Mary. No one wants to be the deer-camp nanny, wagging a disapproving finger. But there was something instructive about the old walls of shame, where you lost a shirttail when you missed a deer. It was as if the community around you came together to say: *Look, buddy. It happens. But from here on out, we expect a little more of you.*

I do not sugarcoat what happens in that moment after I pull the trigger. I want the animal to die as quickly as possible from massive trauma and shock—and I want to be shocked if that doesn't happen.

That's how I can love it all.

My buddy's dad came down with the four-wheeler, headlights slashing the dark. I was crouched by the doe, waiting. Mr. Knight has nurtured and nourished this farm and its wildlife for four decades, but busted knees and hips keep him out of the stands these days. He doesn't hunt anymore.

"Just the one shot?" he asked.

"Yes, sir," I replied.

And I loved the look on his face.

HOLY GROUND

We awoke in the dark to pack the truck and head out. Driving north, through country less settled by the mile, he went over the rules. Again.

"You can't tell anyone anything about any detail of where we're going," he reminded me. "Not the nearest town. Not the name of the creek. No posting on social media. No photos that show horizons or even cliff faces. Close-ups of fish, maybe. But be careful.

"I'm not trying to be a hard-ass about this," he said. "It's just that ..."

He never finished his thought. He didn't have to.

It was a two-hour drive to the trailhead, if you could call it that, and then we hiked with backpacks and fly rods along a series of old roads, foot trails, and game trails. We crawled over downed timber. We bashed through thickets of alder. All the while, my friend knew exactly where he was going. I could have been on the face of the moon. Once, at a large muddy wallow in an aspen grove, he waited for me to catch up.

"Step in my tracks so it doesn't look like a couple of guys are hiking in here," he said. The expression on his face was a mix of conspiratorial frown and sheepishness. "I know it sounds crazy. But trust me. A few more miles, and you'll understand."

And in a few more miles, I did.

My buddy's secret spot turned out to be not a spot at all, but an entire valley, a hidden world revealed after one last sketchy goat-track climb over exposed rock and burnt timber. A creek winked through a broad basin in braided, sinuous sweeps of water clear enough for sight-casting to trout 60 feet away. In years of fishing the creek, my buddy said he'd seen evidence of just a handful of humans. He'd come across even fewer in recent years. Honestly, he said, this creek might not have been fished since he was here a year ago. I let my eyes roam up the stream and past the bends, all still a mile or more away like some lost corner of Middle Earth—a half-real and half-imagined realm of undisturbed wilds. Until I started casting, and there was nothing imaginary about the fish.

After ditching the backpacks, we first hiked past long, sexy runs without rigging a rod. "We're not interested in medium-size trout cruising these runs, like party-goers sampling the bruschetta," my buddy said. Over the years, he'd keyed in on the precise makeup of water that held the largest cutthroat trout—how much timber was just enough and how much wood was too much, how much gravel, how much gradient. "There's typically one really big fish in each pool," he told me. "And he's in exactly the right place, and you'll recognize it and put a cast down the middle, and he'll knock the hell out of it, or we'll keep hiking because the next one will."

And we knocked hell for miles and hiked for more miles, fishing hard for aggressive native cutthroats that slammed garish Chubby Chernobyl patterns in great toilet-flush rises. I know I landed the three largest cutthroat trout of my life, and I'm sure the longest went 21 inches—but I cannot say for sure. Taping a fish here seemed a sacrilege.

That night, we camped under the stars on a gravel bar, drinking gin nosed with spring water from old enamelware cups with battered metal rims that clinked against our teeth. A fire burned in a small stone ring, where bits of charred wood marked my friend's fire from 12 months past.

"This is my church," he said. "This is the place that changed me. The only people I bring here are the ones I think will understand."

The conundrum about a secret spot is that it's something that should be shared—but with the implicit understanding that it isn't to be shared further. It's a gift given with a breath half held because it is wrapped in trust that can be shredded as easily as cheap ribbon. When someone else shows you their secret place—their hard-won, years-in-the-figuring-out trout or duck or buck nirvana—something should happen deep inside you, almost on the chromosomal level. You're not really the same as you were before.

The next night, after another brush-bashing backpack return to the truck, I took stock of my knees and grinned that I'd cheated my orthopedic surgeon out of a beach house again. I tried to parse my sense of near euphoria. It wasn't that I caught the largest cutthroat I'd ever seen. It wasn't that I proved myself tough enough to get into a rough place and fish well and get back out again, even if I limped that last mile to the truck. It was that my friend found me worthy of his spot and trustworthy of his secret. He was willing to take the chance and take me there and know that I would walk out and speak little of the details of that valley, and bury the memory of the trail deep and burn the shovel. Forget the photos and the fish tales. He knew I'd never forget what was most worth remembering: That a place like that still exists.

THE HUNTER'S PRAYER

Give us this day our daily bread . . .

I'm the last one out of the kitchen. When I step into the dining room the lump that has been inching toward the top of my stomach suddenly vaults to my throat, and I have to shut my eyes for just a passing few seconds. Let the wave of emotion settle down. This happens every Thanksgiving.

Give us another dawn with golden light in the decoys, light that lifts our hearts toward heaven . . .

Family rings the table. There is an embarrassment of food. Oddly enough, the food hardly registers. It's the sheer weight of blessing that rocks me back on my heels. Every face reflects a memory of time outdoors: My wife hanging on to the console, the boat bucking in a horrid blow, lightning crackling. My mother beside me at the base of a squirrel tree, white-gray curls barely controlled by a camo cap.

Give us a sunset whose promise is tomorrow. Give us a hunger to taste the wild places that yet remain . . .

And also the blessings left behind by those no longer gathered here. But they still have their place at the table. Sensing this, I shut my eyes again.

Give us this day a glimpse of the glory found in the pool of a stream, in the wild cackle of a goose . . .

Then we join hands—generations linked by intertwined fingers and futures. I sneak in one last look. I bow my head to pray.

Give us this day.

CHAPTER 3

Along for the Ride

ILLUSTRATION BY MICHAEL MARSICANO

FOLLOWING OUR FATHER

Walter DeSales Witt was in a good place: with his back against a hemlock, green boughs drooped with snow all around, like a half-opened umbrella.

He'd wormed his way under the branches, spread out a burlap sack for a makeshift seat, and now he could watch a deep-woods edge where hardwoods transitioned to a stand of hemlocks. It was dark Pennsylvania timber, just the kind of route a big buck might travel.

It was good to be out of the house. No one would ever forget the big storm of December 1974. The snow started falling the night before the antlered deer season opener. It was a Sunday night, and the Witt family was at Grace Brethren Church, in the small town of Meyersdale, Pennsylvania, in their customary pew on the right-hand side, a third of the way back from the pulpit. Eight inches of snow fell during the church service alone. The overnight total pushed 3 feet. It would be nearly two weeks before anyone went anywhere in Somerset County. And in two weeks, buck season would be over.

The Witts, a family of hunters, weren't going to let the season slip away without a try. When the roads were finally cleared enough for travel, Walt, 38, packed his red-and-white Plymouth station wagon with his two boys, Dan, 14, and Mark, 12, and his father-in-law, Roy "Pap" Brown. Now the Witt men were hunting together, on family land, on the very last day of buck season. It was an exciting day. Witt's wife, Cathaleen, had graduated from college just the day before. She was now Christmas shopping with their daughters, Lisa, 9, and Victoria, 17. It had been a tough stretch, raising four kids on $3,500 a year.

For Walt, a ninth-grade earth science teacher and high school track coach, one of the great joys of a few hours in a quiet stretch of woods was the blessing of unfettered thinking. His true calling was sharing his Christian beliefs. In a given year, he might guest-preach at dozens of small Allegheny Plateau congregations. He talked to nearly everyone he met about his faith: the kids on his track team, a lady in the grocery store, a man picking blueberries on a mountain roadside. Tomorrow morning, Walt would speak from the pulpit of Calvary Bible Church in nearby Ellerslie, Maryland. He'd already started writing the sermon, titled simply, "Heaven." The passage he'd chosen spoke of heaven's streets of gold. Of all the blessings of his life, Walter Witt held nothing dearer than the certainty of where he would spend eternity.

Now he peeled an orange, let the rinds fall to the snow, bright orange slashes like leaves curled against the cold, on a carpet of white flecked with the dark needles of hemlock. The day was warming, and as melting snow dropped from the tree boughs the branches would suddenly spring up, dipping and dancing. Each movement would catch Walt's eye, surely bringing a rush of adrenaline. It was just the kind of thing no deer hunter would miss.

One hundred forty-eight feet away from Walt, another hunter watched from the cover of another snowy hemlock. Something was moving in the trees up ahead. There was a patch of fur. It had to be a buck. For 15 minutes, the hunter watched. Then, in the early-afternoon hours of December 14, 1974, the crack of his rifle split the quiet, dreadful woods.

Homecoming

Walt, "Pap" Brown, and Walt's sons, Dan and Mark, trudged in near silence by the light of the moon on new snow, in single file, breaking through snow clear up to the boys' waists. They huffed under apple and walnut trees, past Brown's spooky cattle barn that the brothers feared even in daylight. Walt dropped his father-in-law off first to take a stand in the woods, then his oldest son, Dan, and Mark last. Dan hunted near a large sawdust pile where his ancestors had buried their ice blocks. Slightly elevated, with a broad forest view, it was a good spot, and he was wide-eyed with the thought of a deer coming through the woods. Mark was just as excited. This was his first deer hunt. He watched his dad walk away, passing behind trees, growing fainter and fainter in the gloaming light in and out of sight. Now he could see his dad, now he could not.

Walt didn't hike much farther. A few hundred yards, maybe, and then he could make out the hemlocks just downhill. This was the spot. He didn't want to be too far away from his youngest son. These were familiar woods to the boys, but with this much snow, well, nothing looked quite right.

On a hot June Sunday afternoon, Dan Witt and I pull off Pennsylvania's Highway 160, 5 miles east of Meyersdale and a few hundred yards from the site of Pap Brown's old farmhouse. Rolling ridgelines unfurl to the horizon, checkerboarded with forest, farm field, and pasture. In a dirt parking lot, Mark Witt and Ron Askey, the Pennsylvania game warden who investigated the shooting of Walter Witt, lean against Askey's truck. They greet us like old friends meeting at the edge of a dove field. Askey is built like a fireplug, with a heavy jaw and gray locks over a ruddy forehead. Mark is wiry and bald with a mustache. He shares Dan's dark eyes but not his laid-back demeanor. Dan describes him as a jokester and prankster and a bundle of energy, but if he has the jitters today, I can't blame him.

In the last 37 years—and in particular over the last half decade—the Witt brothers have experienced a remarkable journey of healing and redemption. Since 2004, Dan and Mark have spoken about their father's death and their personal stories of spiritual renewal at churches and church-sponsored sportsmen's dinners from the mountain hollows of West Virginia to the plains of Alberta. They've written about how losing their father in a hunting accident impacted their growing up, their approaches to hunting, their marriages and family ties, and most emphatically, their relationship to God. Without ever seeking the opportunity, the brothers have found themselves on a path whose turns and ultimate destination they each view as an unfolding miracle.

But there is one thing they have never done: return to the woods where their father died.

A few miles away from Walt's line of hemlocks, along the lower flanks of Wills Creek Mountain, four hunters gathered with their own buck dreams. Two of them had a special reason to celebrate a Pennsylvania hometown sunrise. Twenty-four-year-old Johnston Cutler was just three months out of a two-year stint with the US Army. (This man's name has been changed to protect his identity.) He'd grown up hunting and fishing in the Allegheny woods with his dad, but between his college years and military service, the pair hadn't hunted together in six long years. Now the woods were waking up around the father and son. The plan was to drive deer to a couple of standers, and the young Cutler was happy to be on the shooting end of the arrangement. He slipped into the woods, looking for deer.

For Dan and me, it had been a five-hour drive from his Virginia home to his native Pennsylvania, and despite our chatter about the upcoming deer season and Dan's training regimen for a backcountry elk hunt, the interludes in our conversation had grown longer and more solemn. We wondered if we could find the woods where Walt took in his last view of bare winter trees, where he sat with his back to a hemlock, watching for a buck, listening for a shot that would tell him that one of his boys had downed a deer.

After nearly four decades, nothing would look the same. Askey was 31 years old at the time of the accident; now 68, he has bad knees but plenty of grit. He was astonished when I first contacted him about this story but never hesitated about returning to the scene. By triangulating the memories and recall of the three men, we thought we could get close to the piece of ground where Walt sat. We wondered if we might even find the tree.

After handshakes and small talk, we douse ourselves with bug dope and drop off a long, flat ridgetop into the overgrown fields and woods below. Askey is chatty and avuncular. Mark spins good-natured jokes about his boyhood memories, a broad smile appearing under his aviator sunglasses, but Dan grows somber as the trail falls off the ridge into a mosaic of tangled fields and woods. The brothers point out a few apple trees that still remain from the family orchard. We skirt the site of the old barn. Soon the path enters a grove of birch and maple and locust. In 1974, this would have been open fields. "Corn, mostly," Dan says. "It was great for rabbits." There are bear droppings and deer beds. There are long, quiet moments.

I first met Dan a month earlier, at his home on 21 acres of rolling Blue Ridge woods outside Lynchburg. Married for 25 years, and with two grown boys, he's the assistant town manager of nearby Altavista, a town that reminds him of Meyersdale. "It has that small-town feeling," he says. "The folks are extremely resilient." It's also a location with plenty of access to deer woods, and despite the nature of his father's death, Dan remains a serious hunter. A few days after the funeral, in fact, Dan was up before dawn, dressed in his hunting clothes, heading out for one of the last of Pennsylvania's doe days. His mother stood in the doorway, shaking with fear.

"I lost my husband," she'd said. "I'm not losing a son."

But Dan never lost his desire to hunt. "Mom hated hunting and didn't want us in the woods," he tells me. We're sitting on a sofa in the small living room he's just built for his mother-in-law. "But I'm an introvert. I didn't have a lot of friends. Out in the woods is where I felt I could be me." After Walt's death, Don Imhoff, a family friend who had once run track under Walt's coaching, took Dan under his wing. The pair hunted and fished, ran a trapline together, and took up bowhunting with a shared passion. When Dan started college at Liberty University in Lynchburg, Imhoff moved down with him to take a few college courses. It was a healing friendship.

For the Witt family, there will always be unanswered questions about that day in the deer woods, inevitable appraisals of how and why and what could have led, ultimately, to the firing of the bullet that struck Walt dead. But in the weeks and months that followed the accident, more pressing was the doleful reality of simply rising from bed and making it through the day until it was time again for fitful sleep. This is the story of grief: endless days of dark until slivers of light begin to grow into minutes and then hours, and life becomes life again, never the same, but life with laughter and love where once they could not have been imagined.

As Dan describes those times, those months and years, he sits with his right leg crossed over his left, his foot ticking nervously. The rest of the house is silent; Dan's wife and mother-in-law and sons have retreated to distant rooms to cede us space and quiet. He wears cuffed khakis and a yellow-striped oxford shirt and a black-and-gray goatee. He has dark eyes—dark brows, dark irises—and they are not unfriendly, but they are unflinching. His was a small-town tragedy, and he got through it by getting on. His mother taught school. People pitched in.

But throughout his teenage years, Dan lived with a rising tide of anger. He expressed his anguish on Somerset County's winding roads, pushing his 1973 Plymouth Satellite to 110 miles per hour, then 115 miles per hour, speeding "until something started floating around inside the car or the doors were rattling. I can't tell you how many times I did that. I was daring God to kill me." Dan remembers sitting in church as the choir sang:

Amazing grace, how sweet the sound,
That saved a wretch like me.

"And all I could think was 'You are the wretch, God, for allowing this to happen to my dad,'" Dan says. "I internalized all the anger. It just built up in me."

For Dan, spiritual healing was first revealed in a conversation he had when he was in his early 20s, with a former neighbor named Peter Cabin. At the time of Witt's death, Cabin owned one of the hard-drinking bars in Meyersdale, and when Dan questioned God about his father's death, the question was always the same: Why Dad and not a man like Peter Cabin?

Then one day, while visiting his grandmother, he heard someone calling his name from a nearby house trailer. It was Cabin, and he wanted to talk.

"I knew who he was," Dan says. "And I was thinking, 'You're the one that should be long gone. I should be talking to my dad.'" But Cabin told him an astonishing story. Walt, as it turned out, never passed up an opportunity to share his faith with Cabin, and after the hunting accident, the barkeeper converted fully to Christianity.

"And that's not all," Dan says, shaking his head, amazed at the turn of events even after 25 years. "He sold his tavern. He started preaching. He began a ministry in retirement homes because he felt that those people didn't have much time left before eternity. And for years he helped smuggle Bibles into China. All because of my dad's death.

"When he told me that story," Dan continues, "it was like God hit me right between the eyes with a two-by-four. This light came on of God telling me, 'Dan, if you were in charge of this, if you were God, Peter Cabin would be dead today, and he would have to spend an eternity with no hope. I didn't make a mistake with your dad.' It was an epiphany, and the beginning of the healing process for me a decade after Dad's death."

It was a needed breakthrough, because Dan carried a particular burden about that day in the deer woods. What he remembers most clearly about that snowy Pennsylvania hunt, what he can recall in the most exquisite detail, are those few minutes when he left his stand and tried to follow his father's tracks in the snow, to tell him that he was tired and cold and ready to go home.

"I could see where Dad's tracks turned off into the woods," he says. His foot twitches. "I followed the trail until it got really steep." As he speaks, Dan cups each hand, palms facing downward, and pantomimes the struggling gait of a young boy—each step a short, shallow arc in the air, reaching, stretching, searching for his father's tracks in the deep snow. "It was really hard. I got really tired." His foot stills. There is no sound other than his voice. "I yelled and yelled, but with the snow . . ."

Dan can't count the number of times he has asked himself: What if I had never stopped? What if I hadn't given up? The answers hang in the air, unspoken and obvious. They would have met and chatted. Walter Witt would have scooted over to make room for his oldest son on his burlap sack. For sure, they would have made a meaningful warning fuss.

Dan wipes the palms of his hands down the front of his khakis. He uncrosses his legs, and nods his head. He falls quiet, and for the first time his dark eyes glisten.

———～———

Walt was a patient hunter. He knew this farm well. He knew that deer liked to slip along the edge of the dark timber on their way to bed after feeding near the apple trees his wife's grandparents had planted years ago. It was cold, but there was no rush. He ate a sandwich and a candy bar, sipping water from a ketchup bottle he'd washed and used as a makeshift canteen. There was little money to spare in the Witt household, and you had to make do. But now, with Cathaleen's newly minted education, well . . . life just might get a bit easier.

A Brothers' Mission

The field edge where Walt led his father-in-law and sons is now a faint trail in a scrub of second-growth forest, and we wade through blackberry, ferns, and poison oak. Nothing looks like it did, but neither Dan, Mark, nor Askey is surprised by this. "Some of these pines were knee-high back then," Mark says. "But a lot of these woods were just open fields." As we descend toward Wills Creek, Askey's yellow Labrador retriever, Winchester, runs ahead, tail wagging above thistles and briers. He's the only one of us not on edge.

Within a few minutes, Dan disappears into the woods, calling out deer sign. I follow Mark, who peppers Askey with specifics.

Where did the other hunting party park?
Was somebody else on stand with Cutler?
What witnesses were interviewed?
What did they see?

It's been this way for a long time. While Dan seems resigned to the ultimate mysteries of his father's death, Mark has always pushed for more details, more specifics, more answers. A civilian logistics engineer with the Department of Defense in Alabama, Mark is in charge of support details for helicopter crews in Afghanistan and Iraq, and he takes a critical, analytical approach to confronting the unknown. When the brothers speak at events, Dan opens up with hunting stories and a personal testimony of what his father's death has helped him understand about God. Mark is more evangelistic. He's a kidder with a big smile, but he closes the talk with a sermon's defining motif. Mark isn't satisfied until his listeners grasp his core belief: God presents each person with a decision to make—what will you do about Jesus Christ?

And for Mark, too, anger at God defined his adolescence. For years, Mark wouldn't even talk about the day and would leave the room in a fury whenever his father's death was mentioned. "I was raised in the church," he says. Sweat runs into his eyes as he swats spiderwebs from his T-shirt. "But when this happened, it was like God made a mistake. Because of who my father was, how grateful he was to be a Christian. You don't let good people die."

Healing for Mark came years later, when, in his early 20s, he began teaching a Sunday school class for youth. Reaching out to kids who had their own hurts and questions was a turning point, and even now it appeals to Mark's penchant for directness and absolutes. He doesn't mince words to his students. "I tell my kids to go home and tell your parents you love them, because you might never get another chance. In a cemetery, you see tons of headstones that say stuff to other headstones: I'm sorry I didn't tell you this . . . I'm sorry I didn't say I love you. . . . But it's too late. You don't know if you have another moment."

Mark stops short, and looks up the hill. We can see blue sky winking through the trees, marking the edge of an old field. On that hunt long ago, Mark didn't last long in those snowy woods. Cold and tired, he headed back to his grandparents' farmhouse sometime before noon. He was there when he heard sirens, and learned of the accident.

In 2004, a few weeks before the thirtieth anniversary of their father's death, the minister at Meyersdale Grace Brethren Church asked Dan and Mark to come home and share their story to a congregation that had never forgotten Walter DeSales Witt. Neither brother had ever considered such a public forum. "We looked at it as an opportunity to just let people know we were OK," Dan says. "We figured hardly anybody was going to be there, but it was standing room only." He is still struck with wonder at the response. "The setting of being back home was . . ." His voice trails off to silence. "That night was really emotional."

Word of their presentation spread, and invitations to speak at other churches began trickling in. The Witt brothers visited a small church in West Virginia, then another church back in Meyersdale, and traveled to wild-game dinners hosted by area churches as an outreach effort to men. "You tell a deer hunting story, and it doesn't matter who the person is," Dan says, laughing. "It's a deer thing and hunters who have nothing to do with church will come out of the woodwork to listen." From their first story of homecoming and reconciliation, the brothers' presentation evolved into a testimony of faith and healing and even redemption. "We have a blast telling great hunting stories," Dan says, "but we always share our faith and the importance of knowing where you are going to spend eternity for this very reason: We know first-hand that you never know how much time you have left on this earth."

By now the brothers have spoken at perhaps a dozen churches. In the Edmonton, Alberta, area in July, more than 1,200 people came to hear them over a three-day speaking tour. They published a small tract, titled *Mistaken Identity*, in which they tell of their relationships with both their father and Jesus Christ, and of how, as Dan says, hunting has helped them understand that sharing their faith "is a part of God's plan for us right now, whether we understand how and why or not." Their six-panel pamphlet is unabashedly personal and unapologetically spiritual. Word of it has spread with no advertising or marketing, yet the Witts have gone through nearly 3,000 copies. "People call us up to send more tracts, and I'm like, 'How did you get this?'" Mark says. "I was cleaning up tornado damage in Alabama and some guy walks up to me with one in hand and says, 'This is amazing, I need more of these to hand out.' And I don't even know who these people are."

When Walt moved, his Air Force parka rustled against the rough bark of the hemlock. It was a warm coat, with a hood trimmed with wolf fur. His friends rode him hard about that coat. They told him to think twice about wearing it in the deer woods, with that ruff of gray-brown fur. But he needed it on a frigid day like this. After a few quiet hours, Witt heard men in the woods, on the move, hollering to drive deer. Most of the old family farm had been sold off a few years back, and locals had taken to pushing deer through the big woods. Still, it was hard to imagine anyone else would be here, not with the snow and rough roads.

❧

We search the woods for another hour, pushing lower and lower toward Wills Creek. At some point we lose sight of one another; I'm tangled in the briers that thatch the old road, while Mark and Askey cut a parallel course to both sides. Dan has pushed on ahead when we hear him call out from the woods, his voice clear and determined.

"Mark," he shouts. "Hey, Mark!"

"Yeah?"

"Come here!"

Consequences

Cutler had been on stand for about an hour, listening to the drivers holler through the woods, when movement in the dark timber across the slope caught his eye. He stepped up on a limb for a better view. Something was moving at the base of a hemlock tree, maybe 50 yards away. Something was there. For 15 minutes, eyes straining, Cutler picked apart the tangle of drooping branches and dark shadows. Each time a driver would yell, whatever it was under the hemlock would move slightly, as if turning toward the sound. It's one of the oldest tricks in the book. Most hunters know that a smart buck will do that—lie tight in thick cover and let the danger pass.

If only he could get a better view. About 20 feet from the hemlock, directly in his line of sight, a tree stump jutted from the ground, blocking anything but the faintest motion a few feet above the snow. He didn't have a scope on his rifle, but he could make out a swatch of gray-brown fur, and a black stripe like the ones that lie along each side of a mature buck's nose. Every now and then, it seemed as if a deer's antlers dipped and danced under the hemlock. Otherwise, the animal seemed calm. He might have to shoot just to get it to move. Maybe he could thread a bullet through the branches. If nothing else, that might scare the deer toward his hunting party.

———

There are two verities that every hunter accepts: Once a shot is fired, it cannot be controlled. The projectile will go where the muzzle was pointed until it hits something dense enough to absorb its energy or hard enough to deflect it along another, equally ungovernable, trajectory. You cannot put a bullet back into the barrel.

And there is never an excuse for one hunter to mistake another hunter for an animal. There may be circumstances that confound logic in the field and lead to confusion and misidentification and terrible judgment. But the first rule of picking up a gun is never to point it at anything you do not intend to punch a hole through or kill stone dead.

But it can happen, and it does happen, and every hunter knows this, too. In the US, from 2001 to 2010, 103 fatalities were reported to the International Hunter Education Association in which the cause of the incident was "failure to identify target." According to the National Safety Council, the rate of unintentional fatalities involving firearms dropped 55 percent from 1988 to 2008—and experts point to blaze-orange and hunter-education requirements, as well as tighter restrictions on transporting loaded guns, as lifesaving prescriptions. Still, hunting accidents happen, and there is never an excuse.

———

The drivers were coming. Now they couldn't be more than 150 yards—maybe 200—through the woods. The deer looked like it was staying put, no matter what. For Cutler, it was now or never.

———

On February 6, 1975, in the Court of Common Pleas of Somerset County, Pennsylvania, Johnston Cutler pleaded guilty to "shooting at and killing a human being in mistake for deer," a violation of Pennsylvania's Game Law 825(c). The trial was brief. The court records comprise a short twenty-three double-spaced, typewritten pages. The facts were laid out clearly: Cutler spotting movement in the timber as the drivers approached, the particulars of Walter Witt's makeshift blind in the hemlock boughs, the stump that blocked Cutler's view of Witt's torso and his blaze-orange vest, the terrible confluence of poor choices that led to the fatal shot. Cutler admitted guilt.

Even in her grief, Cathaleen Witt expressed to the young man that she bore him no ill will and forgave him for the deadly mistake that took the life of her husband.

Cutler was sentenced to three years' probation, was ordered to pay $1,000 compensation to the victim's family and the $13 cost of the prosecution, and forfeited his Pennsylvania hunting license for 10 years.

Walt's Place

By now the boys had long since grown tired and cold. Their boots—black rubber galoshes they wore for sledding—were no match for the chest-deep snowdrifts. Mark backtracked to his grandfather's house, but Dan stuck it out longer. On the hike in, he and Mark had quarreled about the fact that Mark got to carry a rifle on his very first deer hunt, whereas Dan had had to wait a couple of years before he was allowed such a privilege. Dan was determined to outlast his brother but now, shivering, he could take the cold no longer.

Dan stood up and followed his own tracks uphill where the snow was even deeper. His father's trail continued on, and Dan struggled to place his boots in the deep tracks. When the trail turned down a steep slope, Dan knew he'd never make it back up the hill. He stood in the woods and called for his father, but the deep snow, the dark timber, and the dripping melt swallowed his cries. He turned around. His father would understand. He headed back to his grandfather's house.

～•～

Dan's shout from the woods brings a catch to our throats. Mark passes me at a half run. The ground falls off more steeply as I stumble over mossy logs; blanketed with 3 feet of snow, this would have been a tough slope for a kid to climb indeed. Then, as the terrain flattens again, I see the first of the big hemlocks, and behind them the darker woods that form an interior edge deep in the forest. Dan is standing beside one of the largest hemlocks we've seen all day. Mark is down on his haunches, under the lower dead branches that droop toward the ground. Stuck into the trunk are two reflective thumbtacks, old and rusty. Some hunter marked this spot, marked this very tree. Any deer hunter worth his salt would know: This is the place to shoot a buck.

Mark finds my eyes. "This is the place," he says. "This has to be it."

He turns to Askey: "Where was Cutler standing? What would he have seen?"

Askey's face is ashen. The drivers would have been moving below us, he says, away from the creek. He remembers going back the next morning and replicating the crime scene with another officer. If this is the tree, there would have been another across the slope, to the right.

From there, Cutler would have watched the woods, deciphering every twitch of every bough.

—~—

Maybe 15 minutes after turning away from his father's snowy trail, walking toward the house, cold and alone, Dan heard a single rifle shot ring out in his dad's direction. The sound was unmistakable, one of those two-part shots—pa-THONK!—that occurs when a bullet hits something. Dan's heart leapt with excitement: Dad just got a deer!

—~—

Mark is at the base of the hemlock now. He shifts his body, pressing his back to the tree, trying to conform as closely as possible to what he imagines was his father's pose in those last moments of his life on earth.

"Is this about right?" he asks. "He would have been facing this way?" Mark shifts his legs so that a rifle might rest across his thighs. He swivels his head right and left. Askey and I say nothing.

"This should be it," Mark says. "This must be it."

The drivers would have been close. The deer would have looked like it was staying put, no matter what. Now or never.

Mark weeps quietly at the base of the hemlock, his body mostly hidden from view, only the rise and fall of his shoulders suggesting the cadence of his sobs. "This is what Cutler saw," he says. He reaches up with his right hand and grasps one of the hemlock's lower dead boughs, a thumb-thick branch that forks into shorter and shorter lengths like an antler. He pulls it down a few inches, then releases it to dance and bob directly overhead. "And then he shot Dad." He watches the branch until it no longer moves.

"This is as close as we're going to get," Mark adds. "Right here."

Dan and I exchange a glance. Mark gathers himself, then gets to his feet and takes a few steps from the hemlock. The woods are silent. No one knows what to say. Except for Mark. He turns to Askey to speak of the verity he lives by.

"OK. If it were you that day, what would have happened?" His glasses are in his hand, and he wipes his eyes with the back of a sweaty forearm. For a moment I'm unsure what he means, but only for a moment. "Do you know where you would have spent eternity?"

If ever a man could be forgiven for taking a moment to himself and putting up an emotional wall against the world, it is this man at this time and place. But Mark Witt is the son of Walter DeSales Witt, and he will not let pass an opportunity to speak. "Would you like to know for sure?" he asks, leaning away from the hemlock tree, toward Askey, his red-rimmed eyes softened by a small smile. "You can. You can know. I can share with you how."

The bullet was a .32 Winchester Special, and it entered Walter Witt's forehead just above the right eye, just below the gray-brown ruff of the fur hood the coroner's report would describe as a "Fur lined Head Dress," and just above the black stripe of his thick, dark sideburns.

Fathers & Sons

This is the hard time. Winter and snow. Family and Christmas. The best of times for a hunter, of course, but in some ways the worst days of the year for the Witt boys. When Walt was shot, there were already presents under the Christmas tree. The funeral was held two days before Santa arrived. Even for these brothers, for whom Christmas is a time of celebration, December brings an upwelling of difficult emotion. "We can ruin it for our families, we know that," Dan says. "Christmas is our wives' favorite time of year, but for us, it can be . . . horrible."

This year, though, there seems to be more light on the path ahead. I spoke with Dan in mid-October, a few weeks after bow season opened in the Virginia Blue Ridge. His elk trip had been a bit of a bust—too hot, too rainy—but he took his son Hunter for the first time, and had a chance to hand out a few *Mistaken Identity* tracts.

"I've been thinking about Moses wandering in the wilderness," he told me. "And Abraham being asked to sacrifice his son, and the stuff David went through. Things were put into their lives that God didn't bring to fruition for years and years. As Christians, we are called to share our faith. This just happens to be my story, and I'm just starting to understand that I don't know all of it. Mark and I just have to be open to what God might have in store."

For now, there are presents under the Christmas trees in Lynchburg, Virginia, and Huntsville, Alabama. Outside the leaves have fallen and the deer are settling down after the frantic weeks of the rut. At home, the brothers are redesigning their inspirational pamphlet with updated photos.

"I keep telling Mark," Dan says, "that we have to have some good photos, and those little Alabama bucks of his don't count."

In two months, they will visit the very church where their father was to preach the day after he died. They will step into the pulpit and tell stories about hunting, about their father, about the faith that sustains them. They will talk about the bullet that changed everything, except for those things that are eternal and unchangeable. It will be a difficult path, but they will walk it willingly. One step at a time. Down a trail made easier by the tracks of their father.

This Man Can Hunt

At 3 a.m. the grandfather clock peals, each baritone chime ringing hollow and pensive. From my place on the couch, the living room feels spare even in the dark—no ottomans, no coffee tables, no rugs. There are footsteps. And the click of a dog's nails on the floor. Under a door, a seam of light flashes yellow-white, glinting in the glass eyes of four mounted deer heads on the wall. The door swings open. "Come on in," Julie Bolender says softly. She is barefoot, in sweatpants and a T-shirt. "He's just waking up."

George Bolender is in bed, on his back, right arm crooked over his eyes to shield them from the light. Julie smiles wanly. She unhooks an overnight urine bag and pulls back Bolender's covers. First, the blue jeans. She lifts his right foot, threads the pants leg on. Now the left. She bends his knees and struggles to get the pants over his calves, his thighs. Bolender exhales. It is not easy on anyone.

Next, the morning exercises. Julie works each of Bolender's knee joints back and forth. She stretches the quadriceps, then the hamstrings. Bolender winces. "Spasms, not pain," he explains, through clenched teeth. "Not really." Artie, a young chocolate Lab, pads over to Bolender's bed, begging for attention. He drapes an arm over the edge of the mattress and rubs the dog's ears with the bone nub at the base of his wrist. Nearby, gray-muzzled Sam never cracks an eye. He is used to this.

Julie bends over her husband, hooks an arm under his shoulder, and lifts Bolender's torso off the bed. Now she can tug the thermal top down. She pulls on superinsulated coveralls. Right leg, then left. Julie is efficient. Each movement is fluid. It is a routine as familiar as dressing herself. Next the boots. Then insulated overboots. Quadriplegics have a diminished ability to thermoregulate, and Bolender has to bundle up in anything below 50 degrees.

It is 3:50 a.m. by the time Bolender is in the wheelchair and Julie cinches the boot straps around the frame to hold his feet steady when he pitches and rolls over rough spots in the trail. Finally it's time to go hunting.

George Bolender is 46 years old, slender and quick to smile and sporting a recently grown goatee. He is thoughtful and friendly and chatty. After all, he says, one thing he has is plenty of time.

Since a horrific vehicle accident in June 1991, Bolender has been a quadriplegic. He still has control of his biceps, but not his triceps. "I can move my shoulders, but I don't have any hands. Below the nipples, I got nothing." Except for pain. At times, his legs and butt will throb with terrific pain. "Of course, you could hit my toes with a hammer," he says, "and I wouldn't feel a thing. It's weird. But that's all a part of it."

The phantom pain, the severely restricted mobility, the constant chills, the odd looks from strangers, the altered relationships, the lost friendships— they are all a part of Bolender's day-to-day life in Ontario, New York, just east of Rochester. But astonishingly, so, too, are long days in the woods. Close shots at black bears. Wild turkeys feeding inside bow range. And whitetail deer on the wall that would turn most walking hunters green with envy.

Hunting with intricately modified bows and guns, Bolender takes three to four deer a season. It's enough to provide venison for his family, a few landowners who give him access to their woods, and a local needy family. He hunts two, three, sometimes four days a week. He does it through force of will and a network of supporters that brings tears to his eyes to contemplate. Julie, one of his sons, or a hunting buddy drops him off in the deer woods. Once at his stand site, he backs the electric wheelchair up against a tree or into a blind built with a backdrop of brush. His companion cocks his bow or racks a shell into the gun chamber, and then leaves. Alone, Bolender hunts. For food. For solitude. For a connection to the wild that he refuses to sever.

———

"Oh, yeah. Let me tell you about that one." Bolender is a good talker, a good storyteller. He rests his chin on his forearm, draped across the top of a kitchen chair. It's early afternoon, and we've both been up since that clock tolled in the middle of the night.

"That one" is a deer anyone would want to talk about. He was in Ohio, hunting a few days of last year's gun season. The day dawned windy. Does and fawns meandered by, then, at midmorning, a nice 8-pointer came through a ravine at 50 yards. To hunt with his Ruger Red Hawk .44 magnum, Bolender utilizes a homemade pistol mount crafted with a pair of car struts to handle recoil. To adjust for elevation, he bumps on and off an electric screwdriver whose gears drive the gun mount up and down. To fire the gun, Bolender sips on a mouth tube, which completes an electrical circuit that involves a solenoid attached to a car-trunk lifter that in turn pulls on a wire wrapped around the pistol trigger. Before he could get on target, the buck heard the whining screwdriver and took off. "There's not a thing I can do about that noise," Bolender says with a shrug, "except keep hunting."

Which he did. Seven hours later a "very big deer" started working his way up the ravine, disappeared, and then popped out of the brush. "What a beautiful sight!" Bolender exclaims. "Eighty yards, quartering away. I put the scope on his shoulder and sipped off a shot."

Nothing happened.

Bolender figured the solenoid was balking. "You know, they're not really made for this kind of thing," he says. "So I tried to free up the solenoid. I beat the crap out of it with my wrists. Two more shots, and nothing. That's when the geese showed up. They were heaven-sent."

With light falling, a flock of geese flew low over the trees. Their honks gave Bolender the cover he needed "to make all the noise I wanted. I uncocked the gun, pounded on the back of the solenoid as hard as I could—which isn't all that hard, of course—worked it back in the mount with my wrists, got the scope back on the deer, and sipped on the straw. All I saw then was muzzle flash. I heard him crash into the thicket. I laid my head back in the chair and almost began hyperventilating. I still remember my big puffy breaths making clouds in the cold air."

The buck sported 14 points, with double brow tines, 5-inch antler bases, and kicker points all over the place.

It was his biggest deer to date. Which is saying something. As does the George Bolender story in general.

—◦◦—

"Unrestrained passenger," Bolender says. "That's the term they use. Throw the keys to somebody else, thinking they're a little less drunk than you are. It's a bad idea."

It was the tail end of a long night of barhopping. His buddy was driving his pickup when they ran off the road. The next few seconds are still a blur, filled in through police reports and a fragmented memory. "We ran the length of a ditch. Went through some mailboxes. Overcorrected and went to the other side of the road." The impact of the ditch threw Bolender's friend through the rear glass, relatively unscathed. "But I'm still in the truck. Next we hit a telephone pole. Then a culvert pipe, and that's when the truck did an endo with a little flip-twist, went 50 feet through the air, and came down on the roof."

The telephone pole had bashed in the roof, and when the truck came to a rest, upside down, Bolender's head and shoulders were nestled in the indentation, between the truck top and the ditch. The rest of his body was still inside the vehicle. "I was folded in half. The only thing I really remember is waking up when they were drilling my head out. When I came to, it was three days later." Bolender's neck was broken between the fifth and sixth cervical vertebrae.

After three months in the hospital, Bolender entered a rehabilitation center in Scranton, Pennsylvania, for six weeks of additional therapy. The sessions were difficult; the life they were designed to prepare him for, painful to consider. After the workouts, be rolled his wheelchair along a bank of large windows that overlooked the clinic lawn. Late each afternoon, deer would step out of the woods to feed. Hunting had been his lifelong passion, ever since he'd hunted pheasants as a child, with a cocker spaniel tied to his belt. "So many times, I went from window to window to watch the deer." He is quiet for a moment. "I'd tell myself: It's never going to happen, George. Forget about it. It's just never going to happen." He would roll back to his room and weep.

But George Bolender wasn't out of the hunting game. Still in rehab, he heard about programs for disabled hunters. Organizations such as Buckmasters Ltd. and the NRA's Disabled Shooting Services department help support a nationwide network of clubs, organized hunts, financial aid options, and consulting services for disabled hunters and shooters. Just a few weeks after his return home, Julie drove Bolender to Syracuse, New York, where a man built adaptive bow rigs for severely handicapped hunters. Within 15 minutes of trying out a bow, Bolender was sending arrows into a bull's-eye.

"I kept looking around at Julie, like, *I just can't believe this,*" he says. "A light went off for me. I could see a world of possibility that I thought had been shut off forever." He'd lost his job as a contractor and faced daunting bills and an uncertain future, but he sold a few guns to pay for a $750 PSE bow and rig. His brother-in-law, Russell Zaft, a welder, upgraded the bow with camber adjustments and an elevation screw. (Zaft has since built all of Bolender's hunting rigs.) In November 1993, Bolender killed his first deer "from the chair," he says, a small buck he took with a 20-gauge shotgun. He'd missed but two deer seasons and has not missed one since. To date, he has taken upwards of thirty-five deer with both bow and gun, plus a 6-foot, 7-inch Newfoundland black bear arrowed from a ground blind at fourteen paces.

As an archer, Bolender has handicaps far beyond his lack of mobility. While he is exempt from that most critical aspect of felling a deer with an arrow—drawing the bow while an animal is in range—it's a minor concession.

Bolender's 70-pound-draw-weight Oneida compound bow is mounted permanently to a universal joint, which is in turn mounted to a system of metal bars and plates that fit securely into the armrest mounts on his wheelchair. A 33-inch-long metal rod is welded to the bow holder at a 90-degree angle. On the end are a standard mechanical release and a small bite plate. With the bow drawn and locked into the release, Bolender aims with his mouth. As he moves his head, the bite plate, metal rod, bow mount, and bow move as one.

To shoot, Bolender must first hook his left arm around the back of the wheelchair—no small feat without the use of triceps and torso musculature. If he doesn't, he will fall over and out of the chair when he raises his right arm, unsteadily, to hook his hand over the metal draw rod and maneuver the bite plate into his mouth. Next, he hooks the back of his right thumb in front of the release. He aims, then fires by flexing his biceps slightly, which pulls his thumb against the release.

He has one shot; he cannot reload the bow. If the deer come behind him, they will walk. If they pass too far to the right or left, they will walk. If the wind shifts and sends the scent of Julie and Attie and Sam and his clothes and the four-wheeler and the wheelchair their way, there is nothing he can do but sit and hunt.

But let a deer walk with its head down, within 35 yards of his chair, and within a field of fire from, say, ten o'clock to two o'clock, and it will most likely hear what Bolender describes as the sound of a hammer hitting a metal pole, which is the sound his bow mount makes when he squeezes off a shot.

It's rarely easy, though. One afternoon we hunt a gorgeous tract of land with Bolender's buddy Paul Juszczak. Cornfields slope away into a tangled bottom, wet and mucky and trellised with deer trails worn down like cow paths. We work on a rough blind as falling leaves signal a shifting wind. Across the path is dense brush, a perfect place to hide the chair. But the swirling air, wrong for just about everywhere, is perfectly wrong for that side of the trail. For 20 minutes Juszczak and I cut and drag brush to break up the outline of two men and one wheelchair. "It's no good," Bolender finally says, shaking his head, and he's right. "Come on. The light's getting lower. Let's just settle down and give it a shot."

So we sit. I go directly behind him. For the duration of the hunt, Bolender holds his mouthpiece between his teeth, something he rarely does. But our exposure demands extreme stealth. We hunt hard, which in this case means we are stone still and stiller, until our legs cramp and the shadows blacken and the wood ducks begin to leave the swamp for some other roost. We hunt hard, which means we don't move a muscle in two hours.

Suddenly I catch a glimpse of movement, off to our left. A nice-size doe makes her way down the wood's path, slowly, feeding. I slant my face away from her approach and tap the wheelchair with the toe of my boot. "Left." I whisper. For long moments I wonder if Bolender heard me. Could he feel the tap-tap-tap? Then I notice that his bow is creeping to the left so slowly that I can only discern the movement by tracking the bow's progress against the vertical tree trunks. He pivots his head to bring his bow toward the deer. Ever. So. Slowly. I grin: The man can hunt.

The day before, in his house after a morning on a different stand, Bolender spoke about what he finds in the woods. "I know there's work that's got to be done beforehand," he told me. "I know I can't do this without a lot of help. But after that, it's just me. All the weight is gone. All the *stuff* is gone. And when I'm out there, I feel total freedom. I'm one-on-one with the animal, and that's what a hunter does."

The doe feeds on chest-high thistles, a step closer, now two. She snips off greenery in the path, then she senses that all is not right. She freezes, head up, ears flared. She has seen no movement—there has been no movement—but something is amiss in the reeds and she knows it. Her tail twitches. When she stamps her right hoof in alarm, my heart sinks. The deer turns and walks away. Bolender never sees her. In a day and a half of hunting, she is the only chance we'll have.

—◆—

Bolender couldn't hunt without a remarkable community of support. His sons, George Jr. and Jessie, load gear, drive the van, and monitor the cell phones when he's in the woods. They clear the ground along hundreds of yards of trails so his wheelchair can pass safely and quickly. His buddies, Paul Juszczak, Jeff Emerling, and Ed Soble, scout new territory, build blinds, take him into the woods, drag deer.

But it is Julie who makes all this possible. "Every move I make," her husband says, "she's got to make two." "A saint," declares Juszczak. "There's going to be a statue of her in a church some day."

She does not like to hear such talk. She waves away the words. *No, no, I'm not like that.* But she is. She has learned to enjoy the walks home in the dark woods. ("They're nice, now, really.") She has learned to blood-trail. ("It's like one of those crime shows, you know? It's a lot of fun to figure it out.") But she does not like the questions, for all the questions lead to the same place: Why?

"Oh, I don't know," she says and looks away. "Maybe it's a little crazy," she says, softly, her voice like an echo. "But everything's crazy."

Another morning, like all the others. She is up, Bolender is dressed, she makes Eggo waffles and coffee. An overnight rain has left the woods a mess. This time they'll have to take the four-wheeler. She hooks up the trailer, loads the ATV, and warms the van.

Later, in the woods, she holds a quiver of five arrows. "Which one?" she whispers. Bolender points with a knuckle. She pulls the arrow from the quiver, tests the broadhead to make sure it's screwed in tightly, tests the nock. He nods. She then nocks the arrow to the bowstring and, standing behind the rig, pulls the bowstring, grimacing, and locks it into the mechanical release. "Is that okay?" she asks. Bolender studies the rig for a moment. "Perfect, pumpkin."

Julie drops a cell phone into the seat, pulls an insulated hood over his head, steps back, takes a look. She tugs on the bottom of Bolender's facemask to pull the eyeholes down just a bit.

"All set?"

"You bet."

She leans down. It's a meaningful kiss, no perfunctory brush of the cheek. I hear their lips smack like the cracking of a twig.

"Have fun," she says, and she turns and walks away. Bolender follows her with his eyes, silent, watching the light of her headlamp wink out behind the trees. For the time being, he will say no more. He is hunting. He is just another man in the woods, searching for peace and quiet and discipline and dignity and that remarkable moment when his life meets the wild and he's got as good a shot as any.

MR. MAC AND THE BUSHYTAIL GANG

Two hundred yards away, on the far side of a veil of ash, hickory, and muscadine vine, a dog breaks into a steady, chopping bark. Ark . . . ark . . . ark-ark-ark! Mac English doesn't miss a beat.

"Whose dog is that?" he asks. He gives a playful smirk. The question is directed at English's grandson Colby, who's having a hard time fighting off a grin of his own. "My goodness," the old man says. "I just know I've heard that dog somewhere before."

The barking grows incessant, more purposeful.

"Could that be my Jack?"

"I don't know, Papa," Colby says. He shakes his head, giving up the fight to keep a smile off his face. "Sounds like some ol' trash dog is ruining my Buckshot's chances again."

English, 77, is lean and wiry with a head of white hair that's easier to follow through the woods than the man himself. He wears denim overalls and a battered hunting coat, and when his dog barks, it's time to go—but not until he's had a chance to rub somebody else's nose in the fact that his dog was first on the job. When you're hunting squirrels with squirrel dogs and the English clan of South Carolina's rolling, red-clay Piedmont, it's sometimes hard to say exactly what the quarry is: a squirrel, or bragging rights as to whose dog treed the squirrel.

<hr />

Once upon a time, squirrel dogs were as common in the South and Midwest as cotton gins and working mules. These small-to-middling-size breeds—mountain curs, treeing feists, Kenner curs, treeing brindles, and the like—were a family staple with pioneer roots. "When our early settlers came into this country," English tells me, "they brought these little dogs with them and they hunted everything. They'd tree a coon or a squirrel, run a deer, run a hog. You couldn't get by without them." Such breeds are a part of American sporting literature as well. George Washington wrote about yellow cur dogs. Abraham Lincoln was a fan; a "short-legged fice" was hot in pursuit of bruin in his poem "The Bear Hunt." These treeing dogs figured in William Faulkner's "The Bear" and Marjorie Kinnan Rawlings's *The Yearling*, and the dog that played Old Yeller in the movie, many say, was a black mouth cur. By the middle of the twentieth century, however, most of these specialty hunters had nearly disappeared, and with them a small-game tradition with a storied past.

But what I find here is a full-blown squirrel dog revival, particularly when it comes to the original mountain cur breed. In 1957, four men who met through an interest in old-time mountain music formed a club to promote line breeding of original mountain curs. Today, the breed is recognized by the United Kennel Club, with dozens of breeders listed in the forty-ninth annual yearbook of the Original Mountain Cur Breeders Association. There are now squirrel dogs from perhaps thirty breeders and bloodlines—a crazy-quilt mix of old-time mountain pride and modern demographics. In fact, squirrel dogs these days are all about the future, as interest in these little hunters is growing by leaps and bounds.

At first, line breeding for squirrel dogs was a mountain-hollow niche that involved a few old-timers determined to hang on to the past. No longer. The Internet has linked squirrel dog fans into a community. Membership on the website Squirrel Dog Central has tripled over the last few years. In North Carolina, my buddy Robert Edwards, who's joined me on this hunt, waited three years for his treeing feist puppy. The dollars involved only strengthen the legitimacy of the trend: These days, a pretty good young dog will run maybe $300.

According to English, "a No. 1 squirrel dog, broke on deer and 5 years old, will bring you $10,000." And English is smack in the middle of it all, with a single-minded obsession with squirrel dogs, squirrel hunting, and the dying art of making a good squirrel meal. Retired for 22 years from his days working in the maintenance department at a nylon plant, he hunts as often as six times a week. Most years his hunting parties will take 300 squirrels or better; his record is a staggering 544. He's a major player in the comeback of the original mountain cur breed, and the star talent in a squirrel hunting video. His phone rings 52 weeks a year with folks wanting a puppy, advice, or a guided day in the woods. And he's equally known for what comes out of his black cast-iron pots as for what goes in them: fried squirrel with biscuits and squirrel-broth gravy, squirrel and dumplings, stewed squirrel with tomatoes, squirrel chowder . . . English is a one-man circuit preacher for the wonders of squirrel.

But right now there's a three-dog racket pouring out of the woods, and already young Colby is 50 yards into the trees. English is right behind him, followed by his son Chad, grandson Chase, family friend Danny Souther-land, plus Edwards and me. It doesn't take long to figure out that before I learn another thing about squirrel hunting with dogs the Mac English way, I'll first have to learn to keep up.

Squirrel hunting with dogs barely resembles my boyhood passion of hunkering down under a huge oak and waiting for targets to appear. It's fast-paced and active, but something else is at work to bolster the future for these dogs, and that's the fact that squirrel dogs and squirrel dog hunting are particularly suited to the exigencies of modern life. Compared with many hound breeds, a 20-pound feist is more family friendly and easier to keep in the house. Some states are lengthening their squirrel seasons to attract more hunters, so opportunities to chase bushytails are now available from summer through the end of winter. And part of the growth in squirrel hunting with dogs is coming from the ranks of coon hunters weary of late-night races and rabbit hunters struggling to find good hunting grounds.

As a kid English hunted squirrels the way everyone else hunted squirrels. "Until I was 8 or 9," he says, "I loved to sneak into some hickory trees before daylight. Back then, everybody still-hunted and we all used shotguns. I didn't know what a .22 rifle was." Then, in 1950, English went hunting with his "first known squirrel dog," and he's never looked back. He founded the South Carolina Squirrel Hunters Association, whose Whitmire, South Carolina, headquarters hosts the squirrel hunting world championship, and he's single-handedly nurtured a squirrel-dogging craze that has helped reshape hunting in the region. These days, there are upwards of thirty hunters with squirrel dogs within a 15-mile radius of Whitmire, and almost without exception there is a connection to English.

"He has people he's never even heard of calling him on a weekly basis," Chad English says. "People in the Walmart stop him in the aisles. 'Are you Mac English? I saw you on the Internet.' We tease him about being a celebrity, but he's not doing it for the attention. He's just doing what he's always done, and he loves to show other people what he loves. And it just seems like it's caught fire."

At the base of a soaring shagbark hickory, Jack, Buckshot, and a yellow cur named Ann are putting up a fuss. Unlike coon dogs, most squirrel dogs are silent on the track. Their job is to find a hot scent trail, narrow it down to the last tree climbed by their quarry, then pin the squirrel to the branches by raising a ruckus that keeps the animal's focus off the hunters below. Now the dogs have their heads back and tails wagging, barking to beat the band, clawing at the tree, then backing off to watch the topmost branches in case the object of their desire starts "topping out" or "timbering," jumping from tree to tree in an attempt to find safe haven. If dogs can smile, these three are. I am, too. After all, four grown men, two kids, three dogs, five guns, and thousands of dollars' worth of high-tech optics and GPS dog collars surround a squirrel in a tree—or at least, a tree that may hold a squirrel.

Much of the intrigue of squirrel hunting with dogs, I'm learning, is the challenge of actually trying to spot a squirrel whose life depends on staying hidden. These little jokers are wizards at disappearing in plain view. To find them, you never look for the squirrel itself. You look for a little piece of swollen limb, the dark spot of an eye, a piece of bark that looks slightly unbarkish, a lump on a branch, the sharp point of a squirrel's ear sticking out from a piece of moss. And all of this is at 80 feet high or better. But this time, thank my lucky stars, the squirrel is stretched out on a sunny branch like a college kid at Daytona Beach. Not that it's easy. I'd been warned to bring my best game to South Carolina. "That man can read a squirrel dog in the woods like nobody I've ever seen," says Tree Time Kennels owner Russ Cassell, whose original mountain cur, Culbertson's Wild Rose, is a world champion squirrel dog. "It's uncanny to watch, like he knows everything they're thinking."

And English's prowess isn't limited to keeping up with canines. "Mac English has an extreme, over-the-top pride in shooting squirrels in the head," Jim LaPratt explained on the phone a few weeks earlier. A diehard Michigan squirrel dogger, LaPratt runs the website Squirrel Dog Central, the virtual bible of the sport. "He's turned it into an art form."

English hunts with a Ruger 77/22 with a Leupold Rifleman scope and shoots standard-velocity CCI rounds, a load very close to competition ammo. He favors solid bullets over hollow points, because the only sin more unforgivable than missing a squirrel's noggin is ruining its flavorful meat. Before the hunt English warned me: "Boy, you shoot a squirrel and there ain't no need to run up there and jerk him up off the ground and put him in your vest where nobody can see him. We got to inspect him, and this crowd will raise sand if there's a hole anywhere but the head."

My first shot on a squirrel, earlier in the hunt, brought down a heap of scorn from English, and I'm sure it wasn't all in jest. "Oh, Lord," he said, holding my squirrel with two fingers like a soiled diaper. It was a picture-perfect gallbladder shot, with bits of red guts pushed out the far side of the ribs. "Oh, goodness. Somebody else is going to have to carry this. Looking at it just about makes me sick." Now I have a rock-steady rest, a squirrel silhouetted against the sky, and English at my elbow. He's not letting me off easy. "It just don't seem right," he says, "that squirrel sitting out there in the open. Really, you ought to be ashamed taking a shot like that." The crosshairs waver for a moment, and English pours it on. "My goodness, you ought to have some mercy on that poor little squirrel, all stretched out in the sunshine." I let out half a breath and squeeze. "Oh, Lord, look at the squirrel. Glad that ain't my shot. No excuses now." The rifle goes off and the squirrel tumbles. The dogs are barking and my buddies are whooping and Mr. Mac is hoofing it to the tree. It's a small squirrel, a yearling tender as a green bean, and already English can taste it. "That's a fryer, boys! Get the dogs! I don't want a tooth on him!"

———

Training a squirrel dog is as simple a thing as you can imagine, according to English. As long as you start off with a squirrel dog. "About the only thing you can do is get a squirrel dog that comes from squirrel dogs, and get that puppy in the woods," he says. "If squirrel hunting's in him, it'll come out. And if it ain't, well, you got a long road ahead." There are ways to tip the odds in a hunter's favor. Many tie a squirrel tail to the end of a cane pole and run it up, down, and around the base of a big tree, with the puppy in hot pursuit. Others live-trap a squirrel and place the trap and squirrel on the ground and open the door in front of the puppy. "That young dog sees that squirrel going up a tree," English says, "and most times, that will do the trick." The end result is to get a dog "just pure eat up with squirrel," English says, and watching what happens then is the great delight of squirrel-dog hunting.

Early the next morning, we're hunting a big swath of Sumter National Forest—open bottoms along timbered creeks thick with vines and scattered pines in the hardwoods. I lean against a big beech tree, its late-winter leaves still hanging on, and watch Buckshot work the woods. He's a 30-pound shorthair vacuum cleaner, muzzle to the ground, sucking up scent. Buckshot runs around a tree (*sniff-sniff*), hops on a fallen log like a chipmunk (*sniff-sniff*), docked tail wagging. He inspects a tree stump (*sniff-sniff*), then a rock pile (*sniff-sniff*). He worms through a copse of cedars (*sniff-sniff*) anywhere a squirrel might run. Now he's off wide open through the woods, nose stuck to the ground, around a white oak (*sniff-sniff*), then a red oak (*sniff-sniff*). Something catches his attention, and Buckshot is on his hind legs, paws on the oak trunk, dancing halfway around the tree (*sniff-sniff*) but whatever it is isn't quite enough because suddenly he's off again, disappearing into the woods.

And when he trees, it's Katy-bar-the-door. A single bark makes us cock our ears toward Buckshot's general direction, and then he opens up with a steady, bawling get-here-and-get-here-fast chop. "Whose dog is that, Papa?" Colby yells as we dash through the woods. Blackjack and Ann are already at the tree, joining the fray. What happens next is just one more aspect to the Mac English aura. At the tree we're all searching for the squirrel, binoculars picking apart each tree fork and knothole. "Can you see him, Mac?" someone asks.

"Naw. Can you?"

"Uh-uh."

"Is that him? See where the tree forks and forks again? Go up the right fork to where that piece of moss is on the trunk. I think I see a little piece of leg right there."

Yes, it is. We all jockey for position. There's only one shot, though, a tight angle to the squirrel's head, flattened against the trunk. And there's not a tree positioned correctly for a rest. Which means it's up to English. Years ago, he and his brother perfected a shooting position, tailored to the demands of a high-angle shot with no rest and no margin for error. Within seconds the man who's nearly 80 years old is on the ground, legs interlocked like a pretzel, gun barrel at a 45-degree angle. This time, it's me who fights a smirk. There is complete pandemonium at the tree—three dogs leaping and barking and clawing, and four hunters looking up in the branches with hands stuck in their pockets—and the old man balls up on the ground. *Crack!* My mouth drops open as quickly as the squirrel drops from the tree. That shooting lane couldn't have been half an inch in diameter, a pinprick of clear sailing between vines and twigs and branches, maybe 170 feet to the target. I look down at English, and he hasn't moved a muscle. Now he's smiling at me. "I do believe that squirrel has a headache."

The Locals

It all started as an Internet date, back in 2005. Josh Pelletier posted a photo of green-winged teal on a local duck hunting chat board, and up popped a direct message from a total stranger: "You don't know me," wrote Cullen Ports, "but I can tell exactly where you killed those ducks. Careful." They met a few days later over a beer at Hooters. It was like a match on Duck Tinder. They've been tight ever since, and from there the gang took shape.

Pelletier knew a pretty cool guy from college, Josh Eddings. That made three. Travis Grimes married Pelletier's sister-in-law, who had been a debutante with Gabe White's wife, so add those two to the mix for a hunting party of five—about as many folks that can crowd into a blind and not flare ducks.

And then there's John Webb.

"No one knows how in the hell we inherited John Webb," White says.

Six it is.

Six friends who hunt, fish, and golf together. Their families vacation together. They watch one another's kids. They even run a small nonprofit, Combat Warriors, guiding soldiers on local hunting and fishing trips. A half dozen buddies tight as ticks, and maybe not so different from close friends all over, with one possible exception: Come September, these guys fully commit to an exhausting, highly coordinated, monthlong regimen of scouting and hunting resident Canada geese that flock up in vast North Carolina farm fields. And they shoot them by the truckload.

Like many other states, North Carolina throws out half the rulebook during its 30-day September goose season. For a month, nonmigratory resident birds can be hunted with unplugged shotguns and electronic calls; shooting hours are extended a half hour past sunset, and there's a liberal fifteen-bird limit. On any given day in September, most of the crew is on the road before dawn, scouting peanuts, corn, soybeans, and swamp roosts across a million acres of the state. They log close to 10,000 scouting miles. They track down farmers, knock on doors, pump every contact they can think of to find birds and lock down fields. They text constantly in a 24/7 group message that will grow to thousands of texts.

My birds haven't moved. Cut corn yesterday so any day now.

2 peanut fields I have are so tight we need tennis rackets but I'm working on both.

Gabe can you ride Delman Road?

I'm near Whitman. Geese in the air I'm chasin.

Cullen what's the report north of bull town, ring in man WTH are you doin. His hungry children can wait. We need long nose geese to kill.

In fact, much of the group's success comes from its enviable closeness; chasing local geese over the last eight years has forged deep relationships. "In the last year," Ports says, "every one of us has brought a new baby home, and every one of us visited the others to see their baby. It's crazy how some of our deepest relationships in this world are based on hunting, but that's how it has evolved. We all have shared values. We know we have something special going on."

Last year, I hooked up with the gang for the full September season. I wanted to see what it took to excel in the increasingly competitive game of resident goose hunting. At month's end I walked away with a new appreciation for the ties that bind the hearts of hunters. That and 40 pounds of goose breasts.

⚬⚬

The geese first appear over the treeline, 600 yards away, one giant wad of ragged lines. In minutes the 200 birds have broken into four smaller flocks, and there are geese behind us, over us, in front, and to the sides. We don't move a muscle. Nellie and Scout thump their tails excitedly in the corn duff, but the dogs can't hear what we're thinking: A couple hundred resident Canadas honking overhead is the last thing we want to see.

Three times the birds circle as we clench shotguns and pray: Please, please, please. Then, one by one, the flocks peel off and set their wings for the next field over. Ninety seconds tick by while every single goose is sucked away, and the sky overhead empties. We lie in the blinds, heartsick. Days of scouting, hours of effort, and we may as well go get a biscuit.

Eddings hollers from inside his field blind: "I. Hate. Big. Groups."

"That many eyeballs," White says from the layout next to mine. "It wasn't going to happen."

Just then the blind at the end of the line bursts open. Pelletier unfolds his lanky frame, stomps the cornstalks off his body, and paces off 50 yards downwind. He's the de facto leader of this band of hunters, a biologist for the US Army Corps of Engineers and a Zink/Avian-X pro staffer, and he doesn't take failure lightly. He paces. He throws cornstalks into the wind. He glowers.

"Dude hates to lose," White says. "He'll freaking drive us nuts obsessing over what went wrong. Glad I'm not riding home with him."

The fact that it takes work to dial in on resident Canadas may come as a surprise to some. These birds have long been disrespected as golf-course geese and sky carp. They deserve some of that scorn, nesting in skanky city ponds and waddling around mall parking lots to scavenge trash. But in sprawling agricultural landscapes such as eastern North Carolina, resident Canadas are a wild and wary bunch.

"It's not like Nebraska where there's a new flock every five days," Ports says. "These birds know every rock in every field. We've been hunting some of the same flocks for five years, and by now they know us by name. Resident geese used to be the dumbest animals on the planet, but those days are over."

Killing such homegrown birds requires a helicopter mom's approach. The group is in near-constant contact, so as soon as birds are spotted, somebody will call somebody who knows somebody. Within 15 minutes of a flock's landing, the group typically has a landowner's name and address figured out. With the birds found, they rescout to pinpoint landing zones and wait till weather conditions and flock movements are perfect before bringing in a trailer of layout blinds and full-body decoys.

"Trying to pull resident geese 150 yards is like trying to pull them 3 miles," Pelletier says. "If you want to kill twenty or thirty geese, you need to be where they were putting their feet down the past three days."

Just as important is knowing exactly when to pull the trigger on a hunt. This time of year, farmers are heavy into harvest, and freshly cut fields crop up constantly. Geese are shifting from smaller family groups to larger wintering flocks, and feeding dynamics and preferred fields can change in a matter of hours. The group's 24/7 text chatter keeps eyeballs on multiple options, monitoring the flocks so they can make the call to hunt as bird numbers max out before the entire flock moves elsewhere to feed.

All the effort, the patience, and the miles pay off. Over the past eight years, the group has averaged 250 geese a season. A good day's bag is twenty-five. Their one-day record, with a few other friends in the mix, is an astonishing 105 Canada geese piled up in a sweet potato field. And on most days, the guys are back at work by midmorning.

Of course, every family has its squabbles. Early on one scouting morning Pelletier monitors four guys on the prowl across six counties. It's just a few minutes after daylight, and he's on the phone, riding Ports hard. "Have you gone to the Brown farm yet?" Pelletier asks him. "What?! Lock it down, man. Take a fruit basket. Whatever you got to do. There's a lot of geese in that field." He hangs up but never takes his eyes off the phone. "Where's John Webb?" Pelletier wonders aloud. "What is his deal?"

He punches in a text. *What's happening John what are you doing?*

No response. The phone rings. It's White. He's been on the phone with Webb, who is an hour to the east, looking for a turnaround on the interstate so he can take up the chase on geese flying in the opposite direction. Pelletier fires off another text to see if anyone can give him a hand.

"Bickering back and forth," Eddings tells me later. "That's the only way we know we like each other."

As we watch his field in the early light, Pelletier pulls out a small green notebook. For the past four years he has kept detailed scouting and hunting notes. He jots down field locations, climate conditions, and tick marks for every single bird or group of geese that he sees, how many are in the group, what time they appeared over the trees, and from which direction they were flying. Every hunt. Every scouting trip. Every time.

"Anybody can put out a few decoys and maybe draw a few birds, but that's not what we're about," he explains. "Folks like to see big flights, but I look for waves of five or ten birds coming in a few minutes apart. If forty come in at once and you drop ten, all that means is that you educate thirty, and they'll give you a big circle the rest of the year." It requires discipline, but the group has let eighty geese land in the decoys without firing a shot.

And these days, goose hunters must hunt smarter than ever. More and more hunters are taking a swipe at the growing numbers of resident Canadas. "Five years ago," Ports tells me, "I'd ask a farmer for permission to shoot the 200 geese wearing his peanuts out and he'd say, 'I got geese?' Now, everybody and their cousin buys a dozen decoys and turns into a goose hunter. We know who the young guns are out here, our competition."

The competition is always on their minds, not only because they have to beat them to the birds, but so they can crow a bit about their successes. Every hunt ends with a quick photo session, and the Instagram posts go up in a matter of minutes—showing goose piles carefully arranged so every head can be counted, but without treelines or background buildings that could suggest location.

"There's a couple of groups we have to stay ahead of," Grimes says one morning as he eyeballs truck lights arcing across a nearby field while we pull decoys from the trailer. "It's getting harder, and our lives aren't getting any simpler with kids and jobs and more responsibilities. But I think that's why we like it so much. Nobody is on their own in this deal. We're all in it together."

———

Even a farm-country resident Canada won't turn down an easy meal. That's why we find ourselves pulling on knee boots at 5 a.m. one morning, beside the Dumpsters behind a Dollar Tree parking lot.

Pelletier spotted the flock first—cupping over a Walmart, a McDonald's off their right wing tips, and lighting into a 10-acre cornfield where a scrubby ditch lay along the exact eastern border of the city limits.

Found em. There are 878 gajillion. Someone with a computer call me. Could be dicey.

Jp send me screen shot of field so I can gps.

See that bushy ditch? Could be close enough to make it work.

Hero or zero. Let's watch it.

For a week and a half, Eddings kept his eyes on the birds, watching the numbers build. When the total crested 200, the boys made the call.

It was perfectly safe—but still. Eddings talked to locals and zoomed in on Google Earth to make sure we could set up far enough away from occupied vehicles. Pelletier researched the field on a county GIS website to confirm that it was out of the city's jurisdiction, and called the city police department, the county sheriff, and the state game department to make sure we would be on the up and up. All of that took the better part of a day. No one could come up with a reason that we couldn't drop the hammer on Dollar Tree geese.

The hunt was on.

In the predawn there are peculiar logistics. We have to fine-tune the decoy spread to turn the geese away from the Dollar Tree and persuade them to set their wings outside a couple of self-declared no-shoot zones, due to houses 500 yards away. And we need to get them low enough to take before any cripples can sail across the plane of the city-limits line, 5 feet behind the ditch where we hide. The game warden who comes to check us is so impressed by the attention to detail that he jumps in the ditch with us to enjoy the show. Several small flocks spill into the field. We whoop and holler with each Canada that thumps the ground, amazed that it all came together.

A CrossFit class in neon spandex watches the last few volleys during warm-ups behind the shopping center. We walk out of the field with twenty-two perfectly legal Canada geese, double-timing to the trucks to get the decoys up and the trailer loaded before the morning Dollar Tree shift shows up for work.

"You know who else goes this crazy over resident geese?" Eddings asks as we scramble up a brier bank to the parking lot. "Exactly nobody."

There's more to this September madness than bragging rights on Instagram. I witness it on another hunt, in a sloppy mud pit of a huge cornfield that is a far cry from the civilized Dollar Tree scene. We pile up twenty-one geese—a pretty good few hours, by these guys' standards—but one shot is a goose for the books. With a half dozen guns blazing, it's sometimes difficult to tell who hits what, and on our last volley a wounded goose sails into the woods 300 yards away.

Ports lines up his yellow Lab, Scout, and sends him on the mark. The retriever has been on nearly every one of the group's September hunts. He's traveled on the group's annual road trip to North Dakota, and he was waiting at the house when Ports brought each of his two children home from the hospital. But now the dog is 10 years old, slowed by an old car-strike injury, and almost immediately, Ports is having second thoughts. Retrieves on big-field giant Canadas can be extremely long, and resident birds grow heavy. Ports told me earlier that this was probably Scout's last season on geese.

Now he wonders if he's pushed his dog across the line.

No one says a word, but we all stare at the wood's edge, hearts in our throats. Suddenly, Scout emerges from the trees, goose tight in his jaws. He struggles across a mud-sloppy field but closes the distance. Tears roll down Ports's cheeks. Everyone looks on. Most of these guys have dogs. They know the deal. White steps over and simply claps him on the back. No words. None needed. It's the language of brothers.

◆～◆

In mid-September, Tropical Storm Julia dumps 10 inches of rain on eastern North Carolina. The gang's goose grounds—and family homes—are ground zero for the floods. The texts go out all night long.

My boat just blew ½ down the driveway.

Bad here. 3 inches of water in the garage. Gabe you dry?
18 inches of rain. Siding's coming off now.
River sposed to crest at 32 ft.
You boys in my prayers.

Farm fields are rivers. White's hometown is practically underwater. No one has time to hunt; everyone has a friend or family member dealing with damage from the storm. And there's little to chase since most goose flocks are busted up and scattered. Then, a week after the storm, a text report comes in: Webb's cousin saw a small flock cupping into a peanut field behind Webb's parents' house.

Suddenly, the text string is on fire. Pelletier whips the boys into a scouting frenzy to figure out where the geese are roosting. Webb watches the field for five days as the numbers tick up to 100, 200, and keep climbing. When he figures there are 250 geese feeding in the field, they make the call. After the storm-blasted lull, the guys are ready to shoot.

So, an hour after sunrise, with not a goose in sight, the heckling begins in earnest. No smartphones now. They're giving Webb an earful in real time.

"Where are they, John?"

"We in the right field, John?"

"Zero hour, John."

"When it's your find," Webb tells me through a wad of sunflower seeds, "this is a rough crowd." He hollers down the line: "Y'all have some faith!"

Another 10 minutes.

"Should we just take up, John?"

"Nice scout, John."

I hear Nellie's tail thumping in the cornstalks 10 seconds before I hear the birds.

"Uh-huh!" Webb hollers.

Ports and Pelletier throw up a rolling thunder of cackles and honks. White and I flag like mad. A single flock of 150 birds skirts a treeline 400 yards away and never breaks stride. We wallow so deeply in disappointment that it takes a second to notice: Nellie's tail never stops thumping.

The next flock clears the treeline at half the distance of the first, and there's just enough time to shimmy down in the layout blinds. The first thirty honkers dump air at 75 yards, and when we pull out of the blinds they are 20 yards from our feet. Geese fold like black blankets and crash to the ground. The air above is flecked with hundreds of drifting feathers. Whoops and shouts ring out from a half dozen layouts.

"What do you say now, you freaking haters!" Webb jokes. "I take cash and credit!"

Nellie and Scout vault into action. It's been the toughest year these guys can recall—staying on top of geese through monster storms, six infants, old dogs, grown-up jobs. Now they trade backslaps, six young men shoulder to shoulder in the dirt, all for one, as the sky is dotted with resident geese on the run, honking like wild.

Tough Love

It was his jackleg float tube that really drove me crazy. I'd bought a brand-new camo belly boat for duck hunting—one of the first models that involved more than a Cordura-covered truck-tire inner tube—and my buddy Lee Davis and I had scouted the perfect duck swamp to give belly-boat hunting a whirl. When Davis showed up in the dark, however, he toted a *Beverly Hillbillies* version of my ride. He'd lashed a sky-blue boat cushion into the donut hole of a used inner tube from an 18-wheeler.

"Really, dude?" I said. "I got up at three o'clock in the morning for this hunt, and you show up with a yard-sale boat?"

He just grinned and easily bore it. Davis was used to being chided for leaning on gumption rather than gear. "Man, you don't need all that new stuff," he'd say. "Just tough it out."

Just tough it out. That was his refrain, year after year. Long after the rest of the world had shifted to polypropylene thermal underwear, Davis sported 100 percent cotton waffle weave, despite the fact they stank like a goat's belly after a few hours of hunting. He looked like the lumberjack on those paper towel rolls. I had to have every new flashlight on the market, while Davis was happy with his Rayovac that ate D batteries like jerky snacks. His decoys were anchored with a mishmash of U-bolts and railroad spikes. I swear I remember him once tying a decoy line to a can of beanie weenies. I spent a lot of time with Davis, standing in the dark, shaking my head.

I had Davis on my mind recently for a couple of reasons. For starters, I'd just finished cleaning up the last basement-floor mountain of hunting gear—a nearly waist-high pile of decoys, boots, tree-stand climbing sticks, fetid clothing, and candy bar wrappers that had accumulated like battery-terminal corrosion over the last few months. Like many of us, I've wound up with a ridiculous amount of gear over the years, and I can't wrap my head around why I keep every worn-out and outdated doodad.

In addition to postseason gear sorting, I'd also recently wrapped up reading a book about the ill-fated Donner Party, the Oregon Trail migrants who were snowed in along the High Sierras. They walked until their boots crumbled and their feet turned black. They ate their dogs, then their buffalo-hide blankets, then one another.

I'd never figured Davis for a cannibal, but there was no doubt he was cut from a different cloth than many. He'd played football in high school, a 5-foot, 9-inch atlatl bolt in the cornerback position whom the local paper called "pound for pound the toughest player to wear the Yellow Jacket uniform." He took that approach to hunting. He might not have had the best gear, or been the best duck caller, but he could outwalk, outpack, and outlast just about anybody. Hack through the worst beaver-swamp briers. Haul boats across the mudflats. Stay longer. Never complain. Not rely on stuff. Just tough it out.

What I noticed during all those years I hunted with Davis was that I had to rise to his level. It never occurred to Davis that maybe I was just average, so I grunted it out alongside. We pushed each other. No one was going to quit or cry uncle. I grew tougher—had to be—to hunt with Davis.

We're lucky if we're blessed with field partners who push us to levels of skill, endurance, and pain tolerance that we never would reach on our own. Another who's inspired me is my pal Scott Wood. I've hunted with him when he was so sick that I had to pull over to the side of the road so he could puke out the truck door, wipe his face, then hammer down to the woods. Hard to tell a guy like that that you'd rather just catch a few extra winks in the morning.

Davis's crowning achievement was his country-boy hack of the L.L.Bean town and country jacket. This was the ubiquitous tan corduroy zip-up coat with the knit sleeves and cuffs, designed for casual Fridays and lunch at the golf club. In Davis's hands, it became a blank canvas for a DIY camo job. As I was salivating over the latest love child between Gore-Tex and Mossy Oak, he was in the hardware store aisle, loading up on Rust-Oleum spray paint in flat black and drab green. He went with a vintage pattern, accentuated with a few stenciled leaves. That coat looked like a mildewed rucksack and smelled like a chemical plant, but he wore it for several duck seasons, rain or shine. Wet, the jacket must have weighed 15 pounds, and I'm convinced that he wore it long after he probably wanted to. Same thing with the cotton long johns and the Levi's jeans under his waders. Makeshift gear on the outside came to symbolize steely resolve on the inside. If you're tough enough, what do you care for comfort and convenience?

Of course, Lee broke down eventually. Maybe he didn't have anything else to prove. He bought a decent pair of waders, traded his old over-and-under shotgun or a semiauto, and even sported a few sets of synthetic underwear—although I've long suspected that he picked them from a ski-shop bargain bin.

But for many formative years during which I learned the limits of my own intestinal fortitude—not to mention the limits of my anterior cruciate ligaments—Lee would stage his gear at the edge of the railroad tracks, roll up a flannel shirt to show the waffle weave underneath, and hoist a pack of three dozen decoys that clinked with his junkyard anchors. I'd do the same, grunting, as he'd stop to turn around and shine that big Rayovac in my eyes and call out, "You coming, tough guy?"

BLOOD BROTHERS

The bears don't want to leave the thick stuff. They've been in there for 364 days straight, unmolested, and they're not coming out on their own. If you want a bear from Sliderock Den, a steep tangle of rock and thicket in north-central Pennsylvania, you'll have to roust it out, push it from its bed or off the trails that wind under the rhododendrons like subterranean tunnels. You'll have to drive it to its feet and shoot it on the run.

It is a task that defies imagination. The ground here rises 1,000 vertical feet in a meager half mile. Cloaked in rhodos 20 feet high, the slopes are cobbled in rivers of mossy, loose rock. Surveying the lone stretch of open ground on the mountain, a pipeline cut that runs like a claw mark straight uphill, Pat Weiss counts out fifteen specks of blaze orange strung out in a skirmish line. He is co-captain of the Tau Phi Delta bear drive, perhaps the largest, likely one of the best, and certainly the most storied Pennsylvania bear drive of the last half century. "The bears," Weiss tells me, as he readies to order his men into the breech, "have been in that hellhole all year long, and there's only one day they have to worry about anybody. We're the ones. And today's the day."

The lone professional and social forestry fraternity in the United States, Tau Phi Delta is a fully accredited member of the Interfraternity Council at Pennsylvania State University. In many respects, it's just like the other fifty fraternities at Penn State. Tau Phi Delta has a residence house, a Little Sister program, a formalized pledge process, and regularly scheduled—if, to be frank, marginally successful—mixers with Penn State sororities. Its philanthropy is proven: TPD regularly wins the Penn State "Blood Cup" for best participation in the annual blood drive and is the only Penn State fraternity that has been honored with a city proclamation for its service.

But that's where the typicality ends, for TPD was born and bred and continues to evolve as a brotherhood of diehard outdoorsmen. The frat house boasts a meat pole and freezers for the brothers' spoils. Venison is a dining-hall staple. There's an archery range in the side yard. And for the last 30 years, the so-called Tree House has turned into a de facto hunt camp during Pennsylvania's three-day bear season over Thanksgiving week. Brothers skip class. Alumni show up with cots and sleeping bags. And they do it the traditional way of Pennsylvania bear hunters—a squad of pushers, a squad of standers, and in between a hunk of gnarly Pennwoods.

We'd gathered in the shadow of Sliderock Den in the first minutes after dawn. Twenty-four active brothers and returning alumni were dressed in every permutation of hunting and farm garb, and not a single item of clothing was fresh from the box: blaze-orange bird vests, camouflage deer parkas, brush pants, boots flecked with timber-marking paint, worn-out leather chaps. They wear ankle braces and soccer shin guards and glance nervously at the mountainside, soft and brown and smooth as antler velvet from a half mile away. It's an illusion. "I did this last year," says one brother, shaking his head. "I can't believe anything lives on that f---ing mountain."

Now it's four minutes into the hunt and I have fallen five times and punched a hole in my left thumb that is bleeding down my wrist. I lost sight of my two flankers within 10 seconds of entering the woods, but I can hear their whoops and yells like distant beagles and cowboys: *Aaaa-oh! Aaaa-oh! Woo-oop! Woo-oop!* From knee height to 15 feet overhead, rhododendron branches web in all directions. I drag my gun, push my gun, thread my gun through a mat of wet leaves and veinlike boughs, with broken branches as pointy as stilettos. I worm my way under the really horrible parts spelunker-style, on my back. Then I walk for 40 feet without ever touching the ground, like a monkey through the canopy, crashing, bashing my way along. Rarely can I see farther than 5 feet.

All around me are the cries of a bear drive in action—guys drenched with sweat and dew, screaming out in frustration and resolve as they push for the bear. Every few minutes a cry passes up the mountainside, from one pusher to the next: "Hold the line!" Someone is bogged down in the brush, or sprawled on the rocks, and needs a break. We gauge our progress, and more importantly, the shape of the line by the hoots and hollers of the pushers above and below. It's critical that no one gets ahead, or behind, or moves too close to someone else in the line so as to create a gap where a smart bear could slip through unnoticed. It's a carefully crafted vise that tightens incrementally, step by step, on the bears hunkered down in Sliderock Den.

But those steps get more and more difficult to take. A cold front is moving through, and the mercury is plunging. Now every snot-slick branch is slimed with ice. At times, there's no choice but to shield my eyes with a forearm, cup the rifle's trigger guard with my other hand, and plow blindly forward until my progress is halted by a wall of vines. I cartwheel and karate-chop through the rhododendron jungle for a half hour . . . 45 minutes. Then I sense the vise slowly closing. There's a palpable feeling of anticipation in the wet air, like the scent of game. The standers can't be far. Surely the bears have run out of options. And that's when the shooting starts.

"Nobody shows up here saying, 'I've got to kill a bear,'" Weiss told me on Sunday night, as the TPD brothers and some two dozen alumni crowded into the frat house Chapter Room for a logistics and safety briefing before the next day's opener. "It's all about the we." Weiss is slender and bespectacled and scruffily bearded as if Ted Nugent had inhabited John Lennon's body. The brothers call him "Captain" partly out of respect for his considerable hunting skills and partly as a nod to his no-nonsense way of running the hunt. "I killed a bear on my first post, and I want other people to experience that feeling. That's why I ride these guys so hard to do it right. It's only three days, so we're balls to the wall. If I have to hurt a few feelings to get it done, so be it."

At the moment, the room is little more than a hunt camp. For the rest of the year, TPD takes great pride in keeping the house remarkably clean—it is swept, mopped, and scoured top to bottom seven days a week. Now, double rows of cots line the walls, and the floor is littered with boots, packs, sheath knives, long underwear, bottles of aspirin, and greasy earplugs. Topographic maps spill over a table, held in place with venison salami and cups of stale beer and tobacco spittle. Above it all the faces of bear hunters past grin in framed annual fraternity portraits hanging on the walls.

The origins of the Penn State Chapter of the Tau Phi Delta fraternity reach back to 1922. That year, the eighteen members of a forestry club persuaded the owner of a rooming house to rent rooms only to the club's foresters. Officially, TPD came to life two years later when those young men at Penn State and another small forestry fraternity at the University of Washington hammered out a national charter.

Over the next 50 years, a number of chapters flourished and faded at major universities. A University of Minnesota chapter "literally died out" during and after World War II, says Earl Howar, an alum and executive with the Izaak Walton League of America who serves as the frat's unofficial historian. The cofounding chapter at the University of Washington fizzled away in the 1970s. The brothers of Penn State are the last of the line.

But that doesn't mean they're a dying breed. The fraternity's numbers go up and down, but new pledges find their way to the Tree House every year, and the group has become a brain trust for wildlife conservation. TPD alumni stack the rosters of conservation agencies and nonprofits across the country; they work for just about every Pennsylvania resource agency, the US Fish and Wildlife Service, National Park Service, Rocky Mountain Elk Foundation, and National Rifle Association

No doubt the bear drives have played a part in keeping the group vital. They began in 1974, at brother John Shotzberger's grandmother's farm. "In Pennsylvania, you can't use bait and you can't use dogs," explains Howar. "But here you had a bunch of young, fit college kids who loved nothing better than to go running through godforsaken places. It had a twisted kind of logic to it."

The fraternity's homespun *Bear Drive Chronicles* tells the story of those early, glory days:

- 1974: Three hunters got turned around in a huge snowstorm and were lost for the day. No bears were seen.
- 1975: No bears were seen.
- 1976: No bears were seen.
- 1977–78: Closed season.
- 1979: No bears were seen. The windchill was minus 15, but "a baggie full of old bear shit" was produced to prove that bears had been in the area.
- 1980: A big year for the bear drive. Bob Walley left the beer tap running and drained the keg onto the floor. The sewer backed up into the dining room. Poker games went on all night. The washer broke down, and a flood roared through the ceiling and into the Chapter Room. But the TPD Little Sisters started a beloved tradition of preparing opening day breakfast and lunch, and the brothers finally drew blood: a 402-pound male shot at least seven times before he went down.

In 1987, the year *Pennsylvania Sportsman* magazine declared bear drives "nearly a lost art," Tau Phi Delta went on a tear. They killed bears for the next six seasons in a row. Over the years, the drives grew to be huge affairs, with upwards of fifty participants until the state regulations limited the number to twenty-five. About that time, some of the older alums formed a couple of TPD bear drives in Potter County and Forest County—"the prodigal sons of the north," as one brother describes them.

But the hunts out of the Tree House are only getting better. In 2004, the brothers put four bears on the ground, three in a single first-day drive. Much of the second day was spent successfully blood-trailing the fourth bear through pouring rain. On the third day, shifts of eight men took turns breaking through the rhodos, and they licked their wounds after hauling 1,000 pounds of bear out of the mountains.

Back on the drive, when it finally happens, it happens quickly, with each player isolated in his own world of thicket and fog. No one really knows what's going on. It's only later that the story is pieced together, bit by bit over venison chili back at the frat house, and in truck cabs bouncing over logging roads. One thing is clear: All hell breaks loose at the end of the pushes.

The first animal is just a few yards from the posters' line when Shaun "Slo-Mo" Doran catches a glimpse of black fur. He yanks his gun up, follows the blur, heart pounding, finger wavering over the safety, but he can't get a bead. That's bear No. 1.

A few minutes later, Kevin "Krusty" Walter hears a squirrel in a thicket so dense it couldn't be anything but. The pushers are hollering like madmen just 100 yards away; surely any bear has long since fled. He stretches out on the ground to look under the branches. Four black paws carefully piston up and down through the brush. Walter groans. He killed a bear the year before, and the $800 taxidermy bill nearly broke him. TPD brothers are largely forestry and wildlife management majors who receive a diploma, stiff college-loan bills and, if they're lucky, jobs with salaries that make business majors cackle. Plus, he's engaged. The last thing his fiancée had said to him was, "You're not going to kill another bear, are you?" He had told her the chances of that were like a million to one.

Walter stands up, puts the rifle bead in the only opening he can find, waits until the bear's white-flecked chest blots it out, and pulls the trigger. It's a double lung shot at 12 yards. Bear No. 2. Kill No. 1.

With one bear down, it's a scramble to get the second drive under way. Weiss wades into the disorderly line of hunters, brow furrowed, jaws working on an ever-present wad of Gummi Bears. He orders silence. Two bears have been jumped, and there's a very good chance that more await in the woods ahead.

The second drive is a longer push, and this time I'm covering a post high on a ridge where gusts of wind break against the mountainside. The ghostly hollers of the pushers grow nearer. The vise is closing, the bears' options disappearing by the minute, but there are no bears. I hear shouts ring out— "Posters ahead!"—as the pushers spot gunners and spread the word. It's just about over, and then it begins.

A single shot cracks far below, followed by war whoops that echo up and down Sliderock Den. On the post, Bob "BB Gun" Hivish misses bear

No. 3. It turns and crashes back into the line of drivers. Minutes later, there's another volley from high on the ridge, where a group of local hunters have taken up stands hoping to kill a bear off the brothers' sweat. Bear No. 4, and the second drive is not yet done.

Down by the creek, the posters and pushers who drew low numbers can do little but cheer. One of them has had plenty of experience listening to others shoot. Bob Fitterling is the second man up from the stream. A 1992 graduate and now a forester with the state, Fitterling took part in the TPD hunts for 16 years before finally felling a 460-pound brute in 2003. Fitterling is crashing through brush when he hears an upslope pusher yell, "Bear!" He steps into a rocky opening, racks a shell into his .30/30, and spies bear No. 5 closing the distance at 20 yards. By the time he gets his gun up, the bruin is eight paces away. Fitterling breaks its neck with one shot. Two bears are down.

A few hundred yards away, alumnus Chad Hartzell listens to it all, leaning against a massive hemlock. In eight years of pushing bears for the house drives, Hartzell has seen four animals but never had a shot. This year, he pulled poker chip No. 5, a low post and not a great one, given the bears' predilection for bolting uphill. Hartzell hears someone shout, "Bear in the drive!" but he can't get a fix on the direction. The creek is gurgling, and there's a distant shot—brother Shawn Cable misses a running bear. Then Hartzell hears a twig snap.

He looks up, straight into a sow's face peering out of the rhodos. She is 50 yards away, tops, takes a step closer, and disappears in a gully. Hartzell raises his gun. Unless the bear turns, she will rise from the ditch at 20 paces. The bullet catches her in the chest and flips her backward, silent and still in the wet leaves. Six bears on two drives, and three are on the ground.

An hour after the shot, Hartzell's hands are still shaking as he pulls a gut-hooked fixed blade skinning knife from its sheath. A mob of orange-coated brothers pound him on the back, but he doesn't seem to notice. He looks down at the prize. He whispers, "Thank you, bear."

Back at the house that night, three bruins are hoisted on the TPD meat pole. A few Little Sisters come by to hear the stories. They're in low-rise sweatpants, with navels showing under T-shirts that don't mince words: STIHL LITTLE FELLER, REDNECK GIRL, KISS MY AXE—PENN STATE

TIMBER SPORTS. The brothers are exultant. It will be difficult to top a day like this one.

The joking and sense of family here typifies life at most fraternities, but the brothers of TPD are convinced there is something more at the Tree House, something deeper and more purposeful. With 40,000 students, Penn State is a huge school. "People wonder how they are going to fit in at a place like this," says recent grad Dave Gustafson, "especially guys from a rural background. This fraternity is a lifeline."

That may be because TPD seems so very lifelike to those it attracts. "Spend a little time on college campuses," says Weiss, "and you'll see it everywhere: mama's boys spending daddy's money. Not us. We cut our own wood. We cut our own grass. We make our own repairs. We don't have anyone to bail us out if we screw up." TPD brothers have landscaped the house, put in new windows, retiled the bathrooms, built a brick fireplace. The day before the bear season opener, a half dozen brothers dug out a busted sewer line. "You're never going to feel so close to someone as when you're shoveling out a sewer line, knee-deep in poopwater," says Greg Schaetzle. "That's brotherhood."

And these brothers are keenly aware of their role as stewards of the very ties that bind them. "For us, concern about the future of hunting is not an abstract concept," explains Casey Fenton, the current TPD president. "Don't get me wrong. We don't think we're the solution to declining numbers of hunters. We're just thirty young guys in the subculture of college life who love to hunt and fish, and we want other people to experience what we love so much. But maybe, for now, that's enough."

One thing is for certain: For now, there are three bears to skin and two more days to hunt. After the Thanksgiving break, gun season for deer opens. Then it's time for ducks. Lake Erie steelhead through the winter. Turkeys in the spring. Smallies and trout in the summer.

"Rednecks. Backward farm boys. We hear it all," chimes in Nick Spinelli. "But we almost like it when we're walking across campus and somebody says, 'Look at that weirdo in camo.' You know why? Because once they get to know you, they realize how wrong they are about hunters. They learn that we are a bunch of well-rounded guys, from the country, from the city, who really want to give back to the sports that have given so much to us. If everyone could spend a hunting season at Tau Phi Delta, it would change the world."

THIS OLD BIRD KNOWS TURKEYS

The old man shuffles through the woods ahead of me, making more noise than he knows he should. He is tall and lean and 83 years old, and he carries a battered Winchester 12-gauge autoloader sheathed in peeling camouflage paint. He steps over the merest sticks and branches with difficulty. An hour earlier, in the muted glow of his truck's dome light, he'd catalogued his infirmities as an apology for the slow pace of the hunt about to begin. "I've only got one eye left," he told me, "and I lost my sense of smell years ago." He pointed to a pair of hearing aids. "I can't hardly hear a turkey unless he gobbles in my ear, even with these things."

His excuses delivered, the old man grinned. Just two days earlier, in the woods of Caswell County, North Carolina, a tom turkey made the mistake of gobbling a bit too close to R. Wayne Bailey. "He only sounded off one time, but that was one time too many," Bailey said, his smile stretching a thin face fuzzed with white whiskers. "Ten minutes later he was flopping on the ground."

That was wild turkey No. 239 for Bailey, one of America's preeminent wild turkey field biologists and the point man for turkey restoration efforts across much of the East. Born in tiny Rock, West Virginia, in 1918, Bailey went to work for that state's game department in 1945. He live-trapped his first wild turkey a few years later, capturing the bird with a homemade net jury-rigged from plumbing pipe and dropped from the ceiling of a state park picnic shelter.

By the time he retired in 1980 as the project leader for North Carolina's restoration effort, Bailey had live-trapped hundreds of turkeys in West Virginia and North Carolina and shipped the first wild birds ever released in Ohio, Illinois, Massachusetts, and New Hampshire. He's watched the Eastern wild turkey's rise from near oblivion with the wide-eyed astonishment of a scientist and the appreciation of a die-hard hunter.

Bailey came to turkey science with the heart of a hunter. He grew up gunning for the table—rabbits, squirrels, grouse, ducks, groundhogs, whatever would fill a Great Depression pot. Even then, he says, there was a mystique about the wild turkey. "They were very rare in those days," he says, "but West Virginia still had an open season. My goal was to bag a wild turkey before they became extinct."

By any measure the restoration of the Eastern turkey is one of modern wildlife management's greatest success stories, and one of modern hunting's finest hours. Gunned down to a record low level by 1973, Eastern turkey populations since have been nursed to more than 6.4 million. Tens of thousands of birds were live-trapped and transplanted from state to state, aided to a great degree by the National Wild Turkey Federation.

❧

Bailey's first fieldwork with the West Virginia Conservation Commission involved clipping the toenails of trapped rabbits to mark them for a mortality study, but it wasn't long before he discovered his true aptitude. He was crazy about turkeys: He snared them with drop nets and walk-in wire traps, spending long days in the blind.

Then, during the early 1970s, cannon-propelled nets revolutionized the task of capturing wild animals for study and transport. Thirty feet wide and 50 feet long, the nets were cabled to 5-pound projectiles and launched over feeding turkeys with black powder-powered mortars. A quantum leap over fussy, small-scale drop nets and box traps, the practice nonetheless required stealth and skill. Flocks were lured to the target area with bait. On the day the trap was set, camouflaging the net was critical because turkeys needed to be within 2 to 5 feet of it, with their heads down, for the launch to work efficiently.

And skittish turkeys were only a part of the challenge. Areas that supported populations large enough for successful trapping operations were jealously guarded by locals who were incensed that birds were being removed. Biologists would return to their setups to discover sabotaged nets, equipment, and blinds. Technicians began to cover their tracks. They hauled blinds, nets, and bait into the woods before daylight and varied the routes they used to check on sites, like moonshiners, telling no one about the locations.

Through it all, Bailey never lost his enthusiasm for the birds. "As I sat in the trap blinds, listening to a gobble or even a movement in the leaves that I knew was a turkey, my heart would pound so loud you could hear it," he says.

Up on the ridge we listen to a pair of turkeys gobbling, a half dozen times or more. With each successive call from Bailey, the farthest bird cuts the distance, moving closer to the challenger it detects at the base of the ridge. Bailey leans close. "I think it's going to be a good morning," he whispers, then pauses for a moment. "But it takes a turkey to tell you just how good a morning it's going to be."

BLOOD, SWEAT, AND BEDLAM

After the shot, the world went strangely silent. I heard nothing. Before I pulled the trigger, there was bedlam everywhere: The dogs bayed and snarled in a hellish clamor as the bear, 20 yards away, popped his teeth and smashed brush. There was a single howling yelp as a clawed paw found a hound and sent it cartwheeling. Before the shot, I couldn't hear myself think.

The bear stood, facing away, swatting at the five dogs fanned out in front of him. I was gasping for breath in the thicket. Blood from brier gashes dripped into my right eye. The fight had been going on for 10 minutes already. It couldn't last much longer. I stepped to my left, searching for an open shot, and that meager movement caught the bear's attention. He swiveled his head and found me. Our eyes locked just as the dogs behind him moved, giving me a clear shot. I raised my lever-action and fired at the base of the bear's skull in the exact moment he charged the dogs and bolted, vanishing into the tangled timber behind.

For a long few seconds, I heard nothing. Whether it was the muzzle blast or the adrenaline, I couldn't say. I shook my head to clear my ears, and then I began to hear my heart pounding. The woods crackled with static. Reed Sheffield was on the radio, headed my way. "I don't know," he said into the radio. "He might have missed. Get some more dogs on him."

He pushed past me, barely slowing, and crashed into the brush.

"Come on, Eddie!" he hollered over his shoulder. "Come on!"

Then I heard the dogs. They were back on the bear. Reed was already out of sight. "Come on, Eddie! Can you make it?"

Covering the last 50 yards to the bear had been brutal. I was gassed. My legs quivered, and my shirt was soaked with sweat. When I pulled the trigger, the bruin was on the move, but still the shot felt good. I was convinced I had hit him. I took off running.

I can make it.

⌒

In November 1998, Coy Parton, Dolly Parton's cousin, trucked his bear dogs from the east Tennessee mountains to North Carolina's coastal plain, and he set those Plott hounds loose in woods where you can almost smell the ocean. They cold-trailed a massive set of tracks for nearly 2 miles, then jumped the bear in a thicket of canebrake and pine timber. The bruin turned and fought, then broke and ran. One hunter whiffed a shot, and the bear bolted again.

When the boar was bayed up in a block of woods surrounded by fields, Parton waded in and killed him with a 12-gauge shotgun loaded with 00 buck. The bear was so large, it had to be hauled to a fertilizer company to find scales stout enough for the job. The animal weighed 880 pounds and still stands as the heaviest black bear ever taken in North America.

Parton's feat announced to the hunting world an astonishing fact: Eastern North Carolina's tangled swamp thickets and massive industrial timberlands had turned into the home of the planet's largest black bears. Six-hundred-pound bears are now a benchmark for trophy status there. Hunters have taken nearly two dozen black bears over 700 pounds. And there's a pile of lesser giants as well. According to the state wildlife agency, the 3,200-square-mile Albemarle-Pamlico Peninsula holds the world's densest population of black bears: as many as 8,000. It's not uncommon to see a dozen feeding like deer in a wheatfield.

Not surprisingly, such a trove has attracted a passionate following. Hunters from Canada haul their dog packs to the land of grits and collard greens after northern seasons close. Big money has arrived too: Fully outfitted four-day hunts reach $10,000. And at a time when hunting with hounds has been vilified in many parts of the country, the tradition in this remote, removed region is still strong.

To check out the scene, I planned a four-day swing through Tar Heel bear country, hunting mostly with a father-and-son pair who have deep roots in both hunting and bear-dog training. Ralph Sheffield is 62 years old—stout and sturdy and jovial. He's kept bear dogs since 1975. His son, Reed, 28, is wiry and youthful, studious one moment (he holds a master's degree in business management from England's Northumbria University) yet predatory when a pack of his dogs bays a bear. They live just outside of Vanceboro, deep in the swampy wilds between the Neuse and Pamlico Rivers—about 5 miles from where Parton killed his world-record bear.

Together, the Sheffields have amassed their own impressive kills. Ralph has taken thirteen black bears better than 600 pounds, including a 721-pound behemoth in 1996. Reed killed his first bear when he was 10 and has already put 660- and 695-pounders on the ground. "And that's just the bears we've killed ourselves," Ralph tells me. "I don't know how many 500- and 600-pound bears we've had killed in front of our dogs. Thirty to forty, easy."

Already this year, hunters with the Sheffields have taken sixteen black bears. Seven were by first-time bear hunters—a statistic that gives them great pride. They'd love for me to be their eighth.

Reed held up along a wall of gallberry and listened for movement in the woods. We'd been fighting through the brush for 15 minutes since I had shot. Twice more the dogs had bayed the bear, and both times the bear broke and ran. "You sure you hit him?" Reed asked.

I quickly replayed the scene in my mind, then nodded. Suddenly the dogs' barking quickened.

"They stopped him again," Reed said. He held an electronic dog tracker in his hand, but his eyes bored into the tangle of brambles. "They're looking at him."

A wall of woven briers and bay bushes cut visibility to a mere few feet. The ground was a peaty muck, sucking at every step. Native Americans call these coastal thickets pocosins, which translates loosely to "swamp on a hill." Pushing through them felt like climbing a mountain. I was close to heaving with the exertion of moving forward. *No one in their right mind would try to get through this mess,* I thought to myself.

"Doesn't look so bad," Reed said. "If we're gonna go, we gotta go now and go hard. Next time he runs, he might not stop."

I peered into the woods, looking in vain for a gap. Up ahead, a dog yelped. Another paw swipe had connected. Reed plunged into the brush. I hesitated for a half second, then leaped in behind him.

This was my third day tagging along with the Sheffield crew, and since dawn the dogs had already run three bears. Just yesterday, we'd left the Sheffields' place in the black dark and driven nearly two hours to the marshy peninsula of Carteret County. We'd passed crabbers readying their boats for a day on the water and tourists driving to the Outer Banks ferry. A long-time hunting pal of the Sheffields, Greg Miller, had shot a nice boar, a bit over 400 pounds, when it broke from the brush after a 45-minute chase.

I'd had my own close call on that piece of ground. It was a perfect example of eastern North Carolina's bounty of bear country—5,400 acres of private lands that border the 15,000-acre Cedar Island National Wildlife Refuge. Across a narrow bay was an 11,000-acre Marine Corps bombing range. It was a vast, nearly roadless tangle of salt marsh, pocosin swamp, and longleaf pine forest. Ralph checked a bait barrel he'd sweetened with peanuts a few days earlier. The baits help suck bears out of the pinewoods and pocosins, and they give the dogs a place to start the chase. Last year, the Sheffield party killed ten bears off this one patch of ground. A week earlier, a bear took off on a 6-mile, straight-line run, dragging the dogs along.

Ralph huffed up a steep creek bank, nodding. "Good track," he said. "Big track."

Reed slid out of his truck, jangling with dog chains and electronic collars. The dogs caught the bear scent and filled their boxes with pleading howls.

"Look at these vicious animals," Ralph said as the dogs licked his hands like a bunch of puppies, begging to be picked for the chase. Spook and Bo got the nod, as the others whined in protest. Reed attached their collars, and they launched off the truck, disappearing into the pines and bay bushes in an instant.

The Sheffields typically dribble their dogs out slowly, starting with a pair on a fresh track. "Too many dogs on an old trail can mess it up, and you have to be strategic," Ralph said. And too many hunters moving in too quickly can break up the chase or push the bear too far. "It's kind of like a football game," Ralph continued. "You get both the cornerbacks and the linebackers chasing the wide receivers, it makes 'em think more. More dogs can slow a bear down. But first you got to figure out the game."

What struck me about all of these hunts is how dynamic and fluid each chase can be. During the bear hunt, the dog pack can break up and coalesce time and again, and it's just as challenging to keep track of the hunters. If there are deer hunters at the club, they might join in on the bear hunt. A long chase might draw a few more folks to the woods, while some hunters have to bail for work or home. Folks move in and out, some connected by radios but others just following the sound of the dogs. With hunters spread across miles of woods, and the chase stringing out for an hour or two or five, everyone holds fast to their own strand of the narrative, from their own vantage point, following the bear and the dogs and the plot however they can, and wherever it goes. There's never a single story being written.

When Spook and Bo bawled in unison, Reed cocked his head.

"I'll bet you a dollar they're looking at that bear," Reed said. "Let's go."

We jumped in his truck and spun sand along the two-track, scattering wild turkeys into the woods. Reed stopped the truck and stuck his head out the window. "Still trailing," he murmured as he stomped on the gas. He kept his head out the window, hound dog style, as we bounced and skidded down a sandy two-track. Suddenly, he slid to a stop.

"Listen," he said. "Listen."

The dogs had opened up again. They were close. Reed put a finger to his lips and eased out the door, leaving it open. I did the same. We stepped carefully through the low pocosins 30 feet off the two-track. The dogs went silent, but the brush 80 yards in front of us rustled and swayed. Reed pointed. I nodded and eased the hammer back on the .30/30, muffling the click with the palm of my hand. Each heartbeat thumped like a toilet flush. I snugged the rifle into my shoulder and saw a smudge of black.

But then the dogs bawled, so close that I knew it couldn't be the bear. I lowered the muzzle just as Smoke and Rusty shuffled into the open. Smoke looked at me, tail wagging, and gave me a great, boisterous where'd-he-go bark. I lowered the rifle hammer and let the shivers work their way down my arms.

That was three days ago. Now, I plunged through the brush, trying to keep Reed in sight, as the dogs' bedlam rose. Sweat poured off my brow, but the shivers had returned.

"Come on, Eddie! Come on!"

— ~ —

When Ralph Sheffield first started bear hunting, in 1973, eastern North Carolina's rough coastal swamp-woods were even rougher. Commercial timber harvest had yet to open up the woods with logging roads and skidder trails. His favorite haunt, the famed Holly Shelter Game Land, was 70,000 acres of thicket hell.

"When you left the road, the next road in front of you was 4½ miles away," he told me. At the time, he was a 16-year-old powerlifter, tough as nails. "I could roll," he said. "I was just hard muscle and speed, and I had no fear. And that's what it took. Many times, I spent the night beside the bear I'd just killed, waiting for the sun to come up so I'd know which way to walk out."

At the time, bear hunting with hounds in eastern North Carolina was a bit of a patchwork endeavor. Few hunters owned even a single dog. A pack was simply pulled together from whatever hounds showed up for a hunt. Hunters were divvied up by physical abilities. Some were the dog men, handling the pack. Older gentlemen were put on the ground crew, tasked with getting the dead bears out of the woods. Anyone could shoot, but a few, such as Ralph, were known as the killers—tough and strong enough to push through towering thickets of briers and brush to get to bayed-up bears. After his first couple of hunting seasons, Ralph's mentors gave him a pair of bear dogs—a Plott hound named Stud and a Plott-Walker mix called Boney.

"For the first time, I owned something," he said. "There hasn't been a day since that I didn't have a pack of my own."

On the evening before our first hunt, I met the Sheffields at their dog kennels behind Ralph's house. Despite their wide-ranging hunting habits, Ralph and Reed rarely spend a night away from home. "Family men," Ralph told me. Reed had recently married and was building a home on a piece of land behind his parents' house, where the woods give way to the Neuse River lowlands.

Still, the Sheffield kennels serve as a de facto bear camp for the loose group of hunters who move in and out of their clan. Between them, the father and son hold memberships in eight different hunt clubs across hundreds of square miles of the coastal plain. The smallest is a few thousand acres. The largest, up near the Virginia state line, is better than 30,000 acres. "We roam pretty far," Reed says. "We take this kind of serious, you know."

There might not be a grand lodge on their property—much less a bunkhouse for a couple of buddies—but standing there in the kennels, as the dogs watched their masters' every step, I sensed a sort of gravitas to this place. Whatever happens out in the woods, whatever happens in the thick of the fight, starts here.

Today, the Sheffields keep about fifteen adult dogs at a time, mostly Plott hounds and English coonhounds and a mix between the two, plus some treeing Walkers. They breed for the long term and pair dogs carefully.

"We want 'em hard and tough, but we want 'em smart," Ralph told me. "I like a dog that's got grit but isn't overly aggressive. Some hunters are proud of their vet bill, but that's not the line we breed. We don't get a dog killed but every couple years, if that."

Part of the thinking behind breeding dogs this way is the sheer intensity of the Sheffields' approach to hunting. They train the dogs nearly year-round, running across a vast mosaic of public and private lands. Then, come hunting season, there's barely time for a nap. "When you take three weeks of vacation and hunt every day," Ralph explained, "you've got to have strong dogs—and a lot of them."

With the dogs whining in the background, we leaned against the pickup trucks to plan the next day's hunt. It would be my first time bear hunting, and Ralph was adamant that I only pull the trigger when it felt right. "I'm not going to tell you when to shoot," he said. "I'm not going to tell you what a big bear is."

He asked me if I noticed the whitetail in his living room. It was a small 5-pointer, and it caught my eye given Ralph's reputation for quarter-ton big game.

"Let me tell you what I think makes a trophy animal," he said. In 1963, the day before deer season opened in Georgia, his stepfather, a man he called Papa Jim, bought a Montgomery Ward 12-gauge shotgun and a box of No. 1 buckshot at the Fort Benning PX. The next day he killed a little buck with it—his first deer ever—and never fired the gun again. It sat in Papa Jim's closet for decades, but the story of its one-shot kill was a bit of a family legend.

"About five years ago," Ralph said, "Papa Jim shows up with that shotgun and gives it to me for my birthday. And the first day of deer season that year, I walked out to hunt and that little buck on my wall was the first deer that showed up. On the very first day I owned the shotgun. I carried No. 1 buckshot—just like happened to him."

He held my gaze. "You understand what I'm saying? I once killed a 14-pointer in West Virginia that won a county big-buck contest. But that's not the deer on my wall. Big don't have anything to do with trophy. It's all about the animal's story."

"We got to get there, Eddie!" Reed shouted. "Come on!"

My legs burning and briers tearing at my face and neck, I lowered my head and bulldogged through a shrub jungle of bamboo brier and fetterbush. Wrist-thick pond pines grew tight as bristles on a brush. I fell into a 6-foot-deep V-ditch carved into the peat and grabbed a thorny stalk of devil's walking stick to pull myself out.

Up ahead—100 yards or 500, it was difficult to tell which—the baying of the dogs grew more frenetic. Once again, they'd turned the bear. Pulled by the sound of the hounds, Reed vanished. I threaded my rifle through the crosshatched saplings and sank to my knees in a dark muck of peat. I clawed at the ground, dragging myself clear with my elbows. *I've got to get there. I want my bear.*

The gunshot caught me by surprise.

For just a moment, the world seemed stunned into silence. Reed was no longer hollering from the woods. The dogs held their breath. But, again, the interlude lasted but a split second. Soon the hounds traded their chops and bawls for a guttural din. It expanded into a possessive, growling snarl. I slowed my pace so I could catch my breath. I knew what I was going to find.

The black bear was dead in a 20-foot-tall thicket of river cane, the reeds beat down in a wide circle, with the swarm of dogs going crazy over the mound of black hide. A couple of hunters dragged the hounds off by the collars, snapping their heavy leather-and-chain leads around a nearby tree.

"He was all but dead when they caught him," one hunter said graciously. "I just finished him off."

I heard the whine of an ATV, then more shouts as the various factions of the hunting party converged from all directions. Machetes whacked at shrubs and vines, clearing a trail for the drag out to the road. At any moment, other hunters would push through the cane, angling for a look at the bear, wanting to hear the story. I gazed down at the still, black form. I didn't have long before the entire party was around.

I handed off my rifle and knelt by the bear. It took both hands and all of my strength to turn the animal over. In an instant, I found what I was looking for: a deep gash across the base of the neck, the vertebrae smashed, a sheen of dark blood. I traced a finger across the bullet's path, felt the torn flesh and jagged bone. He couldn't have gone much farther. How he got this far was a wonder.

The group closed in. Everyone wanted a look. A bear hunt like this, with hounds and trucks, a long chase with fits and starts, is a community affair. Everyone played a role. Now we'll share the story like we'll share the meat, passing it along time and again. But backing away to give them room, I touched my fingers to my forehead, to leave a bloody smudge. From my bear.

THE RITUAL

They're in shirtsleeves now, the trees nearby hung with camo packs and blaze-orange hoodies. It's hot work, dragging a deer, no matter the weather. Bill Stoner holds the buck's hind leg, while his brother, Doug, unzips the belly.

The instant I stepped out of the cedar swamp, I could tell this was a moment for the ages. The 5-pointer is Doug's first buck. His first deer. After eight years of trekking to his family camp on Drummond Island, off the northern Michigan shoreline, 8 dirt miles from the nearest hardtop road, Stoner has connected with a beauty. His brother's presence is just icing on the cake: It's the first time they've ever deer hunted together.

Working as a team, they roll out the entrails, cut the windpipe, and prop the chest open with a stick. As steam rises from the open maw of the cavity, Bill drags a thumb through the deer's chest, painting his finger with the blood pooled between the ribs. Doug sits quietly. He knows what is to come.

This tradition—marking a hunter's face with the blood of a freshly killed animal—is rooted in the story of St. Hubert, a seventh-century Frenchman who, before his religious conversion, chased deer pretty much 24/7. On one Good Friday, while the rest of his village was at church, Hubert was afield when the stag his hounds had cornered turned to face him, a crucifix illuminated between the antlers. The buck spoke with the voice of Christ, and Hubert's life changed forever. He entered the priesthood, died in 727, and is the patron saint of hunters. For many years, a kill was marked with three crosses of blood on the forehead and cheeks of the hunter: one for the crucifix between the Christ-buck's rack, one for each of the antlers.

These particulars might be lost on the Stoner boys, but they know of this ancient rite, and if ever there was a time and place for it, this is it. Bill steps over the deer's body and paints a single stripe of blood on his brother's forehead. No video cameras. No empty platitudes. No fist pumps or Facebook postings. Doug nods slightly, looks down at the deer, and pats a shoulder—once, twice, thrice. A coincidence, perhaps.

Doug will return to camp with pockets bulging with the deer's heart and liver, his forehead smeared with blood, the swipe marked with his brother's own thumbprint. It will wash off, or wear off, in the days to come. At least, on the outside.

Chapter 4

Where the Heart Is

ILLUSTRATION BY MICHAEL MARSICANO

THE TAG TEAM

"You're gonna bust those goats," Jim Schiermiester said. He was squinting up the ridge, where a khaki arc of sagebrush scrubbed an endless blue sky. Schiermiester has owned this family ranch for decades, so he knows these pronghorns better than most. "Just one of you go."

I followed his gaze to the top of the rise, trying not to look at my son, Jack. He had filled his Wyoming pronghorn tag the day before, and as the shot went off, I was close enough to hear his breathing. That's what he and I had hoped for over the last few weeks while thinking about this trip—each of us sharing that moment: after the stalk, after the crawl, after you will your lungs to heel and you settle the crosshairs.

"You're probably right," I said. "But it's a package deal. Been the point all along."

Schiermiester pursed his lips, then gave a little shrug of his shoulders. The gesture was clear: Then it's all on you.

I nodded at Jack. He grabbed the shooting sticks, and we headed into the wind.

We had rolled into camp, a deep cleft in the undulating prairies two hours east of Casper, Wyoming, three days earlier. A pronghorn was already hanging from a skinning tripod, with another on the ground in line for the knife. Jack's brow furrowed with a mix of excitement and self-doubt. He's taken his share of deer and squirrels, but he's more comfortable with a shotgun than a rifle, and he was already fretting about the long-range shots common on a pronghorn hunt. I tamped down the urge to chime in with an encouraging word. Some doubts are best faced alone.

What Jack really wanted to do for his first college fall break was hunt ducks in the famed prairie potholes. We'd talked about that for years. He'd never had a school break long enough for us to freelance for migrating birds streaming south from Canada, and I'd promised him that we would strike out for the North Dakota prairies during his freshman year. But then I received an invite to chase speed goats across the Wyoming plains, bunk down in wall tents, and sleep under the prairie moon. And sure, bring the boy along, what's one more in the truck?

He'd read up on tactics and techniques, texting me questions about bullet drop and wind drift while walking to class. I gave him a copy of Jeff Cooper's *The Art of the Rifle* and told him to concentrate more on trigger pull and breath control than ballistic coefficients. The pronghorn is an animal to be hunted, not sniped. They live in a world scored with creek bottoms and pocked with red rock, all of which can be used against them. Glassing for mature goats, then planning and executing a long-range stalk, is a piece of theater. From a distance, you pick apart the ground, plotting moves and countermoves, attacks, feints, retreats, and gambits on a game board that stretches from horizon to horizon. If you make it to the foot of the butte, can you cross that open country and stay out of sight? If the buck returns before you get to the does, can you drop into that creek? Can you slide unseen over the top of that gumbo bank? Can you get to the bottom of that ridge? Is the wind the same there as it is here? Meet a pronghorn on his own terrain, and it's pretty much the most fun you can have with cactus spines stuck into your forehead.

That's how Jack's pronghorn rodeo played out, with a few twists. After two busted stalks on our first morning, Jack, his guide, Will Haines, and I belly-crawled to a high ridge overlooking a broad flat where a good buck was bedded down with a scattered harem. After a 45-minute wait, the antelope stood from his bed, and the guide nodded: When you're ready. That's when the animal turned his butt to us and sauntered off, not stopping till he had doubled the distance. My heart sank. I could feel Jack's sweat.

A few feet from my son, I watched through binoculars. When he shot, the bullet puffed dirt in the red bank behind the antelope, and for a heart-sinking moment all seemed lost. The wind muffled the rifle report, and for a few seconds the antelope seemed confused, unclear where the danger was located. But there's a reason why you keep your eye in the scope after every shot and focus on the animal, not your shortcomings. Suddenly, the antelope decided en masse to put some prairie between them and the bullet's impact. They bolted—and angled hard toward Jack.

He racked another round into the Savage as Haines helped settle his nerves. "Let 'em come, buddy," he said. "Stay with them. It's just getting better." The buck stopped and Jack fired, dropping his first pronghorn at 231 yards.

In a hunter's life, there is only one first Western big-game kill, and for a hunter from the East, particularly, it carries a certain weight, a kinship with all those pioneers and big-game hunters who have stalked and crawled across the pages of countless books and magazines. Jack kept his eyes in the scope, watching the pronghorn as Haines pounded his back. A half minute passed before his eyes found mine in the sagebrush.

With Jack's buck in a cooler and the focus squarely on me, there was a marked change in his demeanor. Part of it was the way a punched tag lightens the psychic load of a hunt, but something else was going on. I sensed it in the way he offered to drag my pack when he insisted on leading the final crawl to the ridge. His mannerisms turned slightly solicitous, almost paternal. He wanted me to shoot my pronghorn as badly as I'd wanted him to connect with his. He wanted to lead me to the kill.

I had fretted about how the years would change our hunting relationship. Jack and I had bonded over uncountable sunrises. He's been hunting with me since he was 7 years old, and in recent years was my most steady companion. But the burden was on me to let go and let him roam. He was no longer reliant on my truck, my gear, and my blessing to hunt—although a Wyoming antelope trip is a significant enticement to an unemployed college student. But in that moment, with the grit and sweat and an animal on the line, he wasn't asking for permission. I sensed it immediately, and I thought: *Maybe this was the answer.* Maybe I had led the charge for so long that I'd forgotten what it was like to share every aspect of the hunt.

We walked up the slope, stooping low near the top, and then went to all fours. Jack ground his thigh into a cactus and rolled over in pain. I waited while he pulled out the largest spines, his pants spotted with blood, before we belly-crawled the last 40 feet to the crest. Schiermiester was right: There was thin cover, and what little sage fringed the ridge was barely a foot tall.

"Let me take a look," he said. "Hold tight."

I nodded. He moved up the last few feet, dragging his legs to keep his butt to the ground, face turned sideways to lower his profile another half inch as he made his way to the tallest clump of sage on the ridge, barely large enough to hide a human head. He glassed the saddle for a minute, then slowly slid his hand down his thigh and wiggled his fingers. I belly-crawled to his side, spitting grit from my lips.

Antelope were bedded down 400 yards away. It was a near reprise of Jack's situation two days earlier. I glassed the animals: a nice buck and three does, unalarmed, and for me, at least, out of reach. We watched the group for a couple of minutes, looking for any sign that they might be ready for a stretch and to possibly make their way closer. But they were down for the afternoon. The shot was a no-go.

"Wait," Jack whispered. He peered through the binoculars. "There's another one. Closer."

He gingerly pointed, and I followed with the binoculars and dialed in the focus on an antelope-shaped blob. Black horns rose over a nice buck partially hidden in grass, half the distance of the others and just as content. I exhaled loudly and turned my eyes toward Jack. He was beaming, nodding slowly. I eased my jacket up for a rifle rest but couldn't get enough elevation in the scope. We'd dropped the shooting sticks a few feet downslope—a stupid mistake—and they'd be just what I'd need to raise the rifle for a shot when the antelope stood. And this one was big enough, and meaningful enough, to wait out. Jack inched downslope, backward, while I watched the buck chew cud. Jack snagged the sticks with a foot and drew them to his hand, and just then, the antelope stood bolt upright.

It's not a scientific term, but it's the only word that works: It is absolutely freaky how a big-game animal can sense unseen danger. Jack was below the ridgeline, but there was just enough micro-commotion on our hill, just enough of a change in the distant outline on the horizon, that an animal that had evolved to discern threats from saber-toothed cats and dire wolves had had enough.

The buck stood, motionless, as if he'd been bronzed, with a sprig of grass held tightly in his mouth. I hissed, "Jack! Freeze!" as I raised the gun off the pack, drove my elbows into the dirt, and centered the crosshairs on the pronghorn's neck. The does stood, nervous. The buck stared as if he could look me in the eye through the metal tube. When the does bolted, he turned his head to watch their flight for a scant second and then took a quarter turn and a half step forward, and I knew in the next instant he'd be pushing 30 miles per hour. I pulled the trigger and pandemonium broke out in the grass. Does raced across the open ground like quail flushed wild, with my antelope hard behind them. I pushed up into a sitting position, racked the bolt, swiveled left, and locked my elbows into the angles of my knees. The buck faltered on the run, trailing behind the does as I tracked him in the scope. He stopped for a moment, sagging. I fired again. After the months of planning and the days on the hunt and the long minutes in the dirt, the end always seems to come so quickly.

After we had gutted the antelope and cleaned the blood from our hands, I stood off to the side as Jack paced across the prairie bottom, 50 yards away. He was talking to his mom on the phone, recounting the stalk and crawl, the shot and the kill. I could see him gesturing wildly, his animated voice rising above the wind. A few minutes later, when Jack handed the phone over to me, Julie asked if I'd gotten ahold of myself. Jack was taken aback by my reaction when the antelope fell, she said. I'm typically reserved at the moment of a kill. I rarely fist bump. I'm not much of a hugger over a corpse. I try to stand where the animal was standing and look back to the place where I took the shot and understand on some deeper plane that moment when one life lent itself to another.

"Mom, you should have seen Dad," Jack had told her. "He went nuts. I've never seen him like that."

I smiled. He was right. When the antelope went down hard, a bit of crazy came out. But it wasn't a celebration of the kill so much. I'd stalked and crawled and killed a pronghorn with my son at my side. With my son taking the lead. I'd crossed a dreaded Rubicon, and the view on the far side seemed as grand and promising as the country that lay behind.

Jack was right: I'd never been quite like this.

THE DITCH

The swans come from the east, out of the sun, looping downwind over the field. "Birds, birds," someone whispers from up the ditch, and we lean into the leftover weeds and willow scrub that screen the rim of the drain. Young wheat forms a patchy green skim on the ground, the only color in an otherwise dull winter world of old brown mud, dead grass, and leafless woods. It's hard to describe the hold this place has on me.

The swans bank north a hundred yards away, ragged lines of pearls against the blue sky. Five of us press our bodies into the near-horizontal bank of the ditch, and barely risk a peek from under our hat brims. They are so close. Already, twenty swans have lit in the decoys. We hunted this ditch last year, the year before that, and the year before that. It's like this every year. Though there are fields just like this one unfurled in every direction, tundra swans from the Arctic North seem to be drawn to this one piece of muck by some immutable compulsion.

These birds are on a string, now, sucked into the open field, their landing options limited by a scattered spread of 200 decoys and the live birds already on the ground. "Who's up?" someone whispers. We take turns, shooting one bird at a time, picking singles out of the squadrons overhead. Swan hunting in North Carolina is by public draw, with a one-bird limit, and we're in no rush.

"That's me," I reply. I free my right foot from the muck, and press my left knee deeply into the mud bank of the ditch. I'll need the leverage when I come up shooting.

My guess is that you've driven by this ditch a hundred times. Well, maybe not my ditch—not the Ditch—but places very similar. Your ditch might be some 100-yard-long shelterbelt in South Dakota or a Shenandoah hayfield or a river bottom where an old box blind has stood for years. Your ditch might be even less impressive than mine. But we all have those ordinary places where we've experienced uncommon moments of meaning and substance, some shared by longtime field companions, others where we alone are witnesses. I have my favorite honey holes that consistently produce ducks, deer, or squirrels, but there are certain places I return to year after year because of their emotional weight: the beaver slough where Jack shot

Formal attire in the duck marsh. Jonesville,
Louisiana. 2015. PHOTOGRAPH BY DUSAN SMETANA.

Casting for salmon and rainbows on Alaska's Canning River, the western border
of the Arctic National Wildlife Refuge. 2003. PHOTOGRAPH BY DUSAN SMETANA.

Appetizer time on the Athabasca-Chipewyan reservation. Alberta, Canada. 2010.
PHOTOGRAPH COURTESY OF THE AUTHOR.

A tough pull. Aniak River, Alaska. 2006. PHOTOGRAPHY BY COLBY LYSNE.

The author, left, and photographer Colby Lysne
after a near-drowning. Kipchuk River, Alaska.
2006. PHOTOGRAPH COURTESY OF THE AUTHOR.

Hanging on tight in the Missinaibi River with pal Peter DeJong. Ontario. 2005.
PHOTOGRAPH BY DUSAN SMETANA.

Practice rounds. Gates County, North Carolina. 1974. PHOTOGRAPH COURTESY OF THE AUTHOR.

All eyes on the sky. Great Salt Lake, Utah. 2013. PHOTOGRAPH COURTESY OF THE AUTHOR.

Field & Stream colleague Nate Matthews portaging folding kayaks around Dolans Falls. Devils River, Texas. 2017. PHOTOGRAPH COURTESY OF THE AUTHOR.

Road trip grouse camp on the Charles M. Russell National Wildlife Refuge. Montana. 2012. PHOTOGRAPH COURTESY OF THE AUTHOR.

Drying story notes on the dashboard after a duck hunt dunking in Boston Harbor. 2015. PHOTOGRAPH COURTESY OF THE AUTHOR.

The author taking notes on his first freelance writing assignment. Mount Rogers National Recreation Area, Virginia. 1984. PHOTOGRAPH COURTESY OF THE AUTHOR.

The author's daughter, Markie, and son, Jack, with Markie's first flyrod trout. South Fork of the Flathead River, Montana. 2018. PHOTOGRAPH COURTESY OF THE AUTHOR.

Horsing around with the road crew on a desert duck hunt in alien country. Roswell, New Mexico. 2019. PHOTOGRAPHY BY TOM FOWLKS.

Cover shot posing for a coastal kayaking adventure. Tongass National Forest, Alaska. 2010.
PHOTOGRAPH BY COLBY LYSNE.

Solitude in the Utah high country. 2015. PHOTOGRAPH COURTESY OF THE AUTHOR.

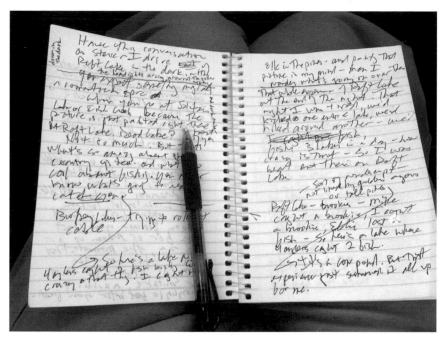

Field notes. Boulder Mountain, Utah. 2015. PHOTOGRAPH COURTESY OF THE AUTHOR.

Duck watching, always. Elephant Butte, New Mexico. 2019. PHOTOGRAPH BY TOM FOWLKS

The author, left, and college pal Lee Davis spray-painted the author's Chevy pickup one opening day afternoon. 1984. PHOTOGRAPH COURTESY OF THE AUTHOR.

The author's strong facial hair game on an Arkansas duck hunt with son, Jack. 2013. PHOTOGRAPH COURTESY OF THE AUTHOR.

Scott Wood waits for reinforcements. Kanairiktok River, Labrador. 2004. PHOTO-GRAPH COURTESY OF THE AUTHOR.

The author, right, with Keith Gleason, the man who taught him how to hunt. PHO-TOGRAPH COURTESY OF MILLER MOBLEY.

The author in his element: In the mud, taking notes. 2019. PHOTOGRAPH COURTESY OF TOM FOWLKS.

Everglades tarpon off Cape Sable. Florida. 2019.

Tundra plane visions of the Arctic National Wildlife Refuge. Canning River, Alaska. 2003. PHOTOGRAPH BY DUSAN SMETANA.

Salmon steaks on gravelbar, many miles from home. Aniak River, Alaska. 2006.
PHOTOGRAPH BY COLBY LYSNE.

The author and his son, Jack, in the Montana backcountry. 2018. PHOTOGRAPH COURTESY OF ANDREW GERRIE.

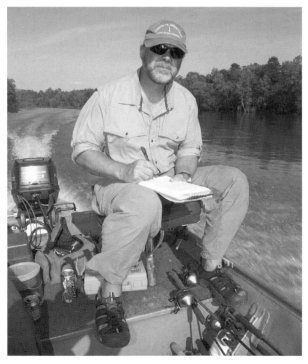

Breaking the mid-note reverie. Altamaha River, Georgia. 2007. PHOTOGRAPH BY COLBY LYSNE.

Flycasting to bonefish in the Everglades backcountry with Capt. Chris Wittman. Florida. 2019. PHOTOGRAPH BY TOM FOWLKS.

The author with a close-quarters Maine moose, taken with guides from Chandler Lake Camps. 2019. PHOTOGRAPH BY TOM FOWLKS.

his first duck, the oak flat where Markie helped me drag an 8-pointer out of the woods, that subtle little knuckle of forest where I first saw two bucks sparring. No one else on earth might find these places remarkable at all. I could never forget them.

This ditch is a case in point. I don't even know the landowner. He's the friend-of-a-friend-of-a-friend. But this land has nourished his own family for generations, and he's happy to pass that blessing along each year when we show up to crash the farm's late-winter swan rodeo. It's this way across the country: Farmers and landowners have no idea that their ditches, scraggly hay bales, and woods corners help produce the kind of moments that endure. We knock on doors and ask for permission, and then we stack up memories we will recall on our deathbeds.

~ ~ ~

In the muddy ditch, we watch the Arctic blanket our world. A mature tundra swan is clad in a thousand shades of white. The birds are so big, so exotic, and so willing to decoy that the temptation is always there to let the birds land, see how close you can get, even if you never fire a shot. Now the swans are lined up as far as we can see: swans in the field, swans in the air with wings set, groups of swans circling overhead waiting their turn, lines of swans in the sky all the way to the horizon. Up to 75,000 tundra swans spend the winter within a two-hour drive of this ditch, three-quarters of the entire population that migrates through eastern America. There are times when it seems as if most of them are overhead.

The flock's bugling whoops echo off the field's sheet water, and I settle on my bird, focusing on a single mature swan on the left side of a flapping line, white as snow, off on its own by a yard or two. The 20-pound bird drops with a ferocious thud as the swans on the ground explode into the air. It's not a challenging shot. It's hardly a difficult hunt, but to be honest, I come for what happens next.

I stand in the ditch, the reeds pulled close to my face, for an hour longer, as hundreds more swirl overhead, sifting down toward the field, and landing just beyond the ditch. There is nothing to prevent me from waking up at 3 a.m., driving two hours from home, setting out decoys in the dark, and standing in the half-frozen water of an unremarkable ditch, just to watch such a spectacle. But I won't. Not without a gun. Nobody does. The cost of admission to witnessing such extraordinary life so close and breathless and wild lies in the stilled form of the huge bird at my feet.

Down the ditch someone calls out: "Who's up?"

More are coming. Always coming. Their cries are deafening. I hear them all year long.

SQUIRREL TOWN, USA

The old man waited for me at the end of the dock, where he'd been pulling *sac-au-lait*—crappies—from the brown waters of Bayou Lafourche. My hunched shoulders tipped him off. "No *écureuil?*" he asked, in the clipped tones of old Cajun French. He was incredulous. This 89-year-old Louisiana papa, with white hair and eyes the color of Spanish moss, had never heard of such a thing. "No *écureuil*," I said, hanging my head. No squirrel.

For 24 hours this kind man and four generations of his family had treated me like one of their own. They fed me stewed catfish and smoked Cajun sausage and fried *sac-cu-lait*. They filled me with wild tales of huge swamp deer and *gaspergou* hooked on trotlines in the bayous. They whipped me in their homemade game of washerboard and brought me a beer every time one hand was empty and baptized me in their family traditions around a campfire. And now I had to own up to Elton (el-TONE) McCauley, patriarch of the McCauley clan of the Ville Platte, Louisiana, Cajuns.

No *écureuil*.

He didn't miss a beat. "Is okay," he declared, this time in broken English. "Guess now we drink the beer and the highball, no?" Then he cackled and clasped me around the shoulders, steering me into the family camp on the high bluffs of the bayou. It was then I began to understand the finer points of Squirrel Day.

Tucked into a landscape of big woods, rice fields, and sugarcane, Ville Platte (population 9,000) lies about 30 miles northwest of Lafayette. It's the seat of Evangeline Parish, named for the doomed heroine in Henry Wadsworth Longfellow's epic poem of the early Acadians, *Evangeline*. The Acadians were French-speaking Catholics that the British expelled from Acadia, a French colony of Nova Scotia, and deported to Louisiana in the mid-1700s. Their descendants are known as Cajuns, and these days Cajun culture is big business in Louisiana. Crawfish restaurants and Cajun dance halls are everywhere, and gas station and grocery store checkouts are piled high with Cajun bric-a-brac from dried alligator heads to cookbooks. But in Ville Platte, Cajun culture has yet to be caricatured or commercialized. It's a place where the old women still speak Cajun French and the old men still cook in black iron pots and even the youngest children know how to bait a trotline.

For years around Ville Platte, the opening day of squirrel season, the first Saturday in October, has been known as "Squirrel Day." Schools close early the day before—some don't open at all—because attendance by students and teachers alike is cut in half. Businesses shutter their windows.

Everybody heads for "camp," they call it, and that can mean a sleeping bag in the back of a pickup truck or a deluxe hunt lodge wired for electricity, with air-conditioning and big-screen TVs. "Squirrel Day is the Cajun Passover," explains Ville Platte native Tim Fontenot. "There's a mass exodus into the woods."

It's lunchtime on Thursday at the Pig Stand, and already the impending squirrel opener is apparent. The air at Ville Platte's most popular diner is spiced with red pepper and smoked pork and a near suffocating dose of perfume. The Sacred Heart Homecoming Court has arrived for lunch, fresh from a pep rally at Crosstown rival Ville Platte High School, and seventeen blondes and brunettes with Barbie hair crowd tables loaded with pig. On Squirrel Day weekend, football games at most Evangeline Parish high schools are bumped up to Thursday night. Play them on Friday, locals explain, and nobody would show. "The day before the hunting season opened you could count on at least 50 percent absenteeism," Bobby Hamlin, the principal at Ville Platte High School, tells me. "Even the teachers played hooky, so it cost the parish a fortune in substitute teacher fees. That's why the schools started closing. They call it 'Budget Day' now, on the official calendar. But everybody knows it's Squirrel Day."

Already hunters are swarming town. At Dalbis Meat Market & Grocery they load up on slab bacon, six kinds of pork sausage, and a heavily seasoned, smoked cut of beef called tasso. Pickup trucks sagging with ATVs clog the parking lot over at Evangeline Bank and Trust Co., where one battered old Dodge is piled dangerously high with sleeping bags, enormous coolers, and a queen-size floral-printed mattress rolled up like a burrito and lashed down with cotton twine. Inside the bank, hunting regulations are taped to the wall. The tellers, loan officers, and even the local VP are dressed head-to-toe in camouflage.

It's the same story at city hall, a looming brick building with Italianate cornices. The clerks working the counters are all decked out in camo, and the mayor is similarly spotted. From city hall, I head over to Cary's Sporting Goods Store, a sprawling collection of buildings on the outskirts of town where Sherry Cary—"Miz Sherry" to seven out of ten customers that walk through the door—holds court. She is petite and pretty, her gray curls gleaming against camouflage coveralls. At Cary's, the few days before Squirrel Day are nearly as big as Christmas. "When the men go hunting, they go crazy," Miz Sherry says. "They're a bunch of little boys—there's no limit to what they will buy."

It is nearly four o'clock, and the door hinges at Cary's are warm to the touch, thanks to a constant parade of customers dressed in everything from worn coveralls to ties and suits. Zydeco music wafts out of speakers hidden somewhere on the other side of the gun cabinets and the mounted head of a 900-pound wild hog. At Cary's you can buy enough cast-iron cookware to sink a skiff, rice cookers, mosquito netting by the yard, plus three brands of squirrel cleaners and two kinds of squirrel calls. Today, of course, the talk is all about squirrels, and it's all in a clipped, fast-and-furious Cajun accent.

Miz Sherry hears it all and grins. "Come Saturday morning you might as well shut Ville Platte down. There won't be a man in town."

The next morning I'm up with the sun to catch Ville Platte's early morning Cajun French radio show, *La Tasse de Kafe* ("A Cup of Coffee"). The topic today is no surprise: Squirrel Day. On the way out the hotel door I pick up a local paper. Squirrel Day's in there, too: "While Hubby is out Hunting Treat Yourself to an Inch Loss Massage," reads one ad. Shoes Unlimited's 20-percent-off Hunting Season Sale is good Friday and Saturday only. At Susan's On Court gift shop, "Squirrel Season is Open with No Limit on the Savings." On the way back into town I happen to glance at the WELCOME TO VILLE PLATTE sign on the highway. There's a squirrel on it, of course.

To be sure, Ville Platteans have taken their lumps about this devotion to squirrels. They've been called crazy, lazy, ignorant, and out of touch for getting so excited about a squirrel. They've been derided locally and nationally. Radio commentator Paul Harvey once took Ville Platte to task for letting something as seemingly meaningless as squirrel hunting season dictate the school calendar. And Ville Platteans are well aware of the derision.

"We know that to a lot of people, this is a joke," says Mark Cary, of Cary's Sporting Goods. "But you know what? We feel sorry for those people, because they don't have the access to the land and the ties to their family and community that we have. Laugh all you want, but if you could see these children in the woods with their daddies and papas and uncles and brothers, you'd understand that the education they're getting about family and culture and community out there is something they could never get from a book."

Ervin McCauley stops, his right boot in midstep, and turns his head to the sky. I follow his gaze. Ervin is 66 years old, the eldest son of Elton McCauley, and shares his father's angular face and the crow's-feet that come from squinting into Louisiana sunrises.

Now he inches his foot down. Beyond the overcup oaks that blot out the sky, a murder of crows is mobbing a hawk, and Ervin uses the raucous cawing to camouflage the sound of his stalk. I match his steps with my own and think: *This is how so many American boys learned to hunt. Following our fathers a few steps behind.*

Suddenly I see what Ervin sees: two squirrels feeding in the withered muscadines. They are coming straight toward us—or toward me, anyway. Somehow, in the last few seconds, Ervin has slipped silently away. He's a dozen yards deeper into the woods now, and for a moment I forget all about the squirrels and marvel at how he's managed to move through woods dry as parchment without crinkling a leaf. I lift my gun and line up the bead and then BOOM! I'm too late.

Ervin steps through a veil of palmetto and spiderwebs with a smile as wide as the Gulf Coast. "I don't know about anybody but us Cajuns," he says with a grin, holding up a beauty of a fox squirrel, grizzled red and black and half again as large as a gray. "But, baby, they is just somet'ing about a squirrel."

In other places squirrel hunting may be considered the pursuit of beginners, a rite of passage to pass right through. But around here people hunt squirrels from the cradle to the grave. Men in Ville Platte talk about the best squirrel hunters just as they fawn over high school football standouts. Elton McCauley was one of the best; everyone knows that. Travis McFarlain, now, that's a dog in the woods, as the locals say. He'll crawl through the palmettos on his hands and knees after a squirrel. David Paul Fontenot teaches at Ville Platte Elementary. "He can go through the woods behind you," Ted Soileau told me earlier, "and you kill maybe two or three squirrels, and he'll get a limit." There's a fellow near Turkey Creek who was born without arms. He's a fanatical squirrel hunter. Steering an ATV with his feet, he watches the trees. When he sees a squirrel he dismounts, lies on his back, and shoots with his bare toes.

Part of this obsession with hunting has to do, curiously, with the oil industry, which employs thousands of Louisianans with shift work that offers frequent weeks off. Also playing a role are Louisiana's famously accessible big woods and sprawling waters. But the strongest force is wholly cultural—and as old as the Cajuns themselves. When the displaced Acadians first arrived in the 1760s, explains historian Carl Brasseaux, "each family received either a saw, axe, or hatchet, plus one rooster, six hens, a gun and ammunition, and a three-month supply of corn. Then they were turned out into an alien land." Those early Cajuns evolved into some of the most skilled outdoorsmen America has known. Their descendants still fit the description.

When we arrive at Ervin's camp, a crowd of Cajun McCauleys are in from the woods. Sons Danny and Kenny have dismantled an outboard motor that refused to start. Its guts simmer in a pot of water on a camp stove. "That's carburetor gumbo!" Danny hoots. Elton, the old man, is hard at work with a fishing rod and two great-grandson apprentices, muttering French encouragement to the shiners he drops through a trapdoor in the boat dock. Another son-in-law, Jay Fruge, is sighting in a pair of .22s. More young boys on ATVs are raising clouds of dust on the dirt road.

From this camp we chase squirrels for the next two days. Fathers and sons pair up. We hunt fox squirrels in the tangled oak and hackberry woods of Bayou Morengo and the Ouachita River sloughs. We go after gray squirrels, which Louisianans dub "cat squirrels" for their mewing calls, in the palmetto-oak forests of the Atchafalaya bottomlands. I hope for a shot at a "chucklehead," a regional variant of the fox squirrel that is darkly furred and seriously oversized. "Those chuckleheads hit the ground," says Jay one night, "and they sound like a 5-pound bag of rice."

To hunt squirrels back home in my Eastern hardwood haunts, I sneak into the woods before dawn, scrape a circle of clear ground beneath a feed tree, and then hunker down for hours on end. Hearing this, the McCauleys stare at me as if I have two heads.

"Not here," Kenny says. "Here you have to creep 'em." It's the Cajun term for still-hunting, with a peculiar twist. Once the squirrel sees you, it's an all-out race through the woods.

"You put the running shoe on 'em," Ervin says.

Danny explains: "That cat squirrel, he's so nervous, he just can't stand it if he sees you. Once he start changing trees, it's time to go, bo. Fast as you can. Get in front of him and let him have it."

We let them have it from dawn to dark, by ATV, foot, and boat. By my third morning in squirrel country I am bleary-eyed and dragging from 18-hour days and poker-filled nights and midnight suppers of squirrels and sausage in onion gravy. Before leaving camp, I shove a two-pack of Alka Seltzer into my pocket. Then once again I cling to the belt of a 66-year-old Cajun racing through the black woods on an ATV.

We park the bike as dawn breaks and chamber the guns. I'd been hunting alone since the first day out, but this morning I follow Ervin through the woods again. It's my last hunt with the McCauley clan, and already I'm feeling a twinge of sadness at having to leave. A few hours earlier Ervin and I stood in the camp kitchen as his family filed into the living room, one by one. "The really serious hunting starts next week," he said, as he scrambled two dozen eggs in a cast-iron skillet. "But for the next few days, this is about something else, no? Squirrel Day is for the family. Seeing my boys all together. Teaching them young kids to creep and how to read sign, see them light up with their first squirrel. You sacrifice a little to get a lot."

SWAMP THINGS

When I'm frog hunting and I catch a bullfrog in a headlamp beam, it just does something to my brain. It opens up a flood of adrenaline and flips a switch from present-day to primeval. I scull the paddle carefully, minimizing the wake that spreads out from the canoe, and hold the light steady as I guide Jack to the sweet spot: 6 feet from the shining eyes and eleven o'clock to the frog. The canoe bumps something underwater, and I suck in a breath. The frog blinks with the muffled percussion but doesn't move. Leaning over the bow, Jack is like an old ship's figurehead, still as a carved mermaid except for the quiver in his shoulders as he grasps the gig. Closing in on a frog may be the most focused Jack and I get all year. This is an evening of frog gigging we'll both enjoy.

There are still places left where a 15-year-old boy frog gigging with his dad is just another summer Saturday night, but Jack and I don't live in one of them. We live in a decent-size town full of decent city dwellers, many of whom consider frog gigging as outdated as bloodletting with leeches. When I mention that I've been slinking along dark pond edges with Poseidon's weapon in hand, I get plenty of looks from folks who can't hide an expression of alarm, if not outright disdain.

Frog gigging? Are you serious? People still do that?

At times, it's kind of fun to live in a place like this.

$$\sim$$

Jack and I slide the canoe into Van's Pond as the first nighthawks swoop overhead, wingbeats ruffling like a deck of shuffled cards. Jack is in the bow seat, headlamp on, with a 12-foot cane-pole gig along the right-side gunwale. There's not much additional equipment for our frog hunting expedition. We have an old pillowcase for the frogs, life jackets, and a small cooler of cold drinks. I have a headlamp, too, and a handheld spotlight tied to a thwart in case the boat goes over. I paddle gently, sweeping the big light along the shoreline. Hundreds of spider eyes reflect the light in green constellations. Water striders scatter. There's a muskrat and snakes. Then a pair of yellow beads, unblinking, appears above the frowny face of a frog chin.

"There he is."

"Got him," Jack replies.

I ease the boat close, keeping my body perfectly still so the canoe doesn't rock. Twenty feet. Ten. Jack raises the gig like a javelin thrower in a Greek tapestry. We're close enough now. When he drives the gig down into the muck, the canoe rocks. "Easy, big man!" I shout. "Watch your balance!" He holds the gig pole with one hand, the gunwale with another. Now comes the tricky part: extricating the frog from the barbed gig. You can't be squeamish. You don't really know if you have frog, mud, or both until you slide your hand all the way down the shaft, feel your way down the gig head, and there—a handful of squirm and wiggle at the bottom of the abyss.

"Yessss," Jack hisses.

By the time we get to the swamp end of the pond, a dozen frogs are lumped in the pillowcase. I ease out of the boat into thigh-deep water and tie the canoe to my waist. From here on out we stalk like herons. Teamwork goes out the window. We are each a one-man hit squad, armed with a headlamp and a gig.

Jack goes a little crazy gigging frogs by foot. He loses sense of time and place, following that mesmerizing cone of light into briery, viney, tangled swamp depths he'd never wade in the bright light of day. I'll turn around and barely see his headlamp, winking in and out behind the trees like a firefly as he plows shoulder-deep in swamp goo with his gig held high. It's as if a switch goes off in his brain. It's good for a boy to be a boy on a hot summer night.

We add a few more frogs to the pillowcase and call it quits. By now we're wet to the shoulders, lashed with vines and bug bitten. We smell like summer garbage. Midnight slipped past some time ago. It will take a scrub brush to clean blood from the canoe in the morning, and I'll be a grouch the rest of the day—grumpy from lack of sleep, a sore back, and the first itch spots of the raging poison ivy rash to come.

We have maybe a dozen and a half frogs in the pillowcase and 10 minutes of hatchet work to ready them for a plastic baggie. I suppose it's not a lot to show for the effort. It will take three times as long to cook those frogs as to clean the bones. But filling our belly was never the point. There are some mighty fine lessons to be learned on a frog pond: Don't fear the dark. Most snakes are harmless. Spiderwebs in your hair, in your mouth, across your face—they never killed anybody. So many of the best waters lie just beyond your fears.

And this I'll admit: I want Jack to be able to say, "I was frog gigging the other night . . ." and grin to himself when he gets those looks.

Frog gigging? Are you serious?

Very.

BITTER COLD

Man, it was cold—14 degrees when I turned off the truck—and as Jack and I dragged the canoe across frozen mud, fangs of hoarfrost scraped the bottom with a ghoulish shriek. We warmed ourselves by cutting river cane and holly, shivering as the morning sun steamed the ice in the slack water by the creek bank. Wood ducks whistled overhead. They'd been pushed out of the beaver swamps where the overnight freeze had surely locked up every inch of open water. This morning, the ducks would have to go to the creek. Which is exactly what we wanted.

Jack had been begging to float hunt for the last couple of years, but I wasn't comfortable with the idea until now. I wait for the rawest, coldest mornings of January to hunt by canoe, and even though I carry spare clothing, hot drinks, and six ways to start a fire, Jack needed to be a bit older before I'd put him in a boat on a frigid winter morning.

I also knew what Jack couldn't yet fathom: There is nothing simple about shooting ducks from a canoe. A brushed-up boat is heavy and unwieldy. Sunlight glinting on a paddle blade will flush birds a football field away. Slip into range, and you still have to make the shot. Bundled up in heavy layers, parka topped with a life jacket, legs folded in the canoe bow, cut brush in your face—there's a lot working against a gunner in a duck canoe. You can't stand. You can't pivot. It's not as easy as you think.

"You ready?" I asked.

"Oh, yeah," Jack said. "Finally!"

The creek unspooled through winter-bare trees, the sun gold on gray trunks. I could read Jack's mind like a book. We all have our sporting fantasies, our visions of what a long-dreamed-for hunting or fishing trip will be. Sometimes the reality lives up to the pictures in our head. Other times, the buck never shows, or the birds never fly. Learning to appreciate whatever the sunrise brings is a journey in itself, and one that can be as crooked as a swamp creek.

This trip, however, seemed to be the lucky strike. Seventy-five yards from the launch, we were into ducks. "One o'clock, Jack," I whispered. He nodded. But neither of us was really ready. We didn't expect birds so soon, and I hadn't yet fine-tuned the camouflage to hide the paddle's movement. Six wood ducks flushed wild, on the edge of range. Jack emptied his gun. Nothing fell.

"Tough shot, bud," I said. "If you need to clear some of that brush, that'd be all right."

He shook his head. "It's OK, Dad. I got it."

I eased the boat downstream.

For the next three hours we bumped birds right and left. Jack rarely had an easy shot. The birds flushed wild or far to one side where he couldn't swing. Shot by shot his frustration mounted, and I cringed as I realized what was happening. Each fresh chance was freighted with the last few years' worth of dreams and anticipation, but each missed shot chipped away at the picture-perfect hunt he'd imagined for so long. He never complained, but the hours were taking their toll. Empty red shotgun hulls rolled around in the canoe, like tattered little remnants of confidence.

Late in the morning, we rounded a bend just as a screeching hawk lit on a low, dead tree branch, maybe 60 yards downstream. I pulled up binoculars—the hawk had pinned three wood ducks under creek-bank brush. Jack slowly swiveled his head and cut his eyes to meet mine. I held up three fingers.

These birds were caught between a rock and a hard place. Our big floating pile of brush made them nervous, but they didn't dare leave the cover. The ducks darted from one side of their sanctuary to the other. At 35 yards away, they could take it no longer. The woodies made a break for it, boiling out of the brush, squealing, wing tips frothing the water. The hawk leapt from its perch, talons extended. I braced the boat with a paddle flat to the water just as Jack swung on the ducks.

Bam-bam! Bam!

The next few moments hung in the air. Jack watched down the end of his barrel, dumbfounded, as the ducks flew away. He couldn't feel my heart breaking.

"I can't—" he stammered. "I don't understand. I was right on them. I know it."

It seemed like the last straw. Slumped in the bow of the canoe, he stared at the shotgun in his hands and shook his head. Sitting behind him, I could see in the set of his shoulders how he was taking the cold, hard lessons of a winter creek. For a moment I thought I might have brought him here too early. Too young. And I knew this: At the moment, it wouldn't do him any good to hear my fatherly insights, to tell him how many empty holes I've punched in a sky full of feathers. "That's OK, bud," I said. "Load up. There's more down the creek."

The words seemed hollow and felt like a meager offering. I planted the paddle and drew it back, moving the canoe toward the inside of the next bend. I was about to tell Jack to shake it off, to stay in the game. I was about to offer up some other empty platitude when he suddenly sat up in the canoe, chin forward, eyes on the river. He broke off a sprig of holly to open up his swing, and gave a firm nod.

"All right," he said. "Let's get 'em."

One day we'll talk about that moment. I suspect that Jack will remember the rest of the morning more vividly than I will, with the hot venison stew on a sandbar, ducks that held so tight in the brush that they flushed 10 feet from the boat, and the time he put it all together—the squirrelly canoe, the off-balance swing, the pull of a trigger, and the splash of his first float duck in the water.

But I'll remember the exact shape of my son in the bow of the canoe—framed in brush, silhouetted in the sun, determined. This is not the time, but I'll tell him one day how proud I was when he let go of disappointment, gripped his gun, and squared his shoulders to whatever the creek would bring.

FAMILY TREES

For the first time in years, things weren't looking good for Fred Silverstein's opening-day streak. Earlier that morning he'd borrowed a shotgun from the USO in Seoul, hitched a ride on an M35 deuce-and-a-half cargo truck, and whistled for a stop in the Korean countryside when he saw ducks dropping from the sky. Now he stood at the end of a dirt path, in front of a small stick hut, flapping his arms with his thumbs tucked into his armpits, and gesturing toward rice fields a couple of hundred yards away. The stooped, elderly farmer who'd answered his knock wasn't sure what to make of the skinny Tennessee boy in army fatigues, holding a shotgun and quacking like a duck. That was in 1962, and Silverstein hadn't missed an opening-day duck hunt in 14 years.

As a kid, he hunted with his dad on Tennessee's famed Reelfoot Lake. Through high school and college, he stalked the green timber and river bottoms of west Tennessee and Arkansas. And as a soldier stationed stateside, getting a weekend pass to go home to duck country was no big deal. Then came the Bay of Pigs incident, and the 22-year-old Morse code specialist was shipped to the US Army's base outside Anjeong-ri, South Korea. Duck hunting got significantly more difficult.

"He had to wonder what this idiot was doing," Silverstein says, recalling that morning half a world away. "He pointed and said, 'Go.' At least, I took it as go, so off I went. No duck call, no decoys—but I was going to hunt. There was no such thing as a duck season over there, but it was opening day for me."

If you give Silverstein credit for his South Korea opener, then this soft-spoken grandson of German immigrants, businessman (he still runs a large bathtub and shower manufacturing enterprise in west Tennessee), and lay rabbi has hunted sixty-five opening days in a row. He may have the longest, deepest, and most historic résumé of green timber hunting in America, especially in the lauded woods of Arkansas. He has hunted most of the most famous pieces of timber—Hurricane Hole, Bayou Meto, TNT, Bayou DeView. He has leased duck ground from the Cache River to the L'Anguille to the Hatchie River of west Tennessee. Silverstein hunted timber before anyone called it timber hunting. Before *Duck Dynasty*, $200 duck calls, and spinning-wing decoys. Before flat ground in Arkansas was worth more filled with water and ducks than soybeans and corn. Before hunting green timber was duck hunting's big deal.

And at 74 years old, Silverstein is still hard at it. Most days during duck season, he's in the woods with his extended family. The man knows the past and present of green timber hunting like few others. It's the future that has him scratching his head.

——

In the gold light of dawn, Silverstein and I share a giant oak, leaning into the gray, fissured trunk, close enough to whisper but with enough room to swing the guns. When I think of flooded timber, this is the scene that comes to mind: A half dozen hunters—sons, grandsons, in-laws—are tucked into the woods on the upwind edge of a timber hole 60 yards wide, knee-deep in the flooded forest. It's a classic piece of green timber, the kind that attracts hunters from around the world.

The first birds are high, flying over outstretched limbs and twigs 100 yards away, but they're close enough to work. While his black Lab, Slate, whines softly from a dog stand pushed into the muck, Silverstein's grandson, Jimbo Robinson, quacks fast and low, a teasing contact call to let the ducks know they have a decision to make, as if to say: *You guys are missing out. Pretty sweet spot down here.*

Six mallards bank and circle downwind, and the calling cuts a pair out of the flock. Robinson has them hooked. The flock circles again, closer, lower, with the pair now right at the treetops. The foursome hangs back, unconvinced. This is the allure of timber hunting—this close, intimate dance with ducks, unfettered by a blind. I drill my eyeballs upward, looking for the birds but not daring to turn my face to the sky. Here they come. The drake scans the hole. I can see his head moving side to side.

Robinson's next calling sequence is slower, more confident, a series of hen quacks with a tailing-off *qwank qwank qwank* in a self-satisfied tone that should turn any bird. *Up to you, but we're fat and happy in this sweet timber hole.*

The pair commits on the third swing—wings set, feet out, skittering through branches and twigs like leaves in the wind. Their decision convinces the four other mallards, now parachuting down 15 yards above the pair. I want to take it all in, but I force myself to keep my head down. We've read the wind, we've fussed with the decoys, we've pressed our faces close to the tree trunks to complete the ruse, and now the ducks hang suspended 30 feet overhead, so close I hear the air rushing through their primaries. We drop the pair with three, four, maybe five guns going off all at once, then knock down two more mallards from the foursome as they claw for daylight. The flooded woods erupt in celebration, but Silverstein remains reserved. "There is nothing more beautiful than those ducks coming through the trees," he says. "I'd rather kill one mallard in the timber than fifty in a rice field."

It's a long holiday weekend, so Silverstein's family duck camp, Snake Island Hunt Club, headquartered in an old country church 15 miles west of Stuttgart, is packed. Silverstein's son, Will, is here with his two young boys, H. T. and Jemison. There's a son-in-law, Jimmy, and three of his kids: Alex, in school in South Carolina; Jimbo, a regional director for Ducks Unlimited; and 9-year-old Jack. Jack has Down syndrome, and the way the extended family folds itself around him—rising early to get him into his waders, taking him to the timber, helping him into the pits—is a defining motif of the club. Later this afternoon, wives, daughters, and other grandchildren will show up at camp. For Silverstein, duck hunting is family time.

That's obvious in the low roar of conversation at breakfast after the morning's hunt. The whole crew crowds around a wide plank table, working over biscuits, eggs, and sausage. There are stories of Silverstein turning the ATV over in a flooded ditch, the morning his boat caught fire, the day the camp caught fire. "He's hunted through every phase of duck shooting you can imagine," Robinson says. "He was here for the point system; he hunted when the numbers were so low the season was down to 30 days and two ducks. He didn't care. He was going, as long as it was legal."

Silverstein loads his coffee nearly white with creamer and remembers his earliest duck trips. "All my first hunts were with my father, up on Reelfoot Lake, and it was just like you hear about," he says. In the 1940s and 1950s, there wasn't a more famous waterfowling spot on the planet than west Tennessee's Reelfoot. "I would walk into the big Samburg Motel with my dad and he knew all those famous guides—Sharpie Shaw, Elbert Spicer, the Hamiltons, the Bunches. I hunted with all of them." Silverstein carried a 20-gauge Winchester Model 12 with a Poly-Choke, but that was his only piece of serious duck hunting gear. He hunted in two pairs of flannel pajamas stuffed under blue jeans, three pairs of socks, and an old army fatigue coat.

After breakfast, we move to the end of the table where Silverstein unrolls a large Arkansas map, the paper peppered with ink circles. He has marked the locations of all the clubs and leases he's had over the years. An accordion file is stretched to its limits, stuffed with plat maps, notes, and photos of old leases and camps. He has three others just like it.

Arkansas's famed waterfowl grounds, he tells me, can be broadly divided into two regions. North of Interstate 40, complex river systems lattice the land—the Black, the White, the Cache, and L'Anguille Rivers. Winter rains flood the streams, and when they spill over the banks they inundate hardwood bottoms. South of I-40, bayous stitch the Arkansas Grand Prairie, land laced with drainage ditches that run for miles and feed many impounded timber plots. In the middle of it all lies Stuttgart, the epicenter of timber hunting.

"I started leasing land back in the '60s, and there was a pretty standard chain of events that happened over and over again," Silverstein says. He and his buddies would hunt a spot for a few years, then get run out of the place. The farmer would either clear the land for planting, or wind up leasing the water to some distant relative. "That was pretty typical for everyone. It was no big deal. We'd just find someplace else."

Those "someplace elses," however, are vanishing in today's new realities of Arkansas green timber hunting. Timberland is under increasing pressure to be used for agriculture, while more and more duck hunters are clamoring for the dwindling number of timber holes left. In the mid-1990s, Silverstein says, farmers figured out they could dig a hole in the ground and lease it for $5,000 a year. "That's when it got crazy," he says. "The really big money just keeps coming in." For example: One duck club recently sold for $8.5 million. This past year, Snake Island lost a hole to another club that offered the landowner twice what Silverstein's group was paying. "It's business, I understand," Silverstein says. "You get outbid. I've had landowners—good friends—call me to say, 'Fred, it's $20,000 versus $40,000. What do you want me to do?' So we're always looking over our shoulders. We know what can happen."

It takes an hour for Silverstein to tell me about all the lands he's hunted. He folds up the maps, then says, "Come on." There's a new place he wants to check out, and there's time to take a look before our afternoon shoot. This is what Silverstein loves most: driving, searching, talking, wondering. Hoping. "One thing hasn't changed in all these years," he says. "There's always a better duck hole somewhere."

In the afternoon we hunt a new piece of timber. Silverstein has glassed these woods for a decade, watching as ducks dump into the trees, but he was never able to secure hunting permission until now. After years of persistence, Silverstein has the OK, just this once, to get a sense of what's there and to feel out a relationship with the farmer. He's excited and a bit jittery. We cut our way through with machetes until the woods open up a bit, and then push through the trees to find an opening that looks large enough to draw birds.

"This is short timber," Silverstein calls. "If the ducks are on the treetops, we're taking 'em."

Jimbo Robinson rings out a reply: "Counting your chickens already, huh?"

This short timber, willow and honey locust instead of the classic tall canopy of oaks and gum trees, is indicative of another challenge facing duck hunters in the Mississippi Flyway: Not only are timber leases harder to come by, but Silverstein worries that climate change is having an even more insidious and long-term effect. Compared with earlier years, water comes later in the seasons to his neck of the Arkansas woods, and stays longer, killing off the timber. Many of the most successful clubs pour fortunes into management— cleaning out the dead trunks and fallen limbs, fertilizing, and pruning. When hunters find a new lease whose younger trees may not offer the traditional big canopy, they still jump at the chance to lock down a timber hole.

"You have to work at finding good woods all year long," Silverstein tells me, as he backs into the root ball of a fallen tree to break up his silhouette. He might have started timber hunting in an era when duck timber wasn't lit up with headlamps three hours before shooting light, but Silverstein isn't living in the past. He's as competitive when it comes to finding new duck ground as hunters a third his age. "The first thing I do every morning is Google duck lease Arkansas." One farm that the club recently leased, Silverstein found on Craigslist.

For a guy like Silverstein, who cares about relationships as much as a heavy duck strap, working all the angles comes as second nature. Every Christmas, Silverstein delivers Tripp country hams, a west Tennessee staple, to his friends and contacts in the Snake Island community. Landowners, farmhands, the people in the general store—he hand-delivers a ham to anyone who has lent him a smile. If the recipient isn't home, Silverstein won't leave the gift on the porch or front counter. It'll sit in the duck club kitchen until he can hand it to someone, personally, and thank him for letting his family be a part of their community. And that's the real clincher for Silverstein: his family. He's killed a pile of ducks. He's gunned with famous hunters. But at Snake Island, he's found a place where the roots feel solid. He's watching his kids and his grandchildren, moms and daughters, learn to love what he loves. He is making plans to enlarge the camp and has a line—or three—on some new ground he might get the chance to lock down. He gazes at the hunters around him. "Look out there," he says. "I've got three generations that hunt with me right here. If I can hang on long enough, no reason I can't make it to four."

It's a long wait in the new timber, but a half hour before shooting light ends, the ducks start pouring over the trees 100 yards high toward some other piece of open water another 100 yards deeper into the swamp. We can hear them landing and quacking, but there's not enough time to move the decoys. Duck shapes dot the sky, buzzing past our spread, then drop into some not-so-distant opening. "There's a million holes in here," Silverstein says. But it's not a complaint. He's looking toward the sound of the ducks, smiling. A million duck holes that need figuring out is just the sort of problem he's happy to fix.

<hr />

I'll be honest: Our second morning in the big timber is a mess. We have quite a crowd. I count eight hunters, plus young Jack and our photographer. One child has already gone in over his waders, and his father has laid him out on a giant fallen tree. He strips off the boy's waders, pants, long johns, and sopping wet socks. Then he removes his own socks, and puts them on his son. All better. There's a fair bit of joke-telling, laughter, and hollering around the timber hole—all in fun, but all quite loud. There's a wooden bench on the hole's shallow side, a good place to stow a pack, but it's mostly to give the kids a comfortable place to sit. Jack has claimed one end. He has his hat in his hand, his blond hair shining, and he's rocking back and forth, smacking the water with a stick, and singing the chorus of "Oh, What a Beautiful Mornin'" at the top of his lungs.

The scene is barely controlled bedlam, and I know that during these most promising minutes of dawn, the odds of a duck dropping in are zilch. I couldn't care less.

Listening to Jack, I sag into a big tree 30 yards away, and my eyes well. The little boy has gone silent for a moment, and he screws his face up with concentration as if he's trying to remember something. Then suddenly it comes back to him, the pieces fit, and he throws back his head and belts out the rest of his homily to sunrise and duck wings and the family that loves him so much they wouldn't dream of not bringing him to the timber:

I've got a beautiful feeling,
Everything's going my way!

I glance over at Silverstein on the far side of the tree. His head is slightly raised, his eyes fixed somewhere beyond the highest branches. The corners of his mouth follow his gaze toward the sky.

I don't say a word, don't move a muscle, afraid to break such a magical spell. There's something powerful about the presence of a man who has sown such a harvest of love, and lived so long and true. For Silverstein, the big questions have largely been answered. He's secure in his place in eternity, in both the spiritual and physical realms, and he knows where his ashes will be spread. They'll be mixed with those of his long-gone Lab, Jake, and scattered in the timber on some opening day to come.

HOMESCHOOL SURVIVAL

"You ready?"

Jack nods.

"Which way are we going?"

"Away from the creek bank, toward the deeper water," I say. "Get clear of the boat so it doesn't knock your noggin." He shakes his head. He's still not convinced that I'm serious about this. "One, two, three!" Together, we jerk to starboard, tipping the canoe over, and roll into the creek. The water isn't frigid—mid-50s, maybe—but it's still a slap to the face. We come up gasping. It takes a slick hand-over-hand pull along an ironwood tree to hoist ourselves out of the water, and we drag the boat from the stream. I'm about to flick a single crayfish off the bow deck when Jack cries out: "Dad, what are you doing? We're trying to survive out here!"

He's right. Keep all the parts. I stuff the crayfish in my pocket and pat a small survival kit that rides on my belt. It carries the basics: space blanket, small folding knife, flashlight and extra batteries, compass, 20 feet of parachute cord, EpiPen and Benadryl, water-purifying tablets, duct tape, lighter, magnesium-spark lighter, and three fire-starting cubes. "Let's go," I say.

———

For a couple of years now, Jack and I had talked about this—pulling off a survival night where we had to tough it out alone, in the woods, with nothing more than a few survival essentials. We are not fooling ourselves: This isn't the Arctic and we're not lost. But I don't want my first crack at building a debris hut to come when I'm hurt, wet, and shivering in the snow. Getting through the night has a lot to do with what you know, I figure, but also how well you can keep your head on straight. Practice might not make perfect, but it should help you power through the dark places and make it to dawn.

Our first chore is the venerated debris hut. I find a downed tree limb to use as a ridgepole and wedge it against the trunk of a fallen pine, then start gathering dead wood for the wall ribbing. Jack's on firewood duty, and I hear him whooping it up at the base of the ravine where he's found the mother lode of fast-firing cedar. After 45 minutes I'm surprised by my slow progress. We have about an hour of daylight left, so I call Jack off of firewood duty. First things first.

Two hours after we dumped the canoe, the shelter is ready. We've worked up a sweat dragging the ridgepole and firewood, and night falls as we nurse a small fire, roasting our lone crayfish on a stick. There's plenty of water, scooped and purified in a bowl I made from duct tape. It's not till I sweep the flashlight inside our hut that I come to terms with the long night ahead.

The forest floor glitters like a green Milky Way. It's the eyeshine of spiders.

Hundreds of them.

—~—

The first few hours go as expected. We squirm on the hard ground. We count coyote howls. Spiders drip down on us like dew. "Living the high life," I mutter. Jack doesn't respond. Hips aching and shoulders sore from the hard ground, I take mental notes of what I've learned so far—what I'd do differently in a true survival situation. I'd try to give myself more time to build a shelter. I didn't treat enough water, and now I don't want to chance a night hike to the creek. And I'm adding a second space blanket to my kit. They're small and light, and I'd be a lot happier with one as a sheet and not just as a ground cloth.

About 2:30 a.m., Jack's restlessness wins over. "I can't take these bugs," he says. "This is horrible. What time is it?"

I keep the truth to myself. "A couple hours to dawn, yet," I say.

"I don't know about this, Dad."

I've spoken with survival experts and survivors, and I've spent enough wretched nights solo in the woods to know that half the battle is a mind game, not whether you can snare a squirrel or wrench water from a vine. Lost or injured, the best course of action is often to find a suitable bivvy spot and stay put. Passing the time becomes the challenge. A positive attitude defends against second-guessing and poor choices.

"Up and at 'em, buddy," I say. "Let's get a fire going. No reason to be miserable while we're out here being miserable."

A half hour in front of the fire, and Jack's eyes start to flutter. "OK," he says. "Let's finish this." That's all it takes—a bit of fire, a warm body to lean against, a few halfhearted jokes, and we're over the hump.

When I wake up hours later, my back feels like a mile of bad road. I piece together the fragments of the rest of the night. At one point we got shivering cold. Jack pulled the space blanket tight like a burrito, but it wasn't large enough for two. He finally gave in and we spooned chest to back, sharing body heat. Whatever it takes. The sandman finally showed up for good.

Now I roll over, expecting Jack, but he's not there. I sit up, bang my head against the hut's roof, and send a shower of dirt and leaves and bugs over my back. When I emerge, Jack is snapping twigs for a fire. A turkey gobbles. It takes a minute to straighten out the rusty vertebrae and stand up tall. Jack looks over his shoulder, face smudged with dirt, and smiles at me grimly.

Next time, we could be truly lost or badly hurt or in some serious trouble of one sort or another. Now I know how to build a better debris hut, and how to barrel through a long, lonely night. More important, next time won't be the first time. I feel very good about that.

END GAME

The shadow is a dead giveaway. It's no more than a dark lump, moving along the shadow of a big red oak draped across the ground like a fallen log. I can't help but grin. This time of year, you rarely see an entire squirrel, and I've learned to look for little pieces that point to the whole: a wisp of tail in a tree crotch, a bump on a log. And I couldn't count the number of squirrels I've tumbled when their moving shadows caught my eye. It can happen anytime in the squirrel woods, but it happens most often on a day like this, late in winter, when trees are bare and the forests wide open and long tree shadows stripe the ground.

The shadow melts away—the squirrel must have moved to the far side of the tree—and now a slash of blaze orange catches my eye. My 12-year-old son, Jack, is on the move, too. This is the first year I've let him hunt outside my immediate grasp. No longer shoulder to shoulder with me at the base of a big oak, he's making his first solo forays through the woods. I remember my own well: A 100-acre wood was a magical world, and a .22 rifle in hand freighted every step, every moment, with promise. I suspect Jack is feeling all of that, too, although it may take him 30 years to realize it.

I don't think there's a better way to wind down a hunting season than to spend a few mornings hunting late-winter squirrels. Some of us never lose our taste for chasing tree rats through the hardwoods, but I'm guessing a bunch of us close that chapter as we move on—and up, we tell ourselves—to deer, ducks, elk, or whatever other game seems to suit our grown-up tastes. That's a pity. The occasional squirrel hunt is like riding a bike with no hands or smooching with your wife in public. If you think those days are past, all the more reason to pucker up.

And squirrel hunting in late winter gives gifts we might have overlooked as kids. Void of leaves, the woods lay bare and open. You can see the crumbled brick chimneys of old farmsteads, the pitch and roll of the land, every branch and twig, a rabbit's briery warren, the deer's bed still warm to the touch. You can see the past, too, if you look in the right places.

As I sit quietly, a highlight reel plays through my mind, flickering scenes of the best of the season now coming to a close. From here I can see the open slash of Black Creek, its banks fanged with cypress knees. I shot a 9-point whitetail there earlier in the year, the last of a heart-stopping trio of bucks that plodded along the creek almost nose to tail, like cows headed to milking. The seep under my feet runs into Meadow Branch, which spills into the creek a couple of stone's throws to the northwest. Jack and I were skunked there earlier on ducks, then whiffed on a string of Canadas that skirted the treetops. Forgettable shots, yes, but what I won't forget was how Jack nearly fell off his bucket and into the creek with a huge backward-leaning dawn yawn. I can see the clear-cut where the beagles ran rabbits. The greenbrier thicket where I shot the season's first meat doe. All this from my winter perch. All things revealed.

But I can barely see Jack now. He moves in and out of sight, a flicker of orange and tan that appears, then disappears, then reappears again, like the windows on a passing train. He's getting out there. I start to whistle him in, then hold my breath. He knows these woods. It's time for him to stretch his wings, as well. It's his last hunt of the season. Soon it will be time to store the rifle and break out the fly rods. A month from now there could be hickory shad in the river, and ancient daffodils pushing up around the crumbled brick chimneys.

The shadow sprouts fine gray fur and a tail, and works its way along a fallen log now, just as I'd hoped. I track the animal through the scope, and when he stops, the crosshairs bump with my quickening pulse. I breathe in, then let half a breath go. Funny, but when a squirrel is headed my way, it never feels like small game.

The Graduate

"I'm gonna ferry across the river," my guide said. "Some pocket water I want you to hit."

"Sounds good," I replied.

I gazed downstream. Montana's Bighorn River is big water, but it was flowing higher than usual, and I hadn't seen much of what I'd call "pocket water" yet. But I kept my eyes open and my mouth shut. It was too early in the float to question the guide. What I did see, however, was a dark gravel bar rising under the drift boat and a plume of water pouring over the ledge into a deep green hole the size of my front yard. I didn't want to scuttle the guide's float plan, but I wasn't going to pass up a giant fishy-looking lair either.

I cast a white articulated fly my guide had handed me earlier, and dropped it into the billowing pillow of water above the gravel bar. The leechlike blob rode the flow like a kid on a pool slide—I could see why he called his creation the Wet Sock—but the second it sank to the green abyss below, a fish hit and bent the rod. Not bad when the first fish of the day is a Bighorn brown trout just a smidge over 16 inches.

"Heck yeah, man!" my guide hollered. "I've been thinking about that pocket ever since we put in."

That's when I nearly stuck my foot in my mouth. *You call that pocket water?* I thought. But the guide was my son, Jack, and we had gone a first hour without a fish—and to be honest, neither of us were sure how this day trip was going to pan out.

Jack had just spent a week at Sweetwater Guide School, a hands-on, dawn-to-dark boot camp for aspiring guides. It was his high school graduation gift—learning how to row a drift boat and field-fix a jet outboard and calm down cranky anglers. Jack had fallen in love with fly fishing when he was 14 years old, wading Montana's Gallatin River. Over the next few years, he pelted guides with relentless questioning from Maine to the Florida Keys. One June, on Idaho's South Fork of the Snake River, he heard that college students worked Western rivers over their summer breaks, shuttling boats and guiding. That was the end of his future as a summer lawn care consultant. With his Sweetwater course now over, he'd bummed a drift boat from an instructor, and I was his first real client.

"Thank you, Lord," Jack said. "I'm not going to lie to you, Daddy. I was getting pretty nervous until you caught that fish."

"You're not the only one, son," I said. "And we need to talk about your idea of pocket water."

When Jack walked out from under the tall Bighorn cottonwoods at the Sweetwater school base camp, I hadn't seen him for a week, but I could tell from his loping gait that Montana had changed him—that a week on the river had given him passage of a sort that he could not yet understand but that I could not deny. He'd been bitten by the West, and wherever his river would run in the future, it would run far from home for at least a portion of his life. This is the cruel contract of parenthood: Give them roots and wings, then pray that the former hold as your child spreads the latter in relentless freedom.

With the monkey off our backs, we settled in for perhaps the finest afternoon of fishing I've ever had. Jack held me in the current seam as I worked the fly all the way down the gravel bar, cast by cast. We caught fish at Grey Cliffs and Suck Hole and Mike's Cabin, and we whooped it up with every strike. *Did you see that? Holy cow, man, did you see that?*

Jack spoke of these places like he might describe the local parks up the street back home. He was fully immersed in the magic of Montana, the fish and the river and the wild country, as the wild dreams of a 14-year-old were coming true right in front of him.

It was just one of those days that leaves you shaking your head and checking your heart. We all get them occasionally, moments in the field when you know that this is one you will carry to your grave. The fish were biting like crazy, yes, and their runs seemed stronger and their spots more finely chiseled than ever in the Bighorn light. But more than the fishing, it was the first day that we'd floated as equals, and the sadness that came with the loss of my little boy was baptized in the gratitude that from this day forward, I would fish and hunt with this man in the boat.

By midafternoon, we didn't have much longer to fish. Soon Jack would have to hit the oars hard; we had a six-hour drive to Missoula still ahead of us. But then he slowed the boat one last time.

"I want you to hit that log," he said. "See it?"

"I think so." It was a giant sculpture of twisted driftwood, 8 feet tall, at least. Who could miss it? But as my mouth opened for a wisecrack, my guide tucked me into range. My first cast brought a ferocious slash from the largest trout we'd seen all day, but the heavy water carried the drift boat too swiftly for a second crack.

Jack slipped overboard and pulled the drift boat 30 feet up current. "I'll hold the boat," he said. "You just catch the fish."

We pulled two more fish from the hole, the second one running wild like a puppy in the yard. The water likely spent, Jack pulled himself back in the boat, rowed clear of the swift current, then stowed the oars and leaned back, soaking in the sun, the moment, the river, and his future, which unfurled just about as far as the next bend in the Bighorn. If there is a finer thing than to be 17 years old on a Montana river, I can only barely imagine what that might be.

"I don't know, Daddy," he said, kicking his Chaco-clad feet on the cooler. He grinned over a grimy sun buff and stroked a 15-day-old beard that I could actually make out in the right slant of sunlight. "I'm thinking of keeping the 'stache, at least. Think I can pull it off?"

I started to taste my foot again, but caught myself in time. I reckon if there's anywhere in this world that a young man can still dream, it's Montana.

CHAPTER 5

Frontiers

ILLUSTRATION BY BRIAN EDWARD MILLER

THE LAST WILD ROAD, PART 1

The last Arctic grayling of the day smacked an olive conehead streamer at 10:30 p.m., just as the first blush of the northern Alaska twilight turned low clouds yellow and orange and pink. The fish was 3 pounds, easy—only slightly larger than the grayling I'd caught a few minutes earlier, and the one landed just a few minutes before that. I trudged across the cobble, scattering salmon fry from the shallows, and sat down in wet sand pocked with bear and wolf tracks. I was tired. Early that morning we'd woken in a makeshift camp perched high on a ridge overlooking the Yukon Flats. We had shared the panorama with a South African couple circumnavigating the world in a customized six-wheel-drive Land Rover, then picked our way north, through dense spruce woods and then alpine tundra, chasing willow ptarmigan with bows and casting dry flies to willing grayling. We hardly blinked when we crossed the Arctic Circle. We never slowed for the scenic vistas marked by roadside signs. Fish. Hunt. Fish some more. No time for tourist stops.

The day before we'd hunted spruce grouse in dense conifer and birch thickets, crossed the Yukon River, changed our first flat tire, and fished along the way, all the while skimmed with a slick of bug dope, sweat, and road grime. And the day before that more of the same.

Now I stretched out on the gravel bar, yawning, and thought: *This is what I came for.* Upstream, the Jim River flowed from the high ramparts of Alaska's Brooks Range; downstream it braided through islands of gravel and sand. I had a tent pitched in the woods a mile away, fish for breakfast, bear spray on my belt, and nowhere else to be. I'd come for the biggest bite I could take out of Alaska in a single two-week period.

And all because of the weirdest, wildest road you can imagine.

⌐ ⌐

Three days earlier, I'd stood in the detailing bay of Gene's Chrysler Center in Fairbanks, Alaska, where gear was mounded up beside two loaner Jeeps. With me were Scott Wood, a friend and fly fishing retailer from North Carolina, and Montana-based photographer Dusan Smetana. It took us two hours to fit it all in: three guns, three bows, eight fly rods, ten reels, a case of shells, three pairs of waders, cold weather gear, rain gear, stoves, food for 14 days, dry bags, cameras, GPS units, binoculars, a satellite phone, a tow strap, and maps galore. On top of one Jeep we bungee-corded two spare tires on rims, 10 gallons of gas in bright red cans, stove gas, and a portage pack of tents and sleeping bags. "The Beverly Hillbillies go to Alaska," I said. "Yeah," Wood countered, "but name one thing you would have left behind." And he was right: We'd be fishing for Arctic grayling and Arctic char, gun and bowhunting for spruce grouse and ptarmigan, driving, hiking, rafting, cooking, and camping. Together or apart, the two of us had hit the roads from Mexico to Canada, in pursuit of elk, ducks, grouse, trout, smallmouth bass, pike, walleyes, barracuda—you name it. But never had we gone after everything at once, and never to Alaska. "It's the ultimate fun-hog trip," crowed Wood, sounding slightly insane.

And it was taking place along the ultimate sportsman's road-tripping road in North America—the Dalton Highway. Thirty years ago, Big Oil built a 414-mile-long gravel road to parallel the Trans-Alaska pipeline, from Livengood to Prudhoe Bay on the Arctic Ocean. Originally called the "Haul Road"—and many Alaskans call it that still—the road was designed for trucking heavy equipment and manpower along the pipeline route. Renamed the James W. Dalton Highway in 1981, after a North Slope engineer, the road bisects some of the wildest country remaining in the Alaskan Arctic, and some of the best hunting and fishing lands in the Last Frontier. To the west lies Kanuti National Wildlife Refuge and Gates of the Arctic National Park. To the east, Yukon Flats and the Arctic National Wildlife Refuge and Preserve. Along the way the Dalton Highway crosses thirty-four major streams and rivers and 800 lesser creeks, their names as enticing as their waters: Yukon. Toolik. Ivishak. Sagavanirktok.

All told, the road accesses nearly 40 million acres of federal wilderness—a region larger than Michigan surrounded by millions more state, federal, and Native American lands.

It's no gentrified byway. Tunneling through caverns of black spruce and white birch, arcing over vast plains of tundra, climbing and descending the mighty Brooks Range, the road is a jumble of mile after mile of gravel, then broken pavement, then new blacktop, then more gravel, plus wash-boarded hairpin turns, 12 percent grades, and asphalt bent into roller-coaster dips by the constant shifting of the underlying permafrost. Tractor-trailers roar up and down the Dalton, groaning with loads of airboats, johnboats, construction equipment, pipe, and generators the size of mobile homes. They spew contrails of dust, grit, and fist-size gravel sheared into shards the Dalton truckers refer to as "arrowheads."

And those are just the man-made hazards. The Dalton Highway climbs from sea level to nearly a mile high clawing its way through the Brooks Range. It can snow any and every month along the road. Ground blizzards make driving impossible. Even on sunny days, harsh winds can sweep across the tundra, closing the highway to all but herds of coastal plain musk ox. Scratch your nose at the wrong time and you might launch into boggy tundra, or into dark spruce woods, or into the utter nothingness that falls away from the road at Atigun Pass. Homemade crosses hammered into the gravel bespeak of dead truckers. Engine parts—and the occasional dead truck—litter the roadside.

We'd scheduled 14 days to mosey up the road. We would make camp in a different spot for 13 nights, sleeping indoors only once. Halfway through the route we'd take a side trip into the Arctic National Wildlife Refuge, courtesy of a bush plane and a 14-foot raft. Back to the road, we would parallel the Sagavanirktok River to the Arctic sea village of Deadhorse, company town for the largest oilfield in North America. All along the way, we kept both hands on the wheel—at least when one of them wasn't holding a rod or a gun.

—◦—

By the time the Jim River receded in our rearview mirror, we'd settled into a daily road-trip regimen: up at six, light the stoves, have coffee followed by a breakfast colossal enough to fuel us till dinnertime. The most precious items in our food stash were a thick sheaf of vacuum-packed country ham and a 5-pound bag of grits. Smetana was a newcomer to Wood's and my back-home staples, and he scraped the sides of the pot and poured leftover fish grease over his second helpings of grits and onions.

"I see you're from the Southern part of Slovakia," Wood quipped the first time he saw this.

"Dixie, take me home," Smetana replied.

After breakfast we bustled to break down the tents, wash the dishes, and pile it all into the Jeeps. Then off we'd go. Hunt, drive, fish till the shadows started lengthening at eight, or nine, or even ten o'clock, and we'd ferret out a campsite away from the thick coat of dust that blanketed every leaf, stem, and designated campground along the Dalton. We pitched our tents atop overgrown trails and in gravel pits and four-wheeled down muddy side roads to tundra bluffs overlooking glacier-fed streams.

An uncountable variety of passions have driven men and women to the foot of the Brooks Range and beyond during the last few centuries—fur, gold, oil, the litmus test of wild country, the chance to camp in a place where it's a good idea to spoon with a semiautomatic shotgun. Alaska itself is an American ideal, a totem of wilderness and self-sufficiency. Even to those who never wish to experience it firsthand, it's a seminal part of the American psyche to know that Alaska is up there, vast beyond description, lush and severe and fertile and stark and somehow set apart. It's a place for dreamers, and along the Dalton Highway, it seems, everybody wears their hopes on their sleeves.

At a small BLM outpost on the banks of the Yukon River, I met a 50-ish Minnesota couple who moved four years ago to a tiny log cabin at the confluence of the Yukon and Hess Creek.

They unabashedly declared that trapping marten in 50-below winters was simply a part of their aspiration of living off the land. The Belgian backpacker hitching on the side of the road had a simple enough dream: seeing as much as he could for as little as he could spend. The grime-encrusted figure on the BMW motorcycle with red gas cans lashed to the seat, the hunters stalking caribou—dreamers all of one sort or another.

It's a stretch to call it a dream, but tops on my Dalton Highway wish list was stalking ptarmigan with a bow, out on the open tundra amid the blueberries, bearberries, cranberries, and cotton grass. North of the Yukon River it's archery hunting only within 5 miles of the road, not a bad idea given the omnipresent pipeline held aloft by heat-resistant trusses that keep it from sinking into the frozen tundra like a piece of hot coal in the snow. Admittedly, locals frequently describe these grouse-like birds as "dumb as rocks," but felling a highly nomadic bird with a bow seemed no more or less crazy than gambling on gold dust or a hole in the ground. Plus, I figured they'd get along well with white flour, black pepper, and smoking hot peanut oil.

Like many northern wildlife species, from lemmings to hares to snowy owls, ptarmigan are everywhere or nowhere. Their populations are extremely cyclical. They range over hundreds of miles of territory. In the historic mining town of Wiseman, 3 miles off the Dalton Highway on the wide Koyukuk River, I talked to a trapper and subsistence hunter, Jack Reakoff, who figured we had our work cut out for us.

"When highly nomadic creatures are migrating, that means there are thousands of square miles of good range utterly vacant," Reakoff said, as he snagged mosquitoes one-handed in a cabin filled with the mounts of Dall sheep and grizzly bear and racks of wolverine and lynx pelts. He is a trim, articulate man, Clark Gable with a wolf-tooth necklace. Reakoff was born in the Brooks Range, the son of an Alaskan bush pilot and guide, and he remembers hearing the chainsaws cutting down the trees for the pipeline, and the road scrapers coming through the woods. "My dad told me then, 'That's the beginning of the end for this country,'" he said, gazing at the cabin ceiling where large Alaskan maps were thumbtacked to the bare wood. Now, when he isn't matching wits with wolves and wolverines, he sits on state and federal wildlife and resource committees. "I'd love to prove my dad wrong."

The country plumbed by the Dalton Highway, he told me as I was leaving, "is a thin slice of everything the interior has to offer—it's an incredible sampling of Alaska. Just bear in mind that it's not the Discovery Channel up here. You can drive for miles and miles during caribou season and not see one. Ptarmigan are no different."

But Wood and I were undaunted. North of the Yukon River, we bird-dogged the tundra like fiends, sweating in day after day of 80-degree heat, thanks to what locals described as "a 100-year heat wave." Near Finger Mountain, a rocky outcrop favored by prehistoric hunters, a pair of peregrine falcons swooped low over the tundra on the east side of the road. Three ptarmigan flushed, and Wood stood on the brakes. "Let's go hunting," he hollered as the door chimed open and we glissaded down the gravel embankment. From the road the tundra looks like a rolling green blanket, as easy to traverse as a putting green. The illusion fades as soon as you put your boots on the ground. Arctic cotton grass grows in dense, foot-high clumps the size of basketballs. Walk on the tops and every third clump collapses. Keep to the spongy spaces between and you trip with comical frequency. We scoured Finger Mountain for an hour, then clawed our way back to the road, birdless. In three days we logged miles on the tundra, marching across the ridges at Connection Rock and Gobblers Knob through rain and fog, sloshing through knee-deep streams in calf-high rubber boots. Nothing. Not a bird.

Then one afternoon, we pulled the Jeeps onto a muddy track that ran beside an airstrip on the Chandalar Shelf, midway up the climb to the Arctic Continental Divide. Draining the headwaters of the Dietrich River, it's a rolling plateau mounded by low, berry-cloaked hills.

It was late and hot and one sore ankle already protested another tundra workout, but we were energized by this new country. We were far into the Brooks Range foothills now, at 3,100 feet, and perhaps the altitude would pay bonus points in ptarmigan.

A third of a mile from the road, Wood hissed, "Birds!" In the instant that I saw them, two ptarmigan silhouettes in the tundra, unmoving. I drew a judo-pointed arrow and settled the 25-yard pin on the bird. A stiff breeze sent tufts of cotton grass tumbling in the air. I moved the pin 3 inches to the left and released. The bird crumpled, and suddenly four more appeared out of nowhere.

With the *twock* of each bowstring, ptarmigan popped up like prairie dogs. We'd draw, aim, and suddenly the target would take off running. I took three steps and tripped, two steps and drew. There were birds down and scattered across a half acre of tundra, and arrows everywhere. Across a shallow gully Wood held up his ptarmigan. "Finally," he hollered over, "the red gods smile!"

In 10 minutes we had seven birds on the ground. We knelt down to study each one, mottled brown feathers going to winter white, snowy feathered legs and feet. We gutted them on the spot, stuffed them into our vests, and headed back to the vehicles. I wasn't sure what to think. Perhaps we'd guessed correctly: that the birds had hung up in the higher passes. That they would seek shade in the unseasonable heat. Or perhaps it was just as Jack Reakoff had said: The Alaskan Arctic gives what it pleases, when it pleases.

—◆—

The climb across Atigun Pass ascends lush moss and lichen-spackled tundra to a moonscape of bare rock and scree piled up in 6,000-foot-high summits. We crawled up the pass in low gear, banks of fog and rain blanketing the slopes in near whiteout conditions. Every few moments the air would clear, and I sucked in breath as giant slopes of black boulders and gray talus rose from the edge of the road, scored by waterfalls pouring off the mountains. "Look at those guardrails," Wood said with a grimace. The aluminum fences were bent and battered by frequent rockslides that sweep across the road. "That's gotta be a drop of 500 feet."

Descending into the North Slope is like entering a different realm. Ridge falls away to serrated ridge, a world of rock and boulders that soon opens to an infinity of peaks clad in tundra and flecked with Dall sheep. Above Galbraith Lake we strung a tarp between the Jeeps and anchored the tents with rocks. It was a good place to dry out, take a breather, and take stock in the trip so far. We'd had fantastic fishing—the trophy grayling in the Jim River, Bonanza Creek's surprise gift of 16-inch grayling smacking dry flies and bream poppers with equal abandon. And I had realized my ptarmigan dreams high on the Chandalar Shelf.

These are classic Dalton Highway moments, but the future of the road will be a test of how much use the region can handle and still remain Alaska. It's easy to argue that one aspect of sporting life along the Dalton Highway calls for more management, not less, or at least an industrial-strength dose of sporting ethics. We'd been warned about the "circus" of caribou hunters that ply portions of the highway. Bob Stephenson, a biologist with the Alaska Department of Fish and Game, had explained: The Dalton attracts increasing numbers of bowhunters because the caribou migrate right across the road, which makes packing out meat a less burdensome task. And a lot of beginning archers use the Dalton because access is so easy. Many hunters figure they can drop off their ethics at the border of the North Slope. "But I wouldn't call a lot of them bowhunters." Stephenson said. "You'll see."

Coasting into the foothills above the flat Arctic coastal plain, we did. I watched as a hunter hopped out of the passenger side of a pickup and used the camper shell as a moving blind as he closed in on a pair of bulls 50 yards off the road. He waved, a goofy *Can you believe this?* grin on his face, as if we ought to join the party.

One day I'd like to kill a caribou. They are the very sinew and tendon of the tundra wild, and stalking one across open country would rank as one of the great experiences afield. But I didn't want these animals to die—not here, not within sight of the pipeline, and certainly not by hunters too lazy or ignorant to refuse to shoot them 20 yards from the road.

After six days of hard traveling, it was high time to take a break. One of the best things about the Dalton Highway is the entrée it provides to even wilder country. Bush planes operate out of dirt airstrips at Coldfoot, Wiseman, Happy Valley, and Galbraith Lake, and from many more backcountry tundra and gravel bar airstrips. From the Dalton you can line up caribou and sheep-hunting trips far into the Brooks Range or up the Ivishak River. Grayling and Arctic char fishing in the Iktilik and Toolik can be world class.

We'd scheduled a four-day raft trip down the Canning River, a waterway that forms the western border of the Arctic National Wildlife Refuge about 65 miles from the road.

After we'd spent two hours winnowing our small mountain of gear into a slightly smaller mountain, our pilot, Tom Johnston, walked up. "Going in the canyon, 900 pounds of bodies and bags is pushing it," he grumbled. "It's a tight squeeze out of there. Not much margin for error. I'd say 800 pounds to get out is the limit."

"So," Wood said, grinning, "as long as we eat all our food, drink all our beer, and shoot all our shells—we're perfect!" I stifled a laugh at the scowl I could feel coming from behind the pilot's glasses. We yanked out a few token items and hid car keys under rocks. Fifteen minutes later we were in the Cessna, with our faces smashed against the glass.

We were ready to slip the leash of the Dalton Highway. We'd started to chafe against the strictures of doing it all: drive and camp and hunt and fish and gawk and drive some more. Sometimes the best place a road trip can take you is to some place far off the road.

Now I watched the plane's shadow below, slipping across the tundra. Somewhere in the mountains ahead was stashed a deflated raft, a jumble of oar frame pipe, and a can of stove fuel. On a piece of paper Wood had scribbled the coordinates of a shelf of tundra for a pickup. We had four days to connect the dots. The char run should be heating up. The ptarmigan should be moving down. We were slightly past the halfway mark to Deadhorse, but the trip suddenly felt as if it were just beginning.

THE LAND OF A MILLION DUCKS

On my knees in the muck, I curled into a tiny ball, or at least as much of a tiny ball as a man in size 12 neoprene waders could muster. I pressed my face so far into the bulrushes that the windblown reeds threatened to slice my retinas. But there were ducks overhead—clouds of ducks, more ducks than I had ever seen in my life—so I took my chances with long-term vision and willed myself not to twitch. Twenty feet in front of me floated a freshly shot shoveler hen, the bird's head propped up with a forked stick. Not much of a decoy spread, but glory of glories, that smiling duck pulled in a lone pintail. Another shot, another forked stick, and I had a pair of real McCoys—and they worked a multiplier effect on incoming mallards. I dropped the nearest greenhead and grabbed another stick. My motley flotilla didn't draw every bird on the pothole, but it didn't have to. All I needed was a few ducks, and they were coming in by the bucketfuls. I couldn't help but laugh out loud at the perfection and completeness of the moment. There aren't many dreams come true in life, so I wallowed in the wonder of this one.

My dream was the dream of every North American duck hunter: Gun the prairie potholes, that sprawling 276,000-square-mile holy grail of duck country. When the last glaciers retreated from North America, they scoured out countless depressions in the Dakotas, northern Nebraska, Iowa, Minnesota, northern Montana, Saskatchewan, Alberta, and Manitoba. Those primeval gouges are now multitudes of potholes, sloughs, and prairie marshes scattered across the landscape. And during fall migration, these prairie potholes are covered with ducks.

Myth holds that hunters can show up in prairie pothole country and leave behind the cares of access, crowded marshes, and paltry flocks. Every farm, this legend insists, is pocked with ponds, and every pond is black with ducks.

In recent years, however, I'd started to hear other tales—that parts of the prairie pothole region were getting crowded. That *No Trespassing* signs were becoming a familiar sight. Between myself and Lee Davis, a college pal and fellow waterfowling maniac, we had 60 years of East Coast ducking experience. But could we show up on the Saskatchewan prairies, find water, find birds, find farmers, gain permission, and finally put it all together in front of a shotgun bead?

To find out, we flew into Saskatoon, Saskatchewan, picked up photographer Greg Sweney, and crammed four dozen decoys, one motorized mallard, decoy sleds, field blinds, camera gear, guns, and a mountain of waders and fleece into a white Suburban. We headed into swales of prairies laden with barley, wheat, peas, and oats. We looked out the windows and shook our heads. "Well, here we are," Davis said. "Now what?"

⌁

On the road, we'd imagined flat land, and there was plenty. But we also found rolling plains with 100-foot contours, ribbons of white-barked poplars and willows, and hunks of wooded country. And hundreds of miles of unmarked dirt roads and gravel paths.

"Saskatchewan has figured out how to save money on road signs," Davis groused during our first full afternoon of scouting. "There aren't any."

But weeks before our trip I'd ordered a pair of 1:250,000 topographic maps and had them laminated. Now 9 square feet of map stretched across the dashboard, and I kept a pen on the grid lines at all times, counting aloud the intersections, circling hidden waterways and potholes tucked out of sight of the road.

While I'd ordered the topo maps, Davis embarked on a more difficult odyssey: securing Rural Municipality, or RM, maps of Saskatchewan townships in our hunt area. RM maps carry landowner data denoted quarter section by quarter section, plus the names at each occupied farmhouse. Davis spent weeks tracking down the charts, and they proved no less helpful in killing ducks than working shotguns. For hours each afternoon we cruised for birds, trying to connect ducks on a pothole to names on a map and a willing farmer on the other end of the phone line.

One particular pothole had us swooning. In the last hour of light one day, we spied a glimmer of water at 300 yards and 35 miles per hour. "Wait! Ducks!" Sweney hollered from the backseat. Davis locked up the truck. Below a low ridge spattered with white boulders, hundreds of birds clotted a 2-acre pothole. WHITE ROCKS! I jotted down on the map. We had found our spot. Next came what we thought would be the hard part.

That night, Davis had phone duty. We listened as he put his Southern charm to good use: "Yes, ma'am, we're up here from North Carolina . . . Yes, ma'am, that's the pothole as near as I can tell from the map . . . Yes, ma'am, I saw that tractor, that's the one . . . Really? You don't mind?" He hung up and danced a little jig. "And I quote," he said, grinning. "Go in there and get 'em!"

Ten hours later we were back at White Rocks. Standard operating procedure for pothole hunting is to show up at sunrise and let the birds leave the roost water, then set up for their return. It's a far cry from our 4 a.m. death marches and fog-shrouded boat rides into duck waters back home.

"I can't get used to hanging out at the truck until half an hour after shooting light," Davis muttered as hundreds of mallards, wigeon, pintails, and teal lifted from the pothole into the sky. "It feels like we're late, and messing up."

Finally I could take it no longer. I picked up a decoy bag. "Right or wrong," I said, "I gotta get in the water." We tossed out every decoy we had, then hunkered down in a stand of reeds some 20 feet from shore.

"Let the games begin," said Sweney. Before our own ripples could dissipate, the ducks came home.

Sweney hissed the first warning. "From the left! From the left!"

"No, they're on the right!" Davis countered. "Man, look at 'em ! They're coming like bees!"

Within a minute we were pinned down by ducks—quacking mallards, wigeon and teal whistling, the sound of wings in every direction. Most of the birds boiled over the ridgeline in front of us and then dropped like rocks for the pothole. We picked out drakes and soon were taking tums. Davis was holding out for a wigeon drake at 20 yards or less. Bam. Next, a pintail. Bam. "If I don't pull the trigger for the next four days," he whispered, "I'll still be a happy man."

Before long we simply put down the guns. We had ducks aplenty for breakfast, lunch, and dinner, and more hours of daylight ahead. Quietly we stood in the reeds and watched them pour in. Sweney shook his head. "It's like five seasons' worth of hunting in a single morning."

"It almost doesn't seem right," Davis added. "The hardest part was crossing a barbed-wire fence."

—◦—

One of the things we most wanted to do was hunt ducks in a field, but after three days of glassing, no dice. We watched small numbers of birds drop into stubble to feed, but there seemed to be no pattern to their choices—why this field when it was surrounded by hundreds more? Then, early one afternoon, we spotted two dozen ducks packed into a wet spot hardly worthy of the name pothole. Except this patch of water was surrounded by a pea field. It was covered in waste grain. Sweney watched the field through binoculars while I scratched my head over the RM map. Deciphering this parcel's ownership proved tricky. Most of the time quarter section boundaries are fairly obvious, marked by a stake in the ground, swaths of grain that run in different directions, or hedgerows. Not this one. It took two farm visits and directions from a kid driving a small tractor to find the right house. A woman came to the door with hands wet from washing dishes and invited me right in. After a brief two-way radio conversation with her husband, on a combine on some distant field, she came back with a nod.

But there was a bigger problem. Sweney and I dragged our gear across the field, scattering ducks like coveys of quail, while Davis hid the truck. When my partner joined us at the edge of the muckhole, I was more than slightly downcast.

"There's good news and bad news," I reported.

"I'll bite. Give me the good news first."

"Okay. They're all ducks."

"And the bad news?"

"Every one of those ducks was a spoonie."

But our hands were tied: We were low on fuel and an hour away from the nearest gas station. Our hunt was here and now, or not going to happen.

For half an hour we stuffed pea stems and chaff into the foliage loops on our field blinds. I crawled inside and closed the doors. Our meager spread of decoys sat motionless in the 4-inch-deep muck, but "Flappy," our motorized mallard, hummed like a high-tension line.

It didn't take long. A pair of mallards maple-leafed into range, and I dropped the greenhead. Then the world turned into feathers.

"Look up, ya'll," I hissed. Already I could see swirling flecks of black stacked up overhead. They were on us so fast we barely had time to pick out targets—mallards in flocks of ten and one hundred, skirting above us so close I could see their eyeballs pivoting, looking for a place to land.

The birds never stopped coming. For 20 minutes we lay in the blinds, silent, watching as hundreds of mallards, pintails, gadwall, wigeon, and shovelers swirled overhead, in range, sometimes mere feet away. Without a word we seemed to be in agreement: Watch and wonder. Make it last and soak it in, because we'd never seen anything like this and we might never again.

Granted, we were the beneficiaries of the wettest spring and summer any farmer in these parts could recall. A late harvest had the fields full of grain. It was astonishing. In two and a half hours, we figured, 3,000 ducks came within shotgun range.

Of course, it wasn't always so easy. We hunted promising potholes that didn't deliver. A time or two we got skunked. But we learned that the prairie pothole formula works: Smile big. Be nice. Never hunt without permission. And spend as much time looking through the windshield as peeking over the edge of a blind.

⸺ ⸺

We'd been saving a Ducks Unlimited Canada marsh for our final shoot, crossing our fingers that no other hunters would stumble across the 25-acre wetland screened by brush and tall pasture. Since it was the day after Canadian Thanksgiving, we wondered if local hunters might have the day off. We arrived well before dawn to make sure we were first in line. We shouldn't have worried about a crowd, because there wasn't another hunter in sight.

If it weren't such a perfect scene, it would be easy to discount the next two hours as just another prairie pothole hunt-of-a-lifetime, albeit the third one of the week. But after five days I was still stunned by the sheer number of birds, at the prairie's windswept beauty, at the kindness of the farmers, at the way the earth trembled when 1,000 birds decided to fly.

Each hunt had its own charms, this one included. Redheads were mixed into the wigeon flocks at a ratio of perhaps one to one hundred, a challenge we couldn't help but take up. We swapped turns picking out these trophy divers, passing up shots of wigeon by the hundreds. "I don't know much about Canadian Thanksgiving," Davis said. "But today should be Wigeon Thanksgiving, because these birds don't know how lucky they are."

I knew how lucky we'd been. After scratching down a double on redhead drakes, it was over for me, and I jacked the shells out of my gun. "I'm gonna give this marsh a rest."

"Don't you have one more duck for a limit?" Davis asked. But there wasn't room in my brain for one more memorable moment. I looked up at the prairie sky. Ducks and ducks and more behind them. "Yeah," I said. "But I'm coming back for that one."

QUEST FOR THE MOTHER LODE

This doesn't feel like fishing. For the hundredth time in the last two hours, I lunge against a makeshift harness, jury-rigged from climbing rope and knotted around my chest. The canoe screeches through black spruce trees and lichen-covered boulders. I take three steps on firm ground and then stumble into a gaping pit camouflaged with bearberry and alpine azalea. Once again, I'm face down in the Labrador taiga, run over by my own boat.

"Aren't we supposed to be looking for trout?" wheezes my buddy Scott Wood. He's a few steps ahead, tied into a similar noose and similarly wrung out from portaging our canoe through the boreal woods. I'm too whipped to reply, but it's as clear as the welts on my face that we have no choice but to pull the boats and push on. Sucking in blackflies, scratched and bleeding, we drag ourselves to our feet so we can drag the boat a few yards more.

It doesn't feel like fishing, but that's exactly what we're doing. And it's all because of a wild-eyed rumor that has drawn us to the far side of the middle of nowhere: that the mother of all brook trout waters may lie somewhere below this hellish, rocky portage.

Or not.

For the last few months we have thought only of Labrador. We pored over charts of the nearly trackless Canadian province. We probed books and magazines and the Internet for meager details about its little-known rivers. We packaged and shipped off a mountain of camping gear and food and fly rods. And then, over the last four days, our foursome of paddlers—Wood, myself, and our pals David Falkowski and Bill Mulvey—endured a mind-numbing travel itinerary from the settled confines of North Carolina to the vast emptiness of the Labrador interior.

First we logged 1,300 miles via commercial airline to Sept-Iles, Quebec, on the shores of the St. Lawrence River. There we crowded onto a railroad passenger car slam full of caribou hunters and Innu natives for a 12-hour, dawn-to-dusk ride to an abandoned mining camp on the Labrador line. This was Schefferville, where the sole recreational opportunity seems to be watching stray dogs chase windblown trash. On day three a rusty school-bus-turned-taxi loaded down with bloody caribou antlers delivered us to a float-plane hub outside the village, from which we finally took to the skies for a 135-mile flight to a skinny lake so far up the Kanairiktok River that it wasn't really a river yet. And that's where the real travel began: From lake to pond to lake to river, by canoe and hiking boots and waders. In the last two days alone we'd hiked 10 miles on this single portage (we dubbed it the Rocky Tangle), humping gear and canoes around a dried-up lake outlet.

All because we wanted to make our own fires and cook our own grub and find our own way. And catch fish that had never seen a boat, a fly, a hook, or a man. Give us time and a good map, we thought, and likely as not we can figure out the rest of it.

⸺ ⸻

Clutched between Ungava Bay and the North Atlantic Sea, Labrador offers perhaps the largest chunk of terra incognita remaining in North America: A half million square miles of taiga, spruce and tamarack woods, and soaring stone ridges that taper into iceberg-laden seas. Three-quarters of the province is entirely roadless.

But the region is crazy with fish stories, especially tales of gargantuan brook trout. Some of the earliest emerged in the 1950s when a young fishing guide named Lee Wulff landed perhaps the best consulting job ever conceived: finding fishing spots for American soldiers just shipped to bases on Labrador's southeastern coast. With a float-equipped Piper Super Cub, Wulff leapfrogged about Labrador's uncountable ponds, lakes, and river systems. He found brookies stacked up like multicolored cordwood and put out the word: Labrador boasted "the greatest brook trout fishing in North America." When Wulff guided Curt Gowdy into the Minipi River basin to film a segment of *The American Sportsman*, trout anglers in the Lower 48 almost swallowed their teeth at the sight of kype jawed brookies the size of an overnight bag.

Understandably, a handful of fly-in guided fishing camps opened up in the Labrador interior, and they now cater to anglers who fork over serious cash for a shot at 5-pound trout by the bucketful. In some Labrador streams it takes a 7-pounder to turn heads. Then, in 1997, a feverish brookie angler named Nick Karas published a 371-page magnum opus, *Brook Trout*. Packed with more breathless reports of the paradisiacal rivers of Labrador, the tome sent new waves of fishermen northward.

Early last summer I'd caught scent of a more recent Labrador fish tale. It was little more than a rumor, really. It came from Harvey Calden, an outfitter who runs remote caribou hunting outposts along the Quebec-Labrador border and a venerated brook trout lodge on Labrador's Little Minipi River. Calden knows the wilds of Labrador's interior waters as well as anyone.

I was looking for a remote stretch of possibly unexplored rivers and lakes that had the makings of a brook trout nirvana. My gang of four had white-water, open-water, and navigation skills. We had more time than money, and we were willing to take our chances on a hunch or a tall tale. Did he know of water that had likely never been fished, never been paddled? And could I talk him into guiding us there?

Calden was as quiet as mist falling on moss. "You're not gonna believe this," he finally said.

Just the year before, Calden had put six caribou hunters on the ground near Morris Lake, a nondescript body of water in the far upper headwaters of Labrador's Kanairiktok River. Waiting on the caribou, the hunters chunked plugs into a typical lake outlet. "Standing on the bank, not even half trying, those guys pulled in 5- to 9-pound brookies," Calden said. "At least, that's what they told me. But no one's been back. Far as I know, there's never even been a boat in that water."

～～

Three months after that tantalizing conversation, I wake to the sound of a tent door zipper. Wood is ready to roar at 5:15 a.m., the Rocky Tangle's torture seemingly forgotten. But I feel like 40 miles of bad road. I pull the sleeping bag over my head and curl my body around knobs of rock and tussocks of blueberries.

In just five minutes, though, I'm climbing into cold waders. As the sun winks through spruce trees, we pick our way across a ledge drop at the bottom of the Rocky Tangle. Fog rises from a slot of water maybe 20 feet by 40 feet. It's the swiftest, deepest run we've seen in three days. My hands are shaking, but I'm not sure if it's from the cold or from nervous anticipation. Months of planning and logistical troubles have led us here. If this river holds scads of big fish, this is exactly the kind of place they'll be—stacked up in pools as they nose upstream during prespawn runs.

It doesn't take long.

Falkowski drops a fly into the water first, rips it crosscurrent, and hangs on as his rod bends double, like a diviner's stick pointing the way to the mother lode. "Three pounds, maybe. Not bad," he hollers as the fish comes to hand. "Of course, it's the largest brook trout I've ever seen in my life!"

In less than 60 seconds, each of us is into a brookie. Suddenly, miles into our route, we're juiced by the hope that there might be just enough fish to justify the difficulty of getting here. After a few more fish we forge onward.

That night we collapse on the rocky shore of an unnamed lake and watch northern lights arc overhead like a lava lamp stretched from horizon to horizon. Mars is up, and Mulvey swears he hears wolves howling. Wood and Falkowski stick their heads out the tent door to catch the sound, but I crawl to my sleeping bag to count the blue-haloed dots on the shimmering flanks of the brook trout that swim through my dreams.

Two days later we're barely 10 miles downstream. Calden described Labrador as "more remote than most of Alaska," and its famously raw terrain has no respect for our planned itinerary. For our first few days we paddled through a flat plain, the scenery an unbroken curtain of spruce and tamarack, blueberries, and Labrador tea. Now the horizon is mounded with high, rocky barrens. We cross lakes in beastly winds, whitecaps slopping over the sides of the canoes, then grind out in bony streambeds where the water dribbles through hundreds of yards of boulder and cobble. We are pulling the boats as much as paddling, but there isn't much point to fretting over what might be around the next bend. Nobody knows, and whatever it is, we'll have to make it through as best we can.

One morning we're out of the tents as a rising sun sends plumes of steam boiling off the ice-slicked canoes. Holding plates of grits and bacon, we huddle over topo maps. By now they are dog-eared, ink-smeared, and smell like fish, but they are no longer lifeless representations of an otherworldly landscape. Paddle stroke by paddle stroke, the maps have come alive. Now we know what an inch of open water on the topos looks like in a headwind, and how the contour lines converge to form bulwarks of mossy rock crowding our route.

Figuring out the lake crossings takes the most head scratching. Orienting the maps to the compass, we cipher out the far shoreline of this morning's puzzler. Somewhere along a distant smudge of green our route pours through a 20-yard-wide outlet and into a narrow gorge. Miss it by just a few compass degrees and we could plunge blindly into any number of lookalike box-canyon coves.

We take a reading and push off. Forty-five minutes later we make land-fall on a rocky shoreline. A solid wall of woods blocks our passage, with no outfall in sight. We pull out the maps and compass, wondering where we've gone wrong.

"We're on a river, and there are still eighty-six wrong ways to turn," says Mulvey. Every lake looks like a Rorschach inkblot. We split up to sortie in opposite directions. Five minutes later Mulvey and Falkowski whistle and wave paddles, semaphoring a find. A small, unmarked island has risen from the lake bottom during low water. Behind it lies a tiny outfall that carries the flow of the entire watershed. We could have lost half a day searching for such a small spigot. Our luck, so far, is holding.

By noon, low clouds spit cold rain as we drop out of the last set of head-water rapids. Rocky bluffs now pinch the waterway into a true, flowing river, its serpentine route snaking into the distance. The tough business of route finding is behind us, but that's only part of the time crunch. The other is that the fishing is only getting better.

We can hardly believe what we're seeing. And catching. Each time the waterway necks down, deep slots and ledge pools serve up bigger and bigger fish. We lean on the paddles to get the slow water over with in a hurry, then scramble to the rapids like kids on recess.

Late one afternoon we drag the boats out of the water above a gorgeous spot. The Kanairiktok spills from one of its uncountable pondlike impound-ments over slick wet ledges, hits a hard bank of rock, and makes a deep turn. The bend is as black as Satan's heart: We know a honey hole when we see one.

"Looks kinda mousy," Wood says, digging through a fly box with a grin on his face. Early in the trip we'd each forked over $6.50 in Canadian change for a large souris vison—a 5-inch-long mink-fur mouse from an old man hawking hand-tied flies on the Sept-Iles waterfront. Wood ties one to a short leader and sends it sailing across the pool. He strips the line twice, and sud-denly a large, dark shadow rises from the pool bottom and pounds the mouse with an audible slurp. Now we beat the water with Canadian mink. "Boys, we got us an old-fashioned lemming hatch!" Falkowski shouts, as the water boils with slashes of bronze and orange.

Standing literally shoulder to shoulder, we pull in fish after fish from 4 to 7 pounds. Three times we fight triple hookups. Once all four lines go live, slashing the water and threatening a macramé of high-dollar nylon. Any-where else and we'd be cursing our neighbor, but here the absurdity of the fishing is linked to the absurdity of the fish—their size, their numbers, the ferocity with which they smack absolutely anything. The females are hammered from verdigris and brass, swollen with roe. And the gaudy, prespawn males have the appearance of a brook trout with its tail stuck in an electric socket. Many are slashed with scars from close calls with pike. "There's nothing but the North Pole between us and Russia and we're standing in each other's waders!" I call out to the guys.

"Don't knock it," Wood hoots, setting a hook. "It's pier fishing, Kanairiktok River–style."

For the next few days we shift into overdrive, scarfing down lunch on the run. We portage and drag and paddle through squalling rain. And we lash the waters with 8-weights and collapse into sleeping bags after ten o'clock dinners. We catch fish with 60-foot casts and just 6 feet from the canoe. Hooked trout run between our legs. Twice I catch a bragging size brookie by walking from pool to pool, dragging my fly behind me.

They hit the traditional northern speckle fare—Mickey Finns and Woolly Buggers, Stimulators and Sofa Pillows. But that's not all. One of my most effective flies is a chartreuse Surf Candy I tied for saltwater false albacore. We catch them on bass bugs, bream poppers, and silverside streamers.

One night around the campfire, our conversation turns to Labrador's esteemed lodges. We've all seen the brochures, plastered with pictures of grinning anglers holding up sag-bellied brookies. Folks take out second mortgages to ply famous lodge waters, but could the holes possibly hold this many fish? Could the country compare to the Kanairiktok's unshaven, unshod grandeur?

"Lodge fishing might be just as good," Falkowski muses as we loll about in the moss, 10 feet from the water. "And you'd definitely have more time to fish. None of this humping through the Rocky Tangle." We all nod. So far we've crammed quality fishing into days otherwise filled with portages, paddling, fire building, fish cleaning, aurora watching, Scotch sipping, and frightfully meager snooze time.

The trout sizzles in the foil. We smell spruce smoke and seared fish and chipotle sauce. The northern lights rain green fire overhead. Falkowski delivers a benediction: "I wouldn't do it any other way."

～✦～

Two days before our scheduled pickup I raise Calden on a satellite phone to pin down a rendezvous point. Wood, Falkowski, and Mulvey mill around, nervously watching spruce trees bend and listening to one side of the conversation.

"We're on the river, Harvey. You there?" The guys all glance my way. "Forty-five to 60?"

Our hearts hit the ground. The forecast for pickup day is for winds in the 50-miles-per-hour range and a cloud ceiling slightly higher than the tree-tops. It's up to us, Calden says, but we know the drill. Missing the floatplane by a single day means missing the once-a-week train, which means begging space on a $4,500 charter flight to Montreal or a long layover in beautiful downtown Schefferville.

We load the boats in stunned silence. We'll be homeward bound come morning, a day earlier than planned.

In our last 24 hours on the water we fish with renewed passion. Each paddle stroke and cast feels like another grain of sand slipping through the hourglass. We take a single break to climb a high ridge of barren rock to gorge on bearberries and gaze over the huge country from which we'd taken but a tiny, tentative bite. And then, too soon and all too unceremoniously, Calden snatches us out of Ethyl Lake in a rising gale.

As we spiral above the river, straining for altitude in a heavily laden de Havilland Beaver, I press my face to the cockpit glass. I can see the big ledge drop we dubbed the Bay of Pigs, where every fish that came to hand seemed bigger than the one before. There's the white-capped lake that nearly sank us, the tributary we'd hoped to explore, and the Rocky Tangle's boulder-studded channel. Now the Kanairiktok's silvery ribbon of river and lake grows smaller and smaller, then disappears at last into Labrador's vernal infinity like a skein of geese vanishing in the sky.

I'm not into head counts on fish, but this trip was different; we knew it would matter. The pace of the action conspired against an exact figure, but best as we can tell, here are the figures: Fishing but a meager portion of each day, we landed 240 brook trout. At least 200 were 3 pounds or better, and 150 topped 4 pounds. We caught a dozen 5- and 6-pound fish and two brutes over 7. Average them out at 4 pounds each, and that's 960 pounds of fish. A thousand pounds of trout.

For weeks those fish would swim in my dreams: huge humpbacked spawning brookies hooked for the first time in their lives. But they are only a part of what will one day, and soon, draw me back to unknown Labrador.

The other part is taped to a wall in a shed behind Calden's floatplane dock, where we dried our gear and picked at scabs while waiting for the train.

It's 7 feet by 4 feet, I'd guess, and on it I could see where the Kanairiktok River spills into the North Atlantic. From there I traced the thin line with my finger, first dipping southwest to Smegamook Lake, then paralleling the Desolation River toward the watershed divide between Labrador and Quebec, where its tiny headwater ponds were marked with minuscule pinpricks of blue.

The tip of my finger covered our entire weeklong route. Which leaves a lifetime of Labrador yet to explore.

GO IT ALONE

The old-timer stepped halfway out of the river cane thicket, where he'd retreated to lick the wounds of the rut. He was alone and reluctant to commit to full exposure. He'd found a welcome sanctuary. The deer looked up the swamp creek and down while I held my breath and narrowed my eyes, but his gaze never settled on my tree. I watched him angle out of the thicket and take a few tentative steps toward the creek. He was in the open now, and I had a bit of time. So I watched. When the old buck put his head down to drink, I eased the rifle to my shoulder and found him in the scope.

Three hours earlier, I had left the house, alone as well. I drove to the farm, shouldered my daypack, and made my way through the black-dark woods. I found the cat-eye thumbtack that marked the turn toward the swamp, found the tree, and climbed it, all alone. Walking to the stand in the dark cleared my mind of deadlines and overdue bills. *Solvitur ambulando*, St. Augustine called it, this mystic healing power of movement. It is solved by walking. In the tree I pulled up my rifle and took a deep breath, listening to my heartbeat downshift. I could hear scattered bird calls in the predawn glow, the drone of insects. That was it. All there was. Me and the dark.

By now we hunters have had the work days, the opening days, the doe days, the rut days, the late nights, the poker nights, the big times at camp. I love the companionship of deer hunting, the camaraderie of hanging stands and clearing shooting lanes. But by now, I'm ready for some time to myself.

Alone, whatever happens is on me. To fidget or not, shoot or not, hit or miss, the blood trailing, the dragging—it's all what I make of it. I love all the rest, but this is what gets me up in the mornings, all alone.

—◆—

A solitary buck, a big buck, this late in the season, had plenty of reason to go it alone, too. The last month had been exhausting, I suspected. He was big enough to have his pick of the does but not without the constant challenge of other bucks that believed their time had come. He walked stiff-legged up the creek. He looked tired and slightly beaten. He had a sag in the belly and was gray around the muzzle. When he turned his head I could see the perfectly symmetrical 8-point rack. He stood there for a long pause, as if gathering his strength. I watched through the scope, my finger off the trigger.

A few months ago, my buddy Scott and I had put this stand up together, and it took us nearly an hour and a half to muscle it into place. The trunk was gnarled with knots and branches. We had to cut our way up the tree, above the canopy of greenbrier and cane, climbing with a linesman's belt, and raising the saws and then the stand with pulleys. We worked together, but all along we knew this was a good place to slip in quietly and go solo.

The buck turned to walk up the creek, through low, winter-dead weeds, quartering away. I've daydreamed about the next few minutes for many hours since: While it seemed as though he walked forever, looking back, moment by moment, I realize I didn't have much time at all. I could hear the gloppy muck sucking at his hooves. He had a front-shoulder limp, worsened by the mud, so he was in no hurry. There was a good 40 yards of clear creek bank in front of him, before the trees closed in, and now that he was in the open and I could see the wide rack, my pulse pounded in my heart, hands, and chest. The old-timer's unhurried demeanor made it worse. I could have shot that buck a dozen times—should have shot that buck long before now, before his saunter up the creek unleashed a torrent of adrenaline. But still I held my fire, and watched him walk.

The creek hooked to the left, and so did the buck. I held him in the scope for what seemed like a very long time, until I knew it was time, knew that if he took another step the angle wouldn't be right and I wouldn't feel good about the shot. I touched off the trigger. He never took another step. On the ground, he kicked once, then lay still.

He was the biggest buck I've taken in 14 years on the farm, but there were no war whoops, handshakes, or empty platitudes for someone else's camera. Alone, I sat in the stand as my heartbeat softened. The climb down, the drag out, the telling and retelling, the cell phone photos—all of that would come, and all of that could wait. I kept the rifle on the shooting rail and my eye in the scope. I knew these few moments wouldn't last, and I didn't want to disturb the quiet, as if it were a startled bird that at any second might flit away. So I sat in the stand, looking at the buck. Just the two of us, alone.

LOS SANTOS DE PUERTO RICO

The saints watched from the crook of a massive, gnarled, and knotted tree: St. Ursula clutched a sword, and beneath her a warrior held her scepter. Ursula, legend holds, was a British princess martyred in Germany in the fourth century, along with as many as 11,000 of her holy companions. Now 2-foot-tall statues of the saints, nestled in an ancient tree at the end of a jungled foot trail, gaze over a wild Puerto Rican river. Rivers of wax from prayer candles flowed like lava down the trunk. A small platter held a smudge of old incense ashes.

"I'm not going to lie," said my son, Jack, as he threaded the tip of his fly rod through the vines dripping beneath Ursula's robes. "This is a little freaky."

But there was nothing to fear. For centuries, the Puerto Rican faithful have placed wooden figurines of saints—*santos*—in their homes as altars for prayer and offering, a tradition born of rural people who had limited access to churches. We passed under the *santos* —Jack, myself, my buddy Nate Matthews, and Craig Lilyestrom, retired director of Puerto Rico's Marine Resources Division—and waded into the clear waters of the Espírito Santo River, four anglers a long way from home, with fly rods and lightweight spinning gear and only the faintest idea of what we were doing.

A slight shiver ran down my spine, and I looked over my shoulder to catch a last glimpse of the *santos*, barely visible in the trees. I wished I had packed a candle in my sling pack. Perhaps I should have hooked a dry fly into the bark below St. Ursula's robe, a token of respect and hope. Given the nature of our quest—to find and catch some of the strangest and least-known fish in America—I'd take all the supernatural help I could get.

◆～◆

I first heard of Puerto Rico's funky fish species on a research trip a decade ago, and I've kept a folder of science papers on the subject ever since. Scores of short, steep tropical rivers fall from the high peaks of the Cordillera Central and the El Yunque rainforest to coastal lagoons ringed with mangroves and sand flats. Within a few hours' hike there are mountain canyons and rich estuaries, and a host of native Caribbean fishes that never see a headline. There's the gem-like sriracha goby that sports suction cups on its fins so it can scale waterfalls in the rainforest. Foot-long freshwater shrimp. The bigmouth sleeper, a fanged fish shaped like a flat torpedo to help it burrow in the river bottom and hang on during the frequent flash floods of the river canyons.

These fish crush baitfish as aggressively as a northern pike, but other than a few locals fishing for the table, no one targets bigmouth sleeper.

And then there's the mountain mullet. This was my holy grail—a catadromous, trout-like mullet that lives in the clear rivers that tumble from the mountains. Google "mountain mullet fishing," and the Internet gives you nearly nothing. There's a blog post from some dude living in a treehouse on the west coast of Costa Rica. A sparse Reddit thread. An 1872 magazine story from Jamaica. Locals call the fish *dajao*, and catch it on tiny pieces of avocado. But recreational fishing is nil. Many Puerto Ricans don't even know this fish exists, much less whether they will take a dry fly.

A few months before my trip, at a pint night for Backcountry Hunters & Anglers, serendipity struck. I ran into Augustin Engman, a post-doc fisheries biologist whose passion was studying the island's native fish, and told him about my Puerto Rico obsession, which was going nowhere. "It's crazy," Engman said. "You wouldn't believe what's down there."

Three drinks into the conversation, I asked Engman: Could a couple of guys pull off a Puerto Rican road trip, part-guided and part-DIY, something that wouldn't break the bank, but would feature a few of Puerto Rico's glamour fish—tarpon and peacock bass, maybe—but roughing it for natives the rest of the time?

Engman lit up with a grin. "I don't think anybody's done that," he said. "Ever."

That was all I needed to hear.

‚ï‚

From San Juan, we coursed east and south—the soaring, vernal bulk of the Luquillo Mountains off our right shoulder. Those high ridges see nearly 15 feet of rainfall each year, all of which thunders more than 3,500 feet to the sea in less than six miles. Clouds were snagged in the mountaintops, and Lilyestrom frowned. "These rivers can spike to fifty times normal flows in a matter of minutes," he said. "If you see the water color up, or leaves and sticks in the main flow, get the hell out."

Our first target was the Sabana River, with headwaters high in the El Yunque National Forest. The big creek falls through tangled greenery, the Cordillera Central high and dark in the background, but getting to the water in the lowlands is a trick. One of the charms of Puerto Rican stream fishing is accessing the stream: We parked at the end of the highway bridge, and macheted through 10-foot-tall brush to the water's edge. Jack was the first to hack his way clear, and he immediately scattered a school of fish from a cobbled flat running clear.

"Silver, and sort of torpedo-shaped?" Lilyestrom asked, pulling thorns from his forearm.

"Yes, sir," Jack replied. "And a spot near the tail."

"Mountain mullet," Lilyestrom said. "Just has to be."

Stoked at our possible good luck, we divvied up the braided channels and each took off in a separate direction. I had no idea what fly to fish, what kind of retrieve to make, or what sort of water to look for to catch a fish that hardly anyone seems to know anything about. Vehicle traffic buzzed downstream, and an occasional car horn blared. But otherwise, I was immersed in an otherworld of clear, running water, gravel bars, and riverbanks clad in a thousand shades of green. Squint, and I might imagine LeTort Spring Run in Pennsylvania or a spring creek in the Rockies.

Starting with a tiny Clouser Minnow, I fan-cast to every pool, riffle, and ledge drop within reach. Silver shapes fled. I switched to a fly that would land with a subtler splat, a little tuft of flash with tiny dumbbell eyes, and slowed down to pick the river apart for where a trout might lie. With close to nothing to go on, nothing is what I caught for nearly an hour.

Then, suddenly, Jack hollered from upstream. "Dad! Dad! Get up here!"

I churned through the current and jogged across a gravel bar, part of me not wanting to miss what Jack might have discovered, and another part hoping he hadn't found himself in some kind of off-the-beaten-path trouble—bayed up by iguanas, perhaps, or with his foot trapped in a truck quarter panel rusting in the river. Instead, he was high-sticking his line for a drag-free drift along an undercut edge of the island. "Dad, it's crazy!" he hollered, as I rounded the bend.

He was talking a mile a minute. He'd learned his lesson from the skittish fish downstream. Casting from his knees, he'd crawled a Crazy Charlie tarpon fly through a slow ledge and pool when the first fish hit. Now he'd already landed two mountain mullet and had another half dozen follows.

"I was so zoned in, I felt like I was 50 miles from the nearest human," he said. "I saw this run and thought: *If this were Montana it would be sick with rainbows and browns.* The first fish took the fly on sort of a super-duper slow swing, so I let the next cast sink to the bottom and WHAM! These fish fight like crazy!"

"Mountain mullet?" I asked.

"I think so," he replied. "Get above me and catch one, then you tell me."

Our gravel bar ruckus, however, had put down every fish in the stretch. We moved up the river, fishing the Sabana as if we were targeting brook trout water back home, crawling up to boulders in the middle of a mountain creek, hopscotching holes to take turns fishing, watching each other's every cast. Every lane looked fishy, every lie, every piece of promising water that gave up nothing was analyzed. When you have no information, all information is valuable.

Jack switched to a double dry-fly rig, his go-to for cutthroat trout as a summer guide in Montana. I tied on a lightweight bead-chain Crazy Charlie, and pinched a bright-orange foam strike indicator to the leader. We were like giddy 10-year-olds that our parents had turned loose on a creek for the first time—except we carried three grand in fishing gear. Moving upstream, I stalked a broad gravel bar where the river took a hard right-hand turn, with two tongues of current cutting through shallow riffles to spill into a dark-tea pool. A retrieve through the far tongue turned up nothing, but on the second cast, I let the current carry the leader into the trough first, trailing the fly, so it would straighten and slingshot the Crazy Charlie deep under the bank.

The fish darted from the bottom of the pool in a silver flash, and the rod jumped.

Jack's fish were hand-size. Not this one. The fish bent the 4-weight rod to the cork. It ran straight upstream, and when it surged over the ledge drop into the riffled shallows above, I gave it all the line it wanted as it rooster-tailed through 4-inch-deep water.

By the time I brought the fish in hand, my own whoops had alerted the team. There was the tail-spot that Jack saw earlier, a charcoal smudge. A blunt head with an omnivore's mouth, ready to scarf down anything from a snail to a floating beetle. And the entire, elliptical, foot-long beast was armored in diamond scales with a bronzed opalescence.

We all gathered on the gravel bar to gawk. "There's probably been less than ten people in all of Puerto Rico that have ever caught a mountain mullet on a fly," Lilyestrom said. "And I'm looking at two of them."

Juiced, we talked about the exultant feeling of catching a fish—even a small fish—in an atmosphere of discovery and even doubt. We've all caught good fish in pretty crazy places. Matthews slings live eels for brute stripers out of a kayak in New York harbor. Jack guides for bull trout in remote Montana. But we were so worried that this wouldn't happen, and that the stories of these fish were little more than myth. And even if they weren't, how could we know if a mountain mullet would eat an artificial fly?

We took a few quick photos, and I released the fish into a slot of clear water in the gravel bar, its scales a prismatic argyle that shimmered with all the colors of this little corner of unknown Puerto Rico—wet rocks, green banks, and blue sky.

"I've got to admit it," Matthews said, "the whole trip felt like we were casting for unicorns. If you told folks back home that you could just park at a bridge, hack your way down to the creek, and basically go trout fishing in Puerto Rico, they'd never believe you."

Of course, we weren't winners everywhere. The next day on the Mamayes River, we roped down a steep bank beside a parking area chockablock with food trucks and locals who eyed us warily. A thunderstorm raged in blinding sheets as I sheltered under a root ball waiting for Jack and Matthews to beat it back downstream before the river rose. On another afternoon we hiked far up another headwater stream to a rumored stretch of river, but other than the 4-inch snook Jack caught to bump up our species list, it was a bust.

But there for a long blissful morning on the Sabana, we had picked the lock on mountain mullet, and while it was hard to say whether we were lucky or good, one thing was certain: We were grateful.

◆

Not that we were chasing spirits and myths alone. Puerto Rico is known for tarpon fishing, and we definitely had glamour shots with big fish on our road-trip wish list. Two days earlier, I'd stood on the bow deck of a flats skiff fishing under a disco ball; my fly line unfurled through a kaleidoscope of color. There was yellow from highway bridge lights, green from the boat's bow beacon, and reds and whites from the nighttime glow of the San Juan skyline.

Captain Angel Munendez stood in the dark behind me, his voice slipping over my shoulder. "Strip the fly like you are writing a new rhythm," he said. "Like you invent something new each time you touch the line, yes?"

It was a beautiful way to think of this tactile connection to the fly, a relationship between the animate and inanimate, and it seemed fitting in the surreal urban wilds of San Juan. Five massive lagoons wind through the city, interconnected with mangrove-lined creeks and canals. At sunset, we would cruise the seawalls of upscale neighborhoods where couples at dinner were silhouetted in their dining rooms a few dozen yards from our casts. We'd duck into side channels where frogs called in the night and music spilled out of waterfront bars. Then we'd round a corner of mangrove canal, and the city skyline rose all around. We had our butts handed to us in that saltwater maze.

At sunrise we'd paddle sea kayaks from the landing at Tarpon's Nest, a boutique hotel that caters to tarpon freaks, into Laguna La Torrecilla with the sound of surf on the far side of the mangroves and white egrets crowding the near shoreline. Huge schools of tarpon would surround us, and fish rolled in every direction, breeching in great toilet-flushes of exploding water 10 feet from the boats. None would eat. As trade winds rose from the east, conditions worsened. Zeroed out in five hours of hard fishing, we headed back to Tarpon's Nest to lick our wounds.

All of which was in my mind as I sent my 300th cast into the disco ball of Laguna San Jose. "It's like roulette," Munendez said. "You cannot know if 5-pound tarpon or 200-pound tarpon is there, but be ready for all."

When the tarpon hit, I can't say if I were inventing something new or simply stripping the fly blindly. But the silver fish leapt immediately in the dark, and I dropped the rod tip to feed slack to the line, and the fish leapt again—this time lit up in the rainbow lights of San Juan.

I felt relief and redemption, two emotions I would come to know well. It would be two days later that I would genuflect to St. Ursula, dipping low under her candle-scented altar above the Espírito Santo River. But in the spangled light of urban San Juan, with the fly line running through the rod guides toward the tarpon in the night, this fish already felt like a blessing.

***

Early the next morning we drove south through Luquillo, past the famed surfing beach with the blue Atlantic stitched with breakers from offshore reefs, to the Fajardo River. We had local intel that the Fajardo was prime hunting grounds for *guabina*, which means "slippery," the local term for bigmouth sleeper. A monster might be 2 feet long, but even the smaller fish have a reputation for MMA-style ferocity that transcends their weight class.

Puerto Rico's natural beauty notwithstanding, you can't discount the reality of its contemporary challenges. Graffiti sprawled across abandoned buildings. Along roads and highways, mind-boggling mounds of trash littered vacant lots, creek crossings, and waterways. An estimated 18,000 tires are disposed of in Puerto Rico every day. There simply is no denying an epic trash problem.

And there are even uglier issues surrounding Puerto Rico's fisheries. Mountain mullet, bigmouth sleeper, and lots of other tropical fish need intact seashore, coastal lagoon, and upland rivers, all of which are under stress in Puerto Rico. Yet fisheries management in the territory is 100 years behind the rest of the country. There are practically zero regulations about fishing licenses or limits. In 2004, when the territory was thinking about passing legislation to require fishing licenses, Lilyestrom literally received death threats. Puerto Rico is much more involved in helping commercial fishermen pillage these resources than supporting what could be a top-shelf recreational destination. A 2011 NOAA report estimated that recreational marine resources on the island could easily bring in more than $70 million a year, nearly ten times what commercial fishing does.

So, Christmas Island, it ain't. Which helps explain the machetes.

Near a Highway 3 bridge overpass, we parked in front of ramshackle abandoned buildings with mangy dogs eyeballing us from the shadows. Jaywalking the highway, we skirted a chain-link fence, stepping around rotting papayas and giant ant mounds. Just past the bridge I dropped down into a tangle of heavy brush, jumbled vines of morning glory, garbage bags, and dirty clothes. The jungle was thick as a kelp forest. I buried my head into my arms and battered through as my buddies waited on the bridge for a scouting report. I felt my way along the concrete bridge abutment, then dropped down into the grotto-like darkness under the bridge.

"I'm at the water," I yelled. "Turn left at the purple panties, then just machete your way down!"

Beyond the bridge, past old car quarter panels rusting in the muck, the Fajardo River flowed along gorgeous banks lined with white-barked sycamores. I struck upstream, and 50 feet from the highway the greenery closed in. Within a few steps I lost Jack in the sawgrass and Matthews in the gloom of the bridge.

I cast to the tail-outs of swift runs and dredged ultralight crankbaits through the deep pools, figuring that the fish that had eluded us so far—bigmouth sleeper—would hunker down in the slower water. I worked pool after pool of nothing. Unsure of my next move, I turned into a side channel and flipped a small crayfish floater-diver plug a few feet downstream, free-spooling the lure under a spiderweb the size of a garbage can and along a dark slash of cut bank. The fish slashed out from under the bank like the head of a state fair whack-a-mole, snatched the crayfish from the surface, and turned back toward its cave.

Once I wrestled it into the open, I couldn't believe the fish was barely 8 inches long. It lunged against the ultralight rod with a cottonmouth's fury. Stick ten fish in a blender and you'd end up with this Frankenstein smoothie of a predator—a trout-like tail with turquoise fin rays, spots like a walleye, and a toothy mouth that made me recoil.

I released the fish with stout forceps, and ten steps away another sleeper crushed the crayfish. I had to run downstream to keep the 4-pound test from snapping. The sleeper wrapped line around a rock then swam to an underwater log. It held fast in the creek, a 14-inch fanged flag in a storm. I set the rod down and went in waist-deep, trying not to think about the old diapers snagged on the bank.

The crayfish came free with a twist. The sleeper had vanished. As I crawled back out of the water, I heard a shout. "You guys need to see this!" Matthews hollered. Once again, I took off running.

My buddy was on his knees in another side channel, wrenching a hook out of a 3-pound bigmouth sleeper. He'd slow-crawled his own crayfish plug up the bank edge and it was smashed by this brute of a bigmouth, which had Matthews's fingers bleeding as he tried to remove the hook.

"Snakehead anglers back home would lose their minds over this!" he said. "Just crazy."

He released the sleeper, and it streaked away. I half-expected it to twist like a rattler and chomp Nate's hand on the way home. Bigmouth sleepers might not win any beauty contests, but they are native fish that need clear mountain water, unpolluted estuaries, and access to the sea. Unlovely they may be, but they are a symbol that all is not lost on Puerto Rico.

With our search image dialed in, I left Matthews to his bleeding fingers. Now I knew where *guabina* lived. And I hadn't caught nearly enough of them.

◆～

We slept in late the next morning, the Atlantic surf rolling just a hundred yards from a hostel we'd booked on the beach at Luquillo. In five days, we'd fished four rivers, the San Juan lagoons, and spent one sunset surf-casting rolling breakers. My body clock was broken, the pieces cobbled together with Red Bull and Starbucks Double Shots. We had a half day left to fish, and felt like we needed a gimme—a guilty pleasure, like a big piece of store-bought cake.

Which is how we wound up hunting peacock bass in golf course ponds that were about as natural as a Hostess HoHo. After all our cerebral, high-minded exploratory adventures, we whacked stocked fish in a high-dollar resort while duffers shot us daggers from the greens.

Gaudy and exotic, peacocks here are a non-native creature that is everything a tarpon is not and all that a mountain mullet might stand against. And we caught whoppers. My largest fish pushed maybe 8 pounds. I remember double-handing the glowing beast, gawking for photos with something that looked like I'd snagged it out of a nuclear power plant silo. Over the photographer's shoulder rose the green-clad mountains of the Cordillera Central, those fragments of the Puerto Rican wild where the mountain mullet and bigmouth sleeper still thrive.

I felt a little guilty. After nearly a week boating, kayaking, wading, and crawling across the northeast corner of Puerto Rico, I had been convinced that this island holds world-class fishing for native fish in unforgettable places.

As I released the peacock back into its artificial home, I made a promise to return and make amends. I'll bring a candle next time, and light it at St. Ursula's feet. On my map I'd marked a stretch of the Espírito Santos that seemed utterly lost to time. It would be a good place to beg the *santos* for a bit of fishing forgiveness.

GIVING UP THE DREAM

All of my hunting life, moose have haunted my dreams. Literally, since I was a child, I have had the same dream. The basic storyline never changes, but as I've matured as an outdoorsman, the details have become more specific and meaningful.

I'm in a canoe—a Maine guide canoe—with a long-shafted beavertail paddle in hand. A lever rifle leans against the bow thwart. My guide and I cruise slowly around a sharp bend in the stream, careful to keep the bow from scraping on the river gravel. Brook trout dimple the water. Mosquitoes buzz. The guide grunts and bellows with a rolled birch-bark call, and the sound seems to skip over the water like a thrown stone, mellowing as it reaches the far shore. I scan the dense woods, picking apart the latticed boughs for the glint of an antler or the horizontal line of a belly or back. In the dream, I am looking for pieces and parts of a moose and then, suddenly, the bull is right there, complete, at the water's edge, silhouetted in front of a sheen of sunlit spruce.

And that's how it ends. Every time. The dream never progresses beyond this point—no matter how many times I have had it, no matter how often I lie in bed trying to fall back to sleep so I can dream my way into slowly reaching for the gun, as the guide braces the boat for the rifle's recoil. Over the years, I came to accept that a moose hunt might be a dream I would never have the chance to live. But if I did, I didn't want to scout from a truck and hunt from a road. I wanted my dream—canoes, remote waters, paddling under the early-morning stars, stalking and calling, and nothing easy.

—◦—

"This wind is killing us," says my guide Peter Koch. Gray clouds race above the serrated firs crowding a narrow, marsh-edged slack in the stream, what Mainers call a dead water. The light is fading, but the far shore is within easy rifle range. "This is the glory hour," Koch whispers, "and nobody can hear us."

This is no dream.

We'd paddled for miles in total silence, communicating in hand signals, hauling the boats across two beaver dams—Koch and I in the lead boat; Sherry Bouchard, another Registered Maine Guide and a longtime friend, and photographer Tom Fowlks in the other. We were worn down before we even started. This was our second long paddle of the day, having left camp at

4 a.m. for a dawn patrol of a distant dead water. Now we've beached the boats and crept across a peninsula of dark forest and bog.

Strong gusts lay the fir tops over like marsh grass. Koch grunts through a birch-bark moose call, and a red squirrel chatters across the water. "He's still there," Koch says, his confidence masked by a furrowed brow, just as the bull answers for the third time.

I silently beg for the bull across the cove to step out and give me a look, even if it's not up close and personal. The bull grunts again, the sound muffled through wind and soaked timber.

"Can you see into the woods?" Koch asks. "Do you have enough light?"

I sweep the scope crosshairs above the water's edge, 120 yards distant. "I'm good."

Koch rakes a nearby birch tree with a canoe paddle, snapping off limbs and shredding bark like a bull moose that's ready for a brawl. More light bleeds from the sky.

"Can you still see? You good? We're dying here."

I search the dark timber. "Yep. But he's gotta show quick."

The third time Koch asks if I can shoot the timber, I answer, dispirited, "No."

"OK," he says. "We're done." There are two minutes remaining of shooting light, but when there's not enough light to shoot, it's over. He doesn't want to push our luck and bust the bull. We have five more days to connect. "We're playing the long game," he says. "Trust me."

And to be honest, on a six-day rut hunt for northern Maine bull moose, I want this to take its sweet time. I would soon learn to be careful what you dream for.

──〰──

Founded in 1902, Chandler Lake Camps and Lodge is one of the oldest traditional sporting camps in Maine, and I've fished for brook trout and landlocked salmon and grouse hunted the big North Woods out of Chandler long enough to count Sherry and her husband, Jason Bouchard, who own the lodge, as friends. I even served as witness to their fireside wedding a few years back. For me, hunting moose out of Chandler was like being hit by happy lightning twice. Drawing a resident moose tag is a near once-in-a-lifetime event, and when Sherry drew her second tag nearly 20 years after her first, she invited me to hunt with her. (Each tag holder can invite a friend to participate in the hunt.) We'd be looking for bulls in the 4 million acres of woods and swamps of the sprawling North Maine Woods, between Moosehead Lake and the Canada border. Good fortune, I knew, wouldn't count for much in those woods. I pored over ballistic charts and hit the gym hard, biking a million Maine miles of imaginary moose trails and logging roads.

Two days into the hunt, though, the weather we encountered was more a hunter's nightmare than lifelong dream. The midnight temperature was 70 degrees, and we ate breakfast in short sleeves. When the rain came it was a hot rain—not the brisk leading edge of a cold front that kicks up the breeding urge—and it was forecast to fall in scattered sheets for the next few days. In a typical year, the peak-rut woods can be a frenzied madhouse of sparring bulls and bellowing cows, but so far we've had only one close encounter.

On our first morning, we paddled for an hour in the dark. No headlamps, no talking. Herons croaked as I mentally tracked each paddle stroke to prevent scraping the hull. I could hear the canoe's V-wake trickling behind me and sense the boat shift with Koch's strokes. Tall brush on each side of the stream darkened the shore, leaving a single lane of silvery light that ran down the center of the creek. I skipped a paddle stroke to wipe away a false tear trickling down one cheek. Heavy mist wetted my face, suffusing the water's surface in a gauzy glow. Suddenly, there was a rustling in the reeds and a low, inquisitive grunt. We all froze, paddles in midstroke, stunned by the closeness of the sound. I could hear the water drip from my paddle blade as a bull moose stepped from the brush, hesitated for a moment, then crossed in front of the canoes at 30 feet. Backlit by moonlight, the massive animal glided through the water almost silently, its black bulk like some ghost ship on the horizon.

It seemed like an omen of good things to come, and for a moment on that misty stream, I wondered if my dream might come true too soon and too easily. But it was the only moose we would see that day. And ever since, finding the quiet bulls in the low marshy country where we've pulled and paddled and humped the canoes has proved another level of tough.

The next morning, as we drive in the dark for another long paddle, Koch talks a mile a minute and has high hopes of getting in front of undisturbed animals. "They've been bedded down, they're soaked, they've got to get food," he says. "They're just like us—they'll want to move around a bit, see what's up. And we'll be right there. We're playing the long game, don't forget that."

A few hours later, Koch is still talking, but in a different language. Days earlier he'd stripped a single piece of birch bark from a tree and stitched it into a megaphone shape with a strip of leather. The call is as much a part of old-school Maine moose hunting as beavertail canoe paddles. With his nose pinched shut to deepen the tones, his guttural bull grunts sound like something bubbling out of a wet hole in the earth—a primeval, nasal belch with a brawler's edge.

But it's his cow bellow that rocks the woods. After stashing the canoes in a marsh, we post up on an edge of alder and scrub juniper, overlooking an open meadow painted with red, orange, and russet fall flowers. Wearing electronic shooting muffs to better siphon the air for a response, Koch lets go with a 40-second wailing, lubricious moan that rises and falls with a quavering fervor. It's the sexiest animal call I've ever heard, urgent and needy. He's silent for a second or two, then grunts softly, as if an answering bull is being reeled in by the hot-to-trot cow.

This is Koch's favored approach: Sort out the squirt bulls and piss off the big boys. He rakes a canoe paddle up and down the lower trunk of a tree, cracking off branches. He thrashes small shrubs, then rakes the ground with paddle and boots. Such aggressive tactics run the risk of pushing off a few animals, no doubt. "A little one, a mulligan," he says. "He'll answer but not come in, because he doesn't want his ass handed to him. But we're not looking for somebody that will talk back and then bail on us. We're looking for Mr. Big."

Sixty moose-less minutes later, though, neither big bull nor runt has responded. It's already our third morning in the woods, and I'm thinking back to that moment on our first day of hunting, when I hoped it wouldn't be over too soon.

In the late afternoon, we paddle up another quiet dead water, probing the bottom with the paddles to find where the deep muck gives way to hardpan, a clue to a possible moose crossing. Woodcock careen overhead, a sign of the turning season, and we take heart. The stream opens into a wide, remote pond, and 15 minutes into an open lake crossing, Koch suddenly wigeonwhistles to halt the boats.

"Cow moose," he says, "right there!"

A big girl is back-deep in the pond, 80 yards from shore. We shift into total sneak mode, feathering the paddles through the water so they don't flash and shine, lying low in the hull. Moose have notoriously poor vision, so we make landfall a few hundred yards from the cow just as she steps onto land, alert but seeming unalarmed. We scramble for the woods, teetering on the tops of shrub hummocks until we get to the dark timber. We're in sign immediately. The woods are latticed with trails, muddied with tracks of moose and bear. Trees are slashed and broken. We sneak 50 feet through the woods, keeping a screen of dark timber between us and the cow. I exchange glances with Koch and Sherry. We can smell moose. We have a live decoy by the water.

Koch picks up an inch-thick branch and snaps it. The wet wood breaks with a subtle pop. "That's all we're listening for," he whispers. It's a sound as subtle as the splat of a raindrop on a sleeve. "You'd think you wouldn't have to listen so hard for a thousand-pound animal, but that's what this game is like."

Deep in woods scored and raked and thrashed with moose, we call, into the falling dark, and listen hard to another nightfall of nothing.

❧

After three days of hunting hard, reality begins to set in. At camp that evening, as I leaf through the current issue of *The Maine Sportsman* magazine, a headline catches my eye: "Canoe Hunt for Moose." Jim Andrews, the author, wrote: "This type of hunting is not for everybody. Canoe hunters see far fewer moose than other hunters do. . . . There's no guarantee of seeing a moose, and waiting for a trophy bull is foolhardy. . . . It takes a certain kind of hunter to decide it's a good idea to punch their once-in-a-lifetime moose permit for this."

I am that certain type of hunter, and while I am loath to give up on the dream—the canoes, the remote ponds, the misty cedar swamps—I can feel time fading. At breakfast the next morning, Jason Bouchard plays the cheerleader. "Day four in the woods," he says. "Time to separate the real hunters from the pretenders."

The ever-cheery Koch weighs in: "Day four—otherwise known as paint-the-ground-red day."

There is reason for optimism: The weather is cooling, and other guides are reporting animals on the move. The urge to breed can't be ignored. "It's not going to get worse," Koch says, before adding a word of caution. "But the reports of moose activity are all from the hardwood ridges."

He lets the line hang in the air with the scent of sausage and eggs. I know what he's thinking. Part of a good hunting strategy is letting the tactics evolve with the ground game. I'm still emotionally and aesthetically tied to the water, but at this point I agree to swap the canoes for boot treads. A mist falls as we all pile into Koch's truck. An hour later, when the headlights cycle off, I hoist my rifle and daypack. As I will discover, if I'd thought the only hard way to hunt moose was by canoe, I was mistaken.

The slope down from the rutted two-track logging trail is cloaked in ferns, vines, and shrub huckleberry. As the terrain flattens, the hard ground turns to a slop bucket of muck that sucks at our boots. In these bogs every footfall sends ripples across the ground. Shrubs shimmer and shake, showering us with water even when the rain slackens. At one point, we're hemmed in on three sides by a nearly impenetrable bog. Koch pushes in one direction, then I attempt another. We each turn back.

"That way is terrible," he says, "and the other way is horrible. In front, it's just a shithole." I catch my breath and wipe blood from my forehead. "Come on," he says. "The shithole it is."

A few hours later, we've climbed out of the swamp to a long, shrubby slope that leads back to the old logging road. Suddenly, moose beds appear like moon craters—first a handful, then by the bucketload. In four days, we've seen widely scattered moose sign. Now, in 100 yards of stalking, we count thirty-four moose beds smashed into chest-high grasses and wild cucumber vine.

Koch is wide-eyed. I'm ready to shoulder the rifle at every twitch of a leaf in the rain. It's coming down even harder now, pelting our jackets so hard we can barely hear each other whisper. But it's the wind, not the rain, that worries me. It's shifted, blowing down the shrubby opening toward the mother lode of moose beds in 30-mile-per-hour gusts.

"That's it," Koch says, leaning close. "We're outta here. We can't take the chance with this wind. We'll slip in tomorrow after it turns. And you can cancel Christmas—you'll have your moose."

Daylight has already begun to fade. There can't be more than 90 minutes of shooting light left. "Man, we are right here," I say, practically pleading. "Right here."

"It's your hunt," Koch counters. "I say we bolt. But you're no beginner. You know the deal."

My legs are quaking from our all-morning bog slog, and I'd love to take a seat and watch a moose come into view through the rain. But Koch is right. Let your guide be your conscience, as a guide friend of mine is fond of saying. I shoulder my rifle and bend my head toward the truck.

On the drive back to camp, though, I'm fighting a full-blown panic attack. My heart is pounding and I'm wringing my hands in the passenger seat. I just can't leave the woods with daylight on the clock. I make Koch pull over at the first decent woods opening, and we all fast-hike into a slash-choked timber cut to sit out the last few minutes of legal light.

<hr />

Bouchard hears it first. During our hike in the next morning, Koch and I are so intent on getting through the brush quietly and making it through the dark to our marked hide on the ridgetop that Sherry has to punch me in the arm to get my attention.

"Bull!" she mouths. She makes a what-the-hell-is-wrong-with-you-guys scowl, and jerks her head toward the dark woods behind her.

The bull grunts again—brrrt. He can't be more than 60 feet away.

For a few seconds, it's a Keystone Cops moment. We're pinned down on the old logging road, a quarter mile from the hide we had marked yesterday. We turn one way and then another, wide-eyed, mouthing words—You hear that? How close? Don't move! We're not sure what our play should be, but then a third grunt seals the deal. The bull is close enough to hear our breathing. I high-step 10 feet away toward the closest copse of shrubs I can reach on the uphill side of the clearing, while Bouchard and Koch hit the ground nearby.

Over the next 24 hours of skinning, butchering, and packing meat—and hashing out the story a hundred times—the next few minutes will come into sharper focus. With my back against tall shrubs, I draw up into a small ball and settle the rifle on my right knee, turkey hunting style. And then two shows play out simultaneously: the one with Koch and Bouchard, and the one that evolves in front of me. Different perspectives of the same reality, as everyone's hopes and dreams take shape.

Koch and Bouchard grunt quietly. As shooting light seeps into the clearing, a yearling bull steps into view, 15 yards away. He grunts in frustration, scenting something unfamiliar, it seems to me, then he turns and bolts into the woods. He passes 12 feet off my right shoulder as I sit frozen in place. Just then, a cow in heat bellows from up the rise.

Bedlam erupts in the woods just behind us—thrashing, grunting, limbs cracking. The furor can't be 30 feet away, and I feel for the scope ring to make sure it is cranked down to 3X, just as another animal bursts into the clearing.

I am gobsmacked by the sight. From the base of the neck to beyond the tip of the snout, the moose's head is swathed in a massive salad of branches, shrubs, and cucumber vine, all raked and torn from the forest up the hill. I nearly panic, unable to see an eyeball or inch of antler, unsure, even, of what I am looking at.

Koch hisses out loud: "Shoot! What's wrong with you? Shoot!"

Then the moose grunts and pounds the ground with a hoof, panting heavily. I snap into focus. He shakes his body as leaves and vines rain to the ground. I can make out a small sweep of palmate antler and three tines, and I know instantly that he is not a huge bull, but I am five days into a six-day hunt. He is so close that the body fills the entire scope. The bull grunts again, bellicose, and I find the daylight under the armpit and shift the crosshairs north.

The moose shudders at the first shot, then bolts down the spine of the ridge, directly between my rifle and the guides. Koch and Bouchard press low to the dirt, worried that either the moose might run them over or my follow-up shot will be headed their way. I follow the bull in my scope, cucumber vine spilling from his antlers with each heavy step, and I let him run far past the spot where my friends lie. The second shot whomps him hard, and he sags. Shoot until you run out of bullets, Jason Bouchard told me earlier. So I do. With the third shot, he stumbles. The fourth puts him down.

For a solid five seconds, I watch the brown body through the scope. The crosshairs seem never to waver. I am surprisingly calm. Then the shakes come—from the cold and the wet, but mostly from the moose.

Over the next few weeks, my sleep will be marked with a new vision of moose. In this dream, the animal appears in the clearing, exactly as before, his head swaddled in greenery. I shoulder the rifle and pull the trigger, time and time again, with no apparent effect on the bull but for this: With each crack of the rifle, a few branches tumble from his antlers. Vines and leaves shake free of the tines. I see the head, the bulbous snout, a glint of eye. Shot by shot, all is revealed, until the bull stands alone in the riflescope—no canoes, no misty lakes, no gravel bars under hoof. Just a moose in the glass, on the crest of the ridge, finally in reach.

LITTLE BIG WOODS

The 7-point buck tiptoed out of the pines as dawn's light set fire to the tree-tops, and I knew in an instant that no matter what happened next, this was one of my best hunts ever. I'd figured him out, right in his own backyard, back in the big woods.

I'd found the sneak trail during one of those midday, midseason speed-scouting trips I tell myself that I shouldn't take. You don't see sign like this as much as you sense its presence, thanks to some primordial brain node that hasn't been scrubbed clean of hunting instinct by smartphone calendar reminders and voicemail notifications. This trail was a little nothing of a track—just a few turned-up leaves and the occasional sprig of snipped-off greenbrier—right where a pine ridge dropped into an open flat of hardwoods.

Between summer feeding and the rut, deer scramble their travel patterns. When the persimmons begin falling, the beechnuts drop, the fox grapes ripen, or the oaks start to rain, this thought keeps me tossing in bed: Somewhere out there a buck—my buck—has scratched out an unobtrusive little wormhole it will use to slip unseen from thicket to mast to swamp bed. On the one hand, it feels wrong to be monkeying through the woods with the season wide open. On the other, that's how you find the wormholes.

Now I watched the buck with my eyes closed to slits. I was nervous about my scent and super aware of any movement. It had been a long walk to get in there, and at one point I'd swapped sweat-soaked clothes for fresh duds. When I tucked into the base of a giant gum tree, there was no treestand advantage, no convenience of a shooting rail, no food plot. Just me, a few square feet of ground kicked free of leaves, and a good feeling inside.

The deer crossed in front of me at 20 yards, then passed behind a stout gum trunk. I raised the rifle and watched him through the scope for another 20 yards. He stood out in relief from the columns of trees in front and behind, like some stag wandering the halls of the Parthenon. I watched his chest rise and fall and saw his whiskers twitch. I shot him at 35 yards, with a lever-action .30/30. He fell in his tracks, and for a long time, I didn't move. I waited for the big woods to go quiet and still. I didn't stand up until a nuthatch flitted in.

Don't misunderstand—I'm happy hunting a cornfield or watching a food plot. But more than anything I like a big chunk of woods where the morning light comes late, the evening gloaming takes its time, and the only opening in the trees marks the edge of the river. Back there, the deer aren't snorting corn like drug addicts or plodding like cattle toward a beanfield. Back there, I tell myself, the deer are at their most primeval: The farther away from a farm path or pasture edge, the purer their behavior.

This is part fantasy, I'll admit. The deer could be moving to the beans a mile away, or toward the corn pile on the neighbor's land. But for those precious moments when the deer appear in the trees and I follow them through the big woods, they are the deer of Crockett and Boone and Natty Bumppo. They are unfettered and untamed, and "all lost, wild America," as Stephen Vincent Benet wrote, "is burning in their eyes."

And here's the beauty of hunting the big woods: They don't have to be all that big to pull off a big-woods hunt in which your quarry acts like deer did back when a cornfield was a quarter-acre plot behind a mud-chinked log cabin. Sure, it's nice to hunt a swath of dark timber measured by the mile and bordered by Canada. But my big woods are no wilderness preserve. They're maybe 300 yards wide and a mile deep, a fringe of ridge oaks and bottomland cypress and gums tucked along a river and a creek. Yours might be a piece of public-land oaks just far enough to keep other hunters at bay. Point is, most of us have places where we can get away from the hard edges of fields and timber cuts—or at least where we can turn our backs and look the woods in the eye.

I dragged the buck to the riverbank, tied a hind leg to a sapling, and gutted it by the water. It was a three-quarter-mile hike to the barn to retrieve the deer cart—and the same back. Four trips, including that first one in the dark. All told, 3 miles of hard work. Through the big woods.

What surprised me the most that morning was this: At one point, hauling that deer cart over downed logs and brambles, I realized I was singing. Sweat-soaked for the second time in three hours, ripped up with briers, late to work and a half mile to go, I was busting it out like a karaoke hero. Part of that joy was a sense of accomplishment, and the happy thoughts of a freezer load of organic, free-range meat. But the larger part was a sense of belonging. I'd met that buck on his own terms, on his own trail, in his own backyard, as far from the taint of humanity as I could muster on my lease. For the moment, I was every bit as wild and free as a buck in the big woods, and I belted it out till the barn appeared through the trees.

THE LAST WILD ROAD, PART 2

I was waist-deep when I heard shouts ringing off the canyon walls. I glanced up from a deep slot of slate-green water and grinned. Fifty yards upriver Scott Wood's fly rod was bent double, the line arcing deeply toward a cliff of black tundra-capped rock. He caught my eye and for a few seconds held the cork handle outstretched in one hand, the rod tip dipping and bobbing. I got the message: This was no grayling.

I reeled up and jogged along the gravel bar with half my line still trailing in the water. Wood's was the first Arctic char of the trip, and I wanted a good look. The char of Alaska's North Slope are little-known fish, spending their summers in the Arctic Ocean and then storming coastal plain rivers in late summer and fall to spawn in gravel beds raked up by glacial melt. This one was a beauty: 8 pounds, give or take, its belly sheathed in orange spawning colors, gemlike halos of purple and pink glittering from its dark flanks.

"This was one hot fish," Wood said, cradling the char underwater. "Jumped four times, and he never gave up." He glanced downstream toward the Shublik Mountains towering over the Canning River. Somewhere behind them, 40 miles away, was a shelf of tundra where our pilot would pick us up in four days. To find it we had topo maps, a GPS, and a crumpled sheet of notebook paper scribbled with coordinates: *6953 039/146 23 242*.

Wood, photographer Dusan Smetana, and I were 65 miles and a $2,000 floatplane ride from the nearest road—which happened to be one of the most famous in all of Alaska. The Dalton Highway is a schizophrenic ribbon of gravel and busted, buckled, and washboarded asphalt that trails the Trans-Alaska pipeline from just outside Livengood (about 75 miles from Fairbanks) to the gritty oil town of Deadhorse. Already we'd logged six days on the Dalton, fishing and hunting our way from the spruce woods south of the Yukon River to the tundra plains that lie within spitting distance of the northernmost edge of North America. When it opened 30 years ago, the Dalton—known then as the Haul Road—opened a swath of Alaskan frontier as wild as any remaining on the continent. Halfway through our two-week road trip, we'd already seen just how wild that country remained. And how much fishing and hunting we could cram into 20 hours of daylight each day.

Our immediate task was to take a big bite out of the backcountry accessed via small airstrips along the road. For our unguided, do-it-yourself float on one of Alaska's most remote rivers, we lashed gun cases, dry bags, and camera gear to the raft stem like toy bags on Santa's sleigh. The boat bristled with rods and bows. We planned to herd a 14-foot raft along wind-whipped flatwater, labyrinthine braids, and deep pools fed by creeks plunging off the Brooks Range. Along the way we'd float through herds of migrating caribou and camp on gravel bars lit up by late-summer lightning storms.

But first I had to gawk at this fish, born and bred and hooked and landed 200 miles north of the Arctic Circle.

Just then a Cessna bush plane roared out of the upstream canyon, blue fuselage against towering black bluffs, fat tundra tires hanging low. It was our pilot of the day before, Tom Johnston, dropping caribou hunters on an upstream stretch of the river. He dipped the plane's wings for a better look at Wood's fish, then turned west to climb into the endless blue sky. It was the exclamation point to a scene of utter Alaskan essence: a kype-jawed Arctic char on the line, grizzly prints in the sand, Dall sheep on the cliffs above, and a bush plane roaring off a gravel bar airstrip, leaving us blissfully behind. Wood slipped the fish into the river, and I headed back downstream. For the moment I was fishless. There was work to do.

⭜

Eighteen hours earlier I'd pressed my face against the glass of that very same bush plane. From 1,750 feet above the Arctic coastal plain I could see the past, present, and future scroll below the Cessna winging east from the Happy Valley airstrip. The tundra was scored with weird geometric shapes—centuries-old ice wedges, ice-filled earthen mounds called pingos, thermokarst lakes trapped atop permafrost craters. I watched the plane's shadow glide across Fin Creek and the Ivishak, Kavik, and Echooka Rivers, the last one a braided plain of gravel choked with a frozen skim of aufeis. And then there was the future, at least in the short term: the glacier-fed Canning River, hemmed in by cliffs 3,000 feet high. During months of discussing logistics with bush pilots, biologists, and locals, one location came up time and time again. If you have only one float trip to make, I was told, make it on the Canning. Flowing down the western boundary of the Arctic National Wildlife Refuge, the Canning held the promise of Arctic char on the line and big flocks of willow ptarmigan.

Now Smetana manned the oars while Wood and I took turns in the bow, lashing the water like mushers gone mad. Wood's first fish came early and easily, and Smetana hooked a deep-swimming hen while I stroked through a swift side channel. Then the Canning went tight-lipped. Mile after mile we floated under soaring benches of tundra. We fished slow, deep holes where fast currents spilled over shelves of gravel, and we waded across roaring main-stem runs that threatened to sweep us downriver with every step. I was feel-ing the heat. Ours was not a group to keep tabs, but the spotlight is on when you're the last man in the raft with nothing to brag about.

Hours later we ground to a stop on a gravel bar, grabbed rods, and split up. I fished my way across downstream channels, pounding every piece of water within casting distance. After a half hour I dialed back the pace, hunt-ing for the sweet spots—current seams, pockets of calm flow, deep troughs—before casting. That's when I put a fly just on the far side of a shelf of gravel and felt the line go taut.

Arctic char are known for violent strikes and brawling leaps that give them a good look at their troubles. But this fish dawdled upstream with a Day-Glo Orange Woolly Bugger stuck in his jaw. I struck again, to make doubly sure. That did the trick. Stripping line from the reel, he rocketed across a barely submerged gravel bar, dorsal fin knifing the air. He stopped only long enough to leap, a thrashing, dark silhouette against pale rock and sand. As he zipped across a second bar, spewing a rooster tail above the cobble, I ran with him over the rocks, rod high, laughing and hooting before halting his run.

Wood was waiting back at the raft. "Did you see it?" I asked. He blinked, uncomprehending, then slowly grinned.

"A dark shadow?" he said. "Hurtling through the sky?"

"You got it," I laughed. "The monkey is off my back."

Over the next three days we floated across a landscape where it seemed that all of Alaska's finest attributes were crowded chockablock one on top of the other. Beneath Mount Copleston a thunderous waterfall poured off the tun-dra into a deep pool where we landed seven char—silver-sided hens and blackmouthed males with hooked jaws. Then the soaring, stegosaurian ridges of the Brooks Range gave way to softer hills nodding with Arctic poppy, which ebbed into recumbent plains of sedge and grass that fell away to the earth's curved edge. Late at night we camped on gravel bars where golden eagles soared low, hunting for ground squirrels. Breaking camp one morning, we found ourselves in a push of migrating caribou. Three dozen bulls, cows, and calves picked their way across an upstream gravel bar. We sat on dry bags and life vests to watch the parade in the gray light of an oncoming rain. Bod-ies crashed into the water, hooves clawing at the gravel for purchase. Three young ones chose poorly. Swept into the swift current at the base of a 40-foot cliff, they retreated midstream, swimming with all their might, only their heads and white tails visible above the water. "What a place for an ambush," Wood said. "Work your way up that gully to the willows, hunker down, and pick your bull."

"Next time," I said. We nodded.

Still, this time, not much went precisely according to plan. We had obsessed over the minutest details of the trip, but so far we'd been blindsided by an Alaskan heat wave and hemmed in by 5 million acres of wildfire. Small-game populations were at an ebb in their boom-and-bust cycle. We worked for every bird and fish.

But the Arctic has its own systems of compensation, and they don't always pay in the expected coin. Day after day of scorching, blue-sky weather came to a halt when we woke up on what was scheduled to be our last morning on the Canning. A dark bank of gray mist and rain cloaked the northern horizon, extending as far east and west as we could see. "There's never been more fog anywhere in the world," Wood fretted as I dug out the satellite phone. A female voice at our pilot's base on Kaktovik Island confirmed our fears: We were fogbound. It could be two hours. It could be three days. Look for the plane, the voice instructed. And don't go anywhere.

We slumped onto a pile of gear. "What now?" Smetana asked. For the moment the answer seemed to be—nothing. Glumly, we dug out the fleece layers that had lain unused in the bottom of our clothes bags. The temperature was dropping as quickly as our spirits. We would look for the plane; we would go nowhere.

Suddenly Smetana sat bolt upright. "Ptarmigan!" he yelled, pointing toward the base of a high ridge of tundra on the far side of the airstrip. "Under those birds!" I looked up just as a pair of falconlike jaegers stooped on a small flock of ptarmigan, causing three to flush. I pounced on the gear mound and dug out my bow. Wood grabbed a shotgun, and we started running.

For the rest of the day we tundra-marched for ptarmigan with gun and bow. We double-teamed the flocks, an archer in the lead and the scattergun as backup when the birds took to wing, watching for hunting jaegers and glassing from windswept ridgelines. We killed ptarmigan on the flat shelf that doubled as the airstrip and far into the tundra, with endless views of the Arctic National Wildlife Refuge.

Back at camp we traded 10 feet of tinfoil for a long slab of caribou backstrap from some hunters riding out the fog a quarter mile away. Then, huddled in the lee of the riverbank, we fried ptarmigan hearts, livers, gizzards, and breasts, and sautéed medallions of rich, dark caribou meat in olive oil and as much garlic as we could dig out of the bottom of the food pack. We pulled up our collars and sprawled out on life vests spread atop boulders. "The best thing to happen to us was missing the plane," Smetana said as we traded shots of whiskey, wondered when we'd make it out, and toasted our good fortune at being marooned in the Arctic.

When we made it back to Happy Valley, I humped the first load of gear from the plane to the Jeep and opened the driver's door. A torrent of stench mushroomed out of the car. Eyes tearing, I found the source: a white trash bag atop my clothes duffel, its soggy bottom bulging with fetid eggshells, old bacon, and the decaying entrails and carcasses of four Arctic grayling. I came up for air just in time to see a cackling Smetana peel off in the Wrangler, laughing and holding his nose. Wood eased into the passenger seat, his face buried in the crook of his arm. "Nice work," he said. With the windows rolled down and the sunroof wide open, we could breathe normally as long as we kept the speedometer pegged above 50 miles per hour.

Happy Valley was one of twenty-nine work camps strung along "Skinny City," the 800-mile-long pipeline construction zone that stretched from Valdez to Prudhoe Bay. The camps had more than 16,000 beds and housed 60,000 workers over a three-year period. Now little is left of them, save for their accompanying airfields and a few maintenance outbuildings. Throughout its planning and construction phase, the Trans-Alaska pipeline and road drew ovations of support and furious opposition. The project was characterized both as a "benign pencil mark across a sheet of paper" and as a "broad and portentous scar across an empty and innocent land." Once the oilfields at Prudhoe Bay run dry, the pipeline, like the enormous construction camps, will be dismantled and trucked away. But the road will remain, "as permanent as the pyramids," bemoaned one detractor.

In fact, there's a current push to rasp away the rougher edges of the Dalton and make it an even more popular traveler's destination. The entire route is scheduled for blacktopping sometime in the next five years. There are plans for more visitor centers, campgrounds, and surfaces kinder to RVs. Road tripping the northernmost highway in Alaska is never going to be a lark, but now's the time to do the Dalton while it still retains more than a few sharp teeth.

Past Happy Valley, the road began its steep descent into the Arctic coastal plain. Wigeon, mergansers, white-fronted geese, and ducks I took for spectacled eiders cruised roadside ponds. On a pancake-flat prairie we pulled over to gawk at a herd of musk oxen, morose-looking animals that corralled into a circle of hide and horn as soon as we opened the car doors.

On a clear, 80-degree day like this, driving the Dalton can be a cake walk. But soon a gauntlet of tall metal poles cropped up on each side of the road—snow poles, which truckers use to navigate when blizzards roar across the highway. I'd learned about them at a diner down in Coldfoot Camp, 180 miles south, where I'd bought a trucker a cup of coffee and asked him about the crosses beside the road. He ticked off recent accidents like a shopping list. "One guy froze to death after going through the windshield," he said, eyes steady behind boxy wire rims. "The glass just ripped his clothes off, and it was 40 below. Another fellow was ejected, and the truck wound up on top of him. A friend of mine went so far down through the snow that nobody could see him. There's no rhyme nor reason to why some of these accidents happen. You can just vanish out here."

For its northernmost 100 miles the Dalton Highway parallels the Saga-vanirktok River, known simply as the Sag. Braided into dozens of channels, the Sag freezes solid during the winter, except for a few deep channels and holes scoured downstream of gravel jetties built to protect the road and pipe-line. Late in the afternoon we hiked down the spine of a 200-yard-long jetty and cast to grayling holding in the swirling current. Far across the river delta, snow and ice clung to the siltstone and mudstone clefts of Franklin Bluffs.

Wood and I struck out across veins of waist-deep current, but in two hours I landed only a single char, the sole rise of the day. After a last try at a rolling run of boulder-strewn water, we sheathed the fly rods. Hiking back to the car, I hardly felt defeated. In five days of chasing char on the Canning and Sag we'd caught two dozen fish—not as many as we might have landed had the migrations been in full swing, but just enough to remember every single strike, every single run and jump, every fish writhing in my hands.

As we trudged back to the Jeeps, we came upon a burly fellow with a three-button beard, slicing salami on the hood of a late-model Toyota pickup. He'd driven up from Minnesota for a ten-day vacation hunting caribou along the Dalton, only to sit in Coldfoot Camp for six days with a busted leaf spring, waiting for parts. "Four days of hunting ain't what I planned on," he said, grimacing. "But this country don't care much for your plans. You gotta take what you can get."

⸻

Deadhorse, Alaska, is as architecturally honest a town as ever I've seen. It exists solely to support the Prudhoe Bay oilfield, and it is spectacularly ugly: dingy metal buildings behind ranks of tracked orange and red machines, trailers on skis and skids, shipping containers, water-filled drainage pits where a few white-fronted geese dabbled. Beyond town the enormous Prudhoe Bay oilfield sprawls between the city limits and the Arctic Ocean, closed to all but oil company workers and tour-bus tourists who shell out thirty-eight bucks for a van ride around the oilfield.

At the Prudhoe Bay Motel, a low-slung haunt of oilfield workers, we piled our gear into spartan rooms. Cans of air freshener were within reach of each bunk. "They heard we were coming," I said. That night I stretched out on a soft bed with clean sheets and a true luxury: a fat pillow that didn't sport a single zipper pull digging into my forehead. I hardly slept at all.

If Deadhorse offers an inglorious end to the 414-mile-long Dalton Highway, it does have one overwhelming saving grace: Take the Dalton to Deadhorse and you have no other choice but to turn around and repeat the process in reverse. The next morning we kicked mounds of dirty clothes into piles and spread out maps on the floor. I felt a flush of renewed enthusiasm. There had to be more ptarmigan on the Chandalar Shelf. Gobbler's Knob, I recalled, looked every bit as good. "And we never did try the Dietrich River," Wood said. Or hike down the Yukon shore to the Ray River. Big pike in there, we'd heard.

We packed the Jeeps and loaded up on snack crackers and peanuts at the Prudhoe Bay General Store. Back in the car I rubbed grit out of my eyes and caught a glimpse of myself in the rearview mirror: a graying two-week beard, cracked lips, bloody line cuts on my knuckles, an infected stove burn oozing on one thumb. As I pulled back onto the highway, I noticed the digital compass on the dashboard. It glowed with a greenish-blue "S." We had three days to retrace our steps—or make new tracks altogether.

"So," I asked Wood. "What do you want to do today?"

INDEX

ACKNOWLEDGMENTS

The fact that there are still magazines being printed, in one form or another, 580 years after Johannes Gutenberg invented moveable type, is an astonishment. And a testament to their irreplaceable storytelling power.

My small role in this history is due to outsized influences from some of the best editors in the business. Colin Kearns, editor-in-chief of *Field & Stream* and my collaborator on this book, has suffered greatly due to my love of compound modifiers and over-the-top flourishes of the keyboard. But when it comes to finding the story, the man can point the way to the heart of what matters like few others. The best of this book bears Colin's mark as much as my own.

I've benefitted greatly from other minds greater than mine. David DiBenedetto, formerly of *Field & Stream* and now editor-in-chief of *Garden & Gun*, has been an unfaltering influence. He and his old boss at both those titles, Sid Evans, first convinced me to write deeply about my hobbies of hunting and fishing, which I was loath to do for fear of ruining my fun. They were right about that, and many other things. Anthony Licata at *Field & Stream* continued their tradition of letting me run amok across the continent. And I can't be more grateful for the photographers whose work often stole the show in my stories. I've shared many a mile with Tom Fowlks, Dusan Smetana, Colby Lysne, and others. And many a laugh and a few good cries.

I am fortunate beyond measure to have fallen in with magazines willing to invest time and treasure in supporting the time-consuming and often expensive pursuit of stories worth telling. That I can occasionally burn two full work days in order to wrestle into place every word in a single paragraph still boggles my mind. I am deeply grateful for the trust these people put into me. And for their grace when I would occasionally blow it.

But mostly, my ability to do what I love has come at no small cost to the one person who made it all possible: My wife, Julie. Sweet woman, I swear, this single thought sustained me across a million miles away from home: Every day I spent on the road was one day closer to coming home to you.